Over Ten Million Served

SUNY series in Feminist Criticism and Theory

Michelle A. Massé, editor

Over Ten Million Served

Gendered Service in
Language and Literature Workplaces

Edited by

Michelle A. Massé

and

Katie J. Hogan

Cover image of the diploma © Felix Möckel / iStockphoto
Cover image of the platter © Anne-Louise Quarfoth / Bigstockphoto

Published by
State University of New York Press, Albany

For information, contact State University of New York Press, Albany, NY
www.sunypress.edu

Production by Diane Ganeles
Marketing by Anne M. Valentine

Library of Congress Cataloging-in-Publication Data

Over ten million served : gendered service in language and literature workplaces /
    edited by Michelle A. Massé and Katie J. Hogan.
        p. cm. — (SUNY series in feminist criticism and theory)
    Includes bibliographical references and index.
    ISBN 978-1-4384-3203-8 (hardcover : alk. paper)
    ISBN 978-1-4384-3202-1 (pbk. : alk. paper)
    1. Women college teachers—Professional relationships—United States.
2. Women college teachers—Workload—United States.   3. Feminism and higher
education—United States.   4. Sex discrimination in higher education—United
States.   I. Massé, Michelle A. (Michelle Annette), 1951–   II. Hogan, Katie,
1960–

    LB2332.32.O94 2010
    378.1'2082—dc22   2009054120

10 9 8 7 6 5 4 3 2 1

For James Catano and Paula Martinac

Contents

PART 2
Non Serviam: Out of Service

PART 3
Service Changes

Acknowledgments

We have been so well served by our friends and colleagues that it's difficult to know where to begin our thanks and how to delimit our gratitude. This project carries not only the traces of every committee, task force, or commission on which we've served but also the memories of those with whom we've served. At the same time, as we have all taught one another about our projects, our institutions, and ourselves through service, we have changed, sometimes as slowly but certainly as surely. as the schools for which we work.

We cannot acknowledge the hundreds of colleagues and friends with whom we've started initiatives, written reports, and proposed curricula over the years. The patina of this particular project, however, was burnished by all of them as well as by those who read materials, encouraged us at every stage, and enthusiastically added their own accounts of service, sometimes with a smile, and sometimes with a curse.

Some of our acknowledgments are individual. Katie J. Hogan thanks Michelle A. Massé for saying "yes," for her support and friendship during difficult times, and for her unwavering commitment to gender justice. Katie also thanks Kathryn Flannery and Sharon O'Dair for graciously inviting her to present her research at their institutions. Rachel Stein, Phyllis van Slyck, Jan Beatty, and Kathryn and Jim Flannery have consistently offered their love and friendship as well as their stories about service, and Katie thanks them with the deepest appreciation. She also thanks her online brief daily sessions writing group—Lisa Brush, Kirsten Christensen, Linh Hua, Anita McChesney, Sara S. Poor, Maggie Rehm, and Donna Strickland—for always being there. To the Carlow feminist writing group—Sigrid King, Jennifer Snyder-Duch, Irene Lietz, Melissa Swauger, Linda Burns, Sylvia Rhor, and Anne Rashid—Katie expresses her heartfelt gratitude for their challenging and thoughtful feedback and warm company. She also expresses her appreciation to the Carlow University Office of Academic Affairs for a course release at a critical stage in this project and to Dr. Karen Kiely and Sara Azarius for their expertise, guidance, and compassion. Andy Hogan, Katie's brother, offered excellent insight on methodological issues related to service, and Debi Carey, Katie's sister, expressed enthusiasm for Katie's latest project. Katie owes the deepest gratitude to her life partner, Paula Martinac, for more than sixteen years of love, fun, struggle, loyalty, and friendship. Her loving support, patience, and expertise contributed to the completion of this project.

Michelle A. Massé's first debt of gratitude for this project is to Katie J. Hogan, whose enthusiasm, fierce commitment, and critical sense were crucial in moving this project from theory to praxis. A fellowship from Rutgers University's Center for Historical Analysis provided the space and time that made undertaking the project possible. Michelle also thanks Devon Hodges and Doris Massé for their unstinting encouragement, laughter, love, and good sense, and the members of her writing group, Kate Jensen, Anna Nardo, and Irene di Maio. Her students have been an insistent reminder that what often passes for learning "professionalism" can be a covert transmission of learning to be silent, work hard, and never complain. And Michelle's final and greatest thanks, always, is to James Catano, as colleague, partner, beloved friend, and endless supplier of commiseration, celebration, and indignation, while sharing service narratives over the years.

Some of our acknowledgments are joint. We especially want to thank not only the contributors to this volume, but Kirsten Christensen, Kate Conley, Linh Hua, Karen Lawrence, Tricia Lin, and Magdalena Maiz-Pena, with whom we served on the Modern Language Association's Committee on the Status of Women in the Profession. Their collegial support in shaping a major project there, along with our collective musings about service for national organizations, helped us articulate and think through some of the issues that led to our developing *Over Ten Million Served*. We would both like to thank Jeffrey Williams for his editorial acumen as well as his unflagging scholarly and personal generosity, a joint gratitude to which Katie adds an individual footnote because of Jeff's friendship and willingness to consider ideas in rough form. We'd also like to thank Jeff for his permission, on behalf of *the minnesota review*, to reprint Katie's essay, "Superserviceable Feminism" (63/64 [2005]: 95–111). In addition, the panels and presentations that the Women's Caucus of the Modern Language Association, the National Women's Studies Association, the Working-Class Studies Association, and Marc Bousquet invited us to give on *Over Ten Million Served* gave us new communities in which we could discuss our ideas, and new ideas with which to refine our original formulations.

Gary Dunham, executive director of State University of New York (SUNY) Press, and Larin McLaughlin, SUNY Press acquisition editor for the Feminist Theory and Criticism series, have welcomed this project from the start and have been quick to speed it on its way. We also extend our gratitude to our two SUNY Press readers for their attentive and thoughtful critical engagement with this project, to Diane Ganeles, senior production editor at SUNY, for shepherding the manuscript through production, and to Michele Lansing for her scrupulous copyediting. Rachel Spear, a doctoral student in comparative literature at Louisiana State University (LSU), has meticulously edited and critiqued this manuscript, which has been improved by every suggestion she made.

As this book goes into the world, we hope that it helps another generation of feminist scholars as they struggle to ensure that their service embodies their own values, their own commitments, and their own activism as they re-form the workplaces of the future.

Introduction

Katie J. Hogan and Michelle A. Massé

Service as Calling

All tenured and tenure-track faculty know the trinity of promotion and tenure criteria: research, teaching, and service.[1] But service, like the Paraclete or Holy Spirit, hovering over everything but never seen, often remains a point of blind faith. Feudal, quasi-monastic understandings of dutiful service animate contemporary higher education workplaces, fueling our unstinting dedication to our orders and our vocations.[2] Almost all faculty do this mysterious "service" work, even though the actual labor of service is rarely tabulated or analyzed as a key aspect of higher education's political economy. The potentially endless list of tasks on campus, ranging from writing recommendations, advising students, and mentoring junior colleagues, through serving on committees and organizing events, to serving on institutional committees and task forces and writing reports, fills our days, weeks, weekends, and years. A good deal of this labor falls through the cracks, rarely finding its way onto a CV or into a promotion or tenure file, rendering this "off-the-books" work invisible. Such invisibility is the focus of this book.

The invisibility of the labor of service is repeatedly reproduced, even in studies of the profession and of higher education. Learning about, research on, and assessment of teaching have undergone a metamorphosis in the last twenty years; evaluation of research has always been crucial. But we lack both qualitative and quantitative understandings of service and know very little formally about its function as part of schools' silent economies. This book explores what service is and investigates why this form of labor is often not acknowledged as "labor" by administrators or even by faculty themselves.

Some academic workers see performing service as an honorable endeavor that creates goodwill and community; for others, service labor is a form of rebellion and workplace transformation; for still others, service work is

1

exploitative and rooted in entrenched structural hierarchies. But for most of us, service is all of these, each response flickering into being at some time during every major service project. This book touches upon many points on this spectrum. Its insights illuminate all professorial faculty experiences with service, but it has a specific focus upon the gendering of service, and a particular emphasis upon service done by women. Exposing the actual labor of service, particularly for women and racial, ethnic, and sexual minorities, helps us understand how this labor then becomes a gendered activity considered appropriate for *all* workers in the group. By examining service as gendered labor and by making the economy of service audible and visible, we can improve the work lives of both female and male academic laborers. Our focus is upon the service labor of the tenured and tenure-track, a decision that at first seems counterintuitive because of that group's privilege relative to non-tenure-track (NTT) faculty. But as that group decreases to less than one-third of the U.S. teaching force in higher education, demand for service that can *only* be fulfilled by professors is expanding, and tenured and tenure-track professors "serve" as the well-fed canaries whose risk marks everyone's danger.

For most U.S. faculty, service is not perceived as intellectual work, and it is often framed as a labor of love instead, akin to the caregiving tasks women perform for their mates, children, places of worship, or community groups rather than as work for which they should be paid and acknowledged. Refusal to perform service can be translated to mean that one doesn't "really care," as Michelle has argued elsewhere, criteria rarely applied to other, non-feminized forms of labor.[3] Belying its graceful disappearing act is the profound reality that service, in all its subtle manifestations—as "administration," "professional development," "faculty governance," "collegiality," "commitment to students," "institutional citizenship," "university-community partnerships," or "social justice"—keeps institutions afloat. Without the labor of service, most institutions of higher education in this country would fold. Service functions as an enormously powerful unregulated economy that coexists with—and maintains—the formal, "official" economy of many institutions, just as women's unrecognized domestic labor props up the formal, official economies of countries the world over. Even when service takes on more tangible, practical forms—for instance, when it is viewed as part of our rapidly increasing "how-to" literature of professional development and touted as a way for junior colleagues to learn about the inner sanctums of the workplace, or when it is promoted as a political strategy to stave off the erosion of faculty governance—the *labor* of service remains largely invisible. Regardless of the guise or manifestation service assumes, it is missing from many faculty contracts, often noteworthy in promotion cases only when disgraceful, and frequently a sop in annual reports where it's unrelated to "merit" raises. In short, service is a workplace puzzler.

When viewed from a gender and class perspective, service emerges as the well-trained handmaid of the academy, quietly going about schools' work while other forms of labor call more loudly for our attention. Schools that ignore or downplay the value of such work while simultaneously insisting upon its performance benefit from the silent economy thus created. Schools that extol the virtues of service, enshrining it in institutional mission statements and in hiring, administrative, and promotion structures, often exploit the idea of service as an ethical virtue rather than as time-consuming labor for which employees should be compensated. This notion of service as moral obligation is particularly difficult for faculty to negotiate at religious institutions, but such lofty ideas about service permeate many institutions of higher education, complicating our critical efforts to demystify its powerful ideology. For instance, how can a faculty member, particularly a female faculty member, ask for compensation for activities that are routinely categorized as an index to one's unselfishness, moral goodness, and dedication to students?

While we believe that service is uniquely vulnerable to these kinds of ideological deformations and manipulations, we are not positing sites of higher education as dark satanic mills. But we are saying that they *are* mills: "knowledge factories," to use Michelle Tokarczyk's and Elizabeth Fay's (1993) phrase, in which we produce some very good things, mills in which many other things—including, sometimes, people—are ground exceedingly fine, but also workplaces in which we *work*. Dismayingly like the clerks at Wal-Mart who "volunteer" to spend off-clock hours restocking, cleaning, or taking inventory, academic workers all too often accept the right of their employers to demand their time. More dismaying still, in most instances the "associates" at Wal-Mart know they're being had: faculty, well-trained to see themselves as disembodied rolling cerebrums or as earnest agents of change, often don't. When it comes to service, faculty are the workers who are potentially so disembodied and alienated that they no longer recognize their own labor as labor.

It may seem that faculty make plenty of noise about service. But complaining about service is not the same as critically analyzing it as a significant dimension of academic labor. Just as a plethora of "women's" magazines, manuals, and advice columns in the nineteenth and twentieth centuries loudly called attention to the domestic sphere while eschewing in-depth study of its relationship to the public economy, so too academic service remains largely unanalyzed. In discussing service as "silent," we are referring specifically to its function as a significant part of academia's public economy: an unpaid form of labor that sustains wage labor while nonetheless not "counting" in an economy that recognizes only paid work. It bears repeating that we also recognize that many of us are women and men who gladly choose service as a way to embody what is most important to us as faculty members. Even a service chosen, however, can become, over time, an involuntary tax to the institution, and service that is imposed from without is more onerous still. And the fact that faculty members may *want* to do service work is irrelevant as the central truth of academic employment, as Sharon Bird, Jacquelyn Litt, and Yong Wang (2004) emphasize: "[That faculty] enjoy the work [they do] is not why they are being paid for doing it" (203).

Doing the University's Housework

Three decades ago, all too many of us assumed that effective teaching was simply the spontaneous overflow of powerful cerebration. Thanks in part to thinkers such as Paulo Freire, Henry Giroux, Ernest Boyer, and bell hooks, that presumption is no longer with us. Service, however, has not undergone the same reconsideration and critical analysis. Ernest Boyer's *Scholarship Revisited* (1990) hit a cultural nerve in its insistence upon teaching as a form of scholarship: service is long overdue for a similar reassessment. Quickly heralded as the bold articulation of a long-known truth—that scholarship is integral to every arena of academic work—the ideals set forth in *Scholarship Revisited* were acclaimed, declaimed, and studied, although all too seldom implemented. Almost immediately upon publication, however, Boyer's insistence upon service as one of these arenas disappeared into the maw of higher education's teaching/research dichotomies, in which research is valued over teaching, and teaching and research together are framed in opposition to service.

Adrienne Rich, in her classic 1975 essay "Toward a Woman-Centered University," demystified service by exposing it as labor. Highlighting the academy's silent dependence upon the unpaid altruism of women as a central dynamic of its political economy, she boldly offered a prescient model for integrating economics, culture, patriarchy, and gender in analyses of higher education. Rich's clarion call for effective and progressive responses to the changing working conditions of higher education remained generally unanswered or unheard though.

That service takes up the bulk of faculty members' time and attention at many teaching schools and particularly at community colleges—where a higher percentage of women and people of color are employed than at research universities—emphatically underscores how little has changed in institutional disciplines since Rich's call to action. In addition, such work, even if it earns one tenure and promotion at one's home institution, rarely garners recognition beyond that institution—it has no exchange value in the academic job market and often eats into time for the research and scholarship that would allow such work to function as the "portable property" that Wemmick, in Dickens's *Great Expectations*, so prudently advocates.

Ironically, silence about service reverberates in texts whose focus is specifically academic "work," repeatedly omitting service as a crucial field of effort while emphasizing teaching. With rare exceptions, such as the "Report of the ADE Ad Hoc Committee on Governance" (Breznau et al. 2001), projects that have made significant contributions to our understanding of "the profession" nonetheless give only the most cursory of nods to service or cut it dead, even while they themselves perform "service to the profession." In otherwise admirable analyses, such as Terry Caesar's (2000) *Traveling through the Boondocks: In and Out of Academic Hierarchy*, Cary Nelson's (2002) "What Hath English Wrought? The Corporate University's Fast Food Discipline," the Modern Language Association's (MLA) "Professionalization in Perspective" (Hutcheon et al. 2002), and several studies that specify "work" in the title, remarkably little notice is taken of who's working in the night kitchen. The conspicuous absence of the labor of service in projects whose titles emphasize the "work" of academia—such as *Academe's* special issue "Rethinking Faculty Work" (July–August 2005)—indicates the need for critical, theoretical, and activist reflection on service. *Over Ten Million Served* sheds light on the labor of service and elucidates its cultural and economic influence in academic workplaces. It challenges the uncritical tradition of seeing service as "natural" and points toward a structural redefinition of this fundamental category of academic labor by bringing together a resonant collection of voices in which professorial workers struggle to articulate what "service" has meant in their lives.

We say "struggle" because, despite the extraordinary collective acumen, experience, and achievements represented by these women and men, the majority display what we have come to call the "service unconscious," manifested in a defensive split between simultaneously held but contradictory beliefs. We know that our behavior sometimes damages us and supports organizational structures that we don't want to reinforce. And yet we nonetheless persevere in these behaviors and articulate their value for the best of all possible reasons: the ways in which "helping" and "serving" please us and fulfill our deepest-held beliefs about the importance of existence in community and the need to achieve change and support for our colleagues and students. We know that service and sacrifice are often necessary in order to bring about more just workplaces, but much of the service we are pressed into is *not* about creating just and fair workplaces, an insight that several contributors to this volume make clear.

We also know that there is something wrong with our collegial definition of "work" as research, implicit in the question we routinely ask one another, "How is your work going?" According to the logic of this formula, teaching and service, which take up the brunt of our weeks, are time-absorbing distractions and not our "real" work at all. We nod ruefully at the troubling inconsistency but continue to ask the question. At teaching institutions, where it is widely assumed that teaching and service eclipse research, it may be more unusual to be asked about one's research. The expectation that faculty members will engage in research and publication at non-research institutions is increasing, though, as a report of the MLA's Task Force on Evaluating Scholarship for Tenure and Promotion points out. The construction of service as altruistic expression exempt from critical interrogation operates at research institutions as well as at teaching schools. In other words, even though in some schools service is touted as superior to research, and at other schools research is constructed as the superior endeavor, the fact is that both service and research are increasingly being conflated as "serving" the institution.[4] The need to recognize service as labor for which one is compensated links the diverse institutions across this country.

Wherever we work, service for most of us is surplus labor that we generate ceaselessly and unquestioningly. Thus the essays in this book explore why this form of labor is often not acknowledged as "labor" by administrators or even by faculty themselves. And although service has its own hierarchy—an exquisite *pilpul* that is often left unaddressed—in general, it is a feminized mode of effort. As Katie rightfully notes in "Superserviceable Feminism," female professors are not the only ones who serve: academic labor is becoming feminized through an intensification of service. We know the following:

- Particular fields are service-intensive, such as composition, language instruction, women's studies, and service learning.

- Other ranks also serve: there are assistants, lecturers, instructors, and graduate students dedicated to institutional service. And they also serve who wait, and wait, and wait for tenure-track jobs.

- There are individual men who are paragons of good citizenship and individual women who are shamelessly self-serving.

Although all ranks of academic workers serve, we focus on professors as a faculty group upon which particular pressures are placed. Regarded less as "stewards of the profession," that resounding Carnegie phrase, than as care-givers, many faculty, particularly post-tenure associate professors, are doing organizational work and administrative maintenance that support both the "younger" generations of scholars and students and the "older" one of full professors. The demand for publication by junior colleagues, as well as their inappropriateness as committee members for many major committees, for instance, often leads to a lessened service load for them. And, as the number of associate professors listed as chairs, directors, and even deans suggests, it is increasingly difficult to recruit senior colleagues for positions of responsibility that were once assumed to be part of that rank's responsibility. Indeed, it was the unique functions of this particular "sandwich generation" academic life stage that particularly interested Michelle when, as co-chair of the MLA's Committee on the Status of Women in the Profession (CSWP), she first proposed the Associate Professor Project, which she oversaw during the first years of its development, and in which Katie participated extensively as a member of the CSWP.

The Association of Departments of English (ADE) Ad Hoc Committee on Governance (Breznau et al. 2001) reports with a note of surprise that in a discussion group made up of recently tenured faculty "the self-descriptions of recently tenured participants revealed an extraordinary degree of administrative responsibility among faculty members who had held tenure only for a year or two. The group included a department chair, a director of undergraduate studies, and an associate dean, as well as many with heavy participation in important committees" (5). The same schools that draw upon their newly tenured faculty often will not promote them for performing the very tasks they're called upon to perform in order to maintain the institution, however: job description and actual tasks are bizarrely awry.

In addition, as the report notes, faculty members who are effective committee members and administrators are turned to repeatedly, which results in an "often uneven distribution of the load of departmental responsibility" (6). Female—or feminized—professors' acceptance of above-average service loads can be forced by external pressure as well as gender socialization and expectations. Such loads can also be embraced, or even sought after, though, because of the faculty member's own definition of professional commitments, justification for not doing other work, internalization of institutional expectations, or naiveté about evaluation criteria.

Service with a Smile

Institutional caregiving, like domestic work, is heavily gendered. Women often find themselves primarily responsible for doing the university's housework as well as the family's, and this "housework," as Dale Bauer and others have called it, constitutes a silent economy that oils the gears of institutional functioning.[5] Like other kinds of work associated with caregiving, such as nursing and teaching, service work, particularly in its most necessary and standard forms, is "feminized" and denied official recognition. We hypothesize that just as women fill the less-prestigious ranks of language and literature units, so too women and minorities are proportionately overrepresented when we start to tally who's doing the institution's housework. In a recent article in *The Chronicle of Higher Education*, Piper Fogg (2003) notes that "women have a harder time than men in turning away colleagues who ask them to contribute time and energy to a cause. Barbara Keating, a sociology professor . . . thinks that is because women have been socialized to be caretakers" (A16). Linda Kerber (2005) also wrote about this in a *Chronicle of Higher Education* essay on academic working conditions, pointing out how women are now starting to speak out about "overloaded service expectations (particularly for women of color)." We see this theme manifested strongly in the essays in this collection.

The statistics of a profession's "feminization," forcefully set forth in a report by the MLA's CSWP, entitled "Women in the Profession, 2000" (McCaskill et al. 2000), underscore the fact that the increasing percentage of women in language and literature workplaces is in many instances related to lessened prestige and salary for women *and* men. Indeed, one can argue convincingly that sectors traditionally referred to as "service" components of departments, such as Freshman English or language instruction, are dour harbingers of the fate that is now threatening many humanities units.[6] Furthermore, early responses from CSWP's Associate Professor Project, open discussion on service at MLA's 2005 Delegate Assembly, and anecdotal evidence suggest that, *pace* Steven Porter's much-discussed 2006 presentation claiming few differences in service loads, the increased demand for service, allied with distributions relative to rank, falls disproportionately upon women and minorities.

Furthermore, women and minorities may be called upon precisely for their embodied representations of "diversity." Schools, sometimes for the best of all possible reasons, are often specifically committed to having female and minority representation on committees, and it would seem that there are women aplenty for such representation. As Marc Bousquet (2008) repeatedly points out in *How the University Works: Higher Education and the Low Wage Nation*, the proportion of female PhDs in major literature and language fields such as English and French passed the 50 percent marker years ago, but the profile of contingent labor is now overwhelmingly female. As Katie (Hogan 2005) argues in "Superserviceable Feminism," little has changed since the deplorably uneven stratification that Florence Howe noted in 1971: "Women and racial/ethnic minorities continue to be overrepresented among tenured faculty in two-year, women's, and non-research/teaching colleges, while these same groups are underrepresented among tenured faculty in elite research institutions and resource-rich public universities" (95).

The hopes once tied to the pipeline theory, which presumed an increase in workplace status and rank once enough female candidates were in place, have ebbed before the realities of slower-than-expected change in the number of women holding professorial jobs and in the skyrocketing numbers of women in NTT positions. Despite women's overrepresentation in poorly paid NTT jobs held by highly educated workers, they remain underrepresented and overtasked in the tenured ranks of the professoriate upon which so many key task forces, commissions, and committees draw.

Gender and Superserviceability

As the traditional research, teaching, and service triad that has structured the work and personal lives of the professoriate for decades is transformed by the service economy of the global marketplace, we are seeing that many more faculty of all races, genders, and backgrounds are increasingly engaged in various kinds of service work. Jobs and institutions are becoming service intensive, the transformation of higher education into a managed, feminized service economy impacts almost every aspect of our working lives, and few faculty members are exempt from its reach and influence. Such seismic changes in academic life converge to demand that we recognize the status of faculty service as an urgent issue for the future of higher education.

In saying this, we are well aware that service expectations remain unevenly distributed in the prestige economy of higher education according to factors such as institutional type, sex, race, ethnicity, and class, as well as category of service, but this intensified demand for service, or superserviceability, transcends institutional type and traditional experiences of service, as Katie explains. Seeing service as labor, and superservice as a manifestation of the speeded-up academic workplace, reveals its link to the new global economy in which we all work.

Once again, however, we find that the speedup in service that is affecting many professorial faculty is largely ignored. Much of higher education has indeed become a franchise for what Cary Nelson (2002) ringingly castigated as "fast food" disciplines: *who* is serving those demanding customers remains an indigestible truth. There are fewer of us even though there is more work to be done. Recently released data from the federal government indicates that tenure-track and tenured faculty comprise a mere 32 percent of U.S. professors, a sobering fact that infuses a new urgency to the question posed in Mary Burgan's (2006) cogent analysis *Whatever Happened to the Faculty? Drift and Decision in Higher Education.* Like many contemporary professional workers in a downsized economy, professors are experiencing intensification in workload, a phenomenon that has been typically discussed in terms of greater publication requirements for tenure and promotion. But service obligations have also mushroomed because of changing accreditation criteria, outcome assessment, post-tenure review, and an increasing reliance upon corporate management models, even though the number of tenured and tenure-track faculty who can do these jobs has shrunk by one quarter to one half at many schools.

Schools that once emphasized teaching and service now want scholarly publication; schools that prided themselves upon their faculty's dedication to research now also trumpet their teaching and warm availability to the community as they market education to undergraduates. Yet the shockingly low numbers of faculty who are tenure-track or tenured make these administratively imposed agendas almost impossible to carry out. And the stark 32 percent figure is still lower in humanities units, whose proportion of NTT teachers is grossly inflated by their bearing the brunt of language, writing, and general education requirements.

In addition, the exhilarating expansion of interdisciplinary programs and centers on many campuses is often followed by the draining reality of no staff support. The challenging work of re-theorizing the boundaries of knowledge and curriculum all too often also means finding not only one's inner secretary but one's inner accountant, one's inner fund-raiser, one's inner IT specialist, and one's inner travel agent. And work that once would have been unhesitatingly identified as an administrator's—labor performed for a wage as part of one's job description—or as a task for highly qualified (if poorly paid) staff has devolved to faculty as the numbers of interdisciplinary programs, initiatives, and mission goals proliferate without a proportionate increase in institutional support. The faces that embody these demographic shifts are increasingly female.

As all of this unfolds on campus, faculty are also encouraged to embrace the service legacy of American higher education through "public engagement" programs and community civic partnerships off campus. Formally initiated with the publication of Ernest Boyer's (1990) *Scholarship Reconsidered*, and more fully explicated in his 1997 article "The Scholarship of Engagement," this movement seeks to broaden definitions of scholarship, community, and service and has spawned an industry of books, articles, and Web sites devoted to the creation of engaged campuses committed to reviving the university's image as good citizen. To our knowledge, none of this work seriously concerns itself with the dwindling numbers of tenure-track and tenured faculty lines or the unethical exploitation of contingent faculty, and none of it takes seriously the central idea of this book: that service, while important, meaningful, and often generative, is labor for which one should be paid. Instead, the emphasis rests on transcending traditional ideas of research and service, a worthy goal that many feminists have applauded, but one that should be met with skepticism when framed using the language of "engaged campus" initiatives. Cloaked in social justice language and beguiled by visions of new relationships between communities and colleges and universities based upon mutual respect, the engaged campus literature is earnest and optimistic, but it glosses over difficult, uncomfortable economic and social realities. It also contributes to a subtle belittling of independent, autonomous intellectual work, a pernicious effect for women and minorities who have struggled for the right to perform that work. In much of this literature, the single-minded scholar who focuses on producing a new book or article emerges as selfish, insular, and elitist. Equally disturbing is the lack of consideration for how the engaged campus movement might play into the university's feminized "service" economy, since service-learning courses and university-community "partnerships" are labor-intensive projects largely carried out by women, graduate students, and NTT faculty.

Increasingly, the very language ascribed to the university is a language of service: faculty members respond to increased demands for endless reports of various kinds; administrators ask faculty and staff to assist them in marketing the public image and mission of the institution; and students are treated as discriminating "customers" to whom faculty and staff must provide academic guidance and personal attention. At the same time, students and contingent faculty serve as cheap sources of campus labor so that colleges and universities can direct funds toward improving campus facilities and sports complexes, all in the name of recruitment, retention, and marketing. And while there are fewer full-time tenured and tenure-track professors to join committees and work closely with administrators and students, the legwork related to these service activities has not decreased. This "servicification" of higher education shifts attention from the production of basic knowledge and bold intellectual inquiry toward a model of selfless serving, helping, and assisting with institutional goals chosen by others for both on-campus—and, increasingly, off-campus—agendas.

Some of our authors, and some respondents to questions about service, rightfully praise the pleasure of service done well and rewarded appropriately. The ADE Ad Hoc Committee on Governance (Breznau et al. 2001) claims: "Service is governance, governance is service" (12), and, in a good workplace that would be all we know and all we need to know. That dictum can be a handmaid's tale, however, at a school in which feminized faculty members serve those who govern.

Over Ten Million Served: Gendered Service in Language and Literature Workplaces theorizes service as a major, yet frequently overlooked, dimension of faculty labor and insists that we turn our critical attention to this essential dimension of labor in the academic workplace. By moving the discourse of service from the familiar framework of complaint and fatigue to a more nuanced feminist analysis of service as work, we open a new window onto the labor dynamics of the contemporary academy. With the ultimate goal of creating immediate and long-term positive change, our contributors consciously demystify service while at the same time offer practical and creative solutions to the problem—and value—of service in language and literature workplaces.

Part 1, "Service Stations," examines what "service" is and where it takes place, at the same time as it explores that fungible term. Although we talk readily about "service," the "service" rubric in U.S. academic workplaces is mostly unexamined, even while service as a category plays a central role in the ongoing restructuring of faculty labor in higher education. Putting service at the center of analysis brings into bold relief questions about an institution's commitment to learning, intellectual culture, and equitable workplaces.

We begin this section with Mary Burgan's essay, "Careers in Academe: Women in the 'Pre-Feminist' Generation in the Academy," which delineates a history of women in the profession in relation to service and the changing profession and urges contemporary faculty members to reclaim service as campus activism in order to respond with dignity and effectiveness to the violent corporatization threatening the profession. In "Superserviceable Subordinates, Universal Access, and Prestige-Driven Research," Sharon O'Dair presents an analysis of the profession in terms of elitism and the voracious investment in prestige and hierarchy permeating the discourse of graduate education and the profession, with significant ramifications for service. Katie J. Hogan's essay, "Superserviceable Feminism," initiates a much-needed discussion of the "servicification" of feminism and women's studies as a powerful manifestation of the gendered working conditions of academe. Hogan diagnoses "superserviceable feminism" as the harbinger of the "servicification" of humanities and of higher education more generally.

Donna Strickland also sees feminized work as foundational in "The Invisible Work of the Not-Quite-Administrator, or, Superserviceable Rhetoric and Composition" and specifically addresses the pervasive ideology that defines composition as administrative service. Drawing on her professional experiences as an assistant professor of composition, Strickland explains that the common misreading of composition studies as administrative service means that service and administrative labor are expected of her, and yet, because she is not officially an administrator, this service work remains largely invisible. In "Foreign Language Program Direction: Reflections on Workload, Service, and Feminization of the Profession," Colleen Ryan-Scheutz offers a similar analysis of the gendered assumptions of service in the context of foreign language administration and argues for necessary changes that will bring to visibility the labor being done in these programs, mostly by women.

This section concludes with Marc Bousquet's essay, "Ten Million Serving: Undergraduate Labor, the Final Frontier," which focuses on the predicament of undergraduate students as poorly paid service workers. It underscores the impact of the contemporary global service economy on higher education in the lives of undergraduates and also illuminates connections between faculty and students by showing how both groups experience a speedup in the context of increasingly limited opportunities for learning, teaching, and research. Bousquet's essay argues persuasively that we are using the ideology of higher education to train "student workers": what they are in fact learning is how to become docile workers in an exploitative, feminized service economy.

Part 2, "*Non Serviam*: Out of Service," features essays about workers saying—or trying to say—"no" to what is in effect mandatory overtime, as well as deciding how, why, and when to say "yes." Given the current economic conditions under which many academics labor, how can "no" be articulated? How can the increasingly powerless minority of tenured and tenure-track faculty assist less secure workers in their efforts to limit service expectations? How can faculty who choose their service as an integral part of their scholarly and pedagogical commitments to their communities ensure that that service will be recognized? These theoretical/empirical/personal questions are thoughtfully addressed throughout the essays in this section. Presenting strategies to delimit service demands that go too far, discussing what to do when "no" is impossible or perceived as impossible, and analyzing the conditions that make "yes" possible emerge here as central concerns.

In "The Value of Desire: On Claiming Professional Service," Kirsten M. Christensen argues that an integral feature of theorizing and practicing service is the conflict between the desire to serve and service overload. Focusing on the concept of overload as one of the most corrosive elements undermining faculty desire, Christensen analyzes how faculty's own desire for service is repeatedly abused and lessened because of the crushing volume of service requested, not because one is dismissive of service. Christensen offers some ideas about what institutions and faculty can do to transform this unhealthy and ultimately self-defeating pattern.

Using a critical perspective on service and challenging the typical framework of simplistic views of service as moral uplift or good work, Myriam J. A. Chancy explores her own professional behavior in relation to service in "Outreach: Considering Community Service and the Role of Women of Color Faculty in Diversifying University Membership." Chancy also questions the nature of the relationship between the university and the community covered under the mantle of service and asks whose unpaid labor is extracted in order for such outreach to be performed. Raising the specter of colonialism and the history of missionary work couched as selfless service, Chancy wonders "Can the University, with all its trappings of elitism, effectively become communal, a community *participant* rather than a removed player interacting with the community as its other?"

Shirley Geok-lin Lim believes in the potential of service to create community, but she ruefully notes that, throughout her career in academe, service's dark side has eclipsed its positive side, as she lucidly explains in

"To Serve or Not to Serve: Nobler Question." Lim's essay uncovers the overloaded burden of service that Christensen's essay delineates and analyzes the colonialism and racism that Chancy's piece invokes. Whether the worker labors at a two-year urban community college in an international city or a top research university on the West Coast of the United States, Lim argues that service is too often overwhelming, particularly for women of color.

In "Not in Service," Paula M. Krebs too describes how although national and/or local institutional service can be energizing and exciting for faculty members, it can devolve into enacting corporate methods of image management and institutional marketing. As one strategy for identifying kinds of service, she proposes a crucial distinction between service organized around creating political change and service that is simply about keeping an institution running more smoothly. What Krebs calls "public service" maps a major route to major change.

Andrea Adolph also insists that not all service is, as she puts it, "created equal." Service learning/social justice projects informed by disciplinary knowledge therefore should be distinguished from "regular service." In "Experience Required: Service, Relevance, and the Scholarship of Application," Adolph looks closely at Ernest Boyer's *Scholarship Reconsidered* and its companion volume, *Scholarship Assessed*, and she identifies one of the key differences between engaged service and traditional ideas of what is rewarded in the academy: one's scholarly expertise. By expanding what "counts as scholarship" and by distinguishing among types of service, Adolph offers helpful strategies for identifying and rewarding service.

Margaret Kent Bass's essay, "Humble Service," further explores the deployment of service, specifically in terms of diversity initiatives, by delineating the linkages and conflicts among Christianity, service, race, racism, and the racist manner in which colleges and universities formulate and carry out such initiatives. As an African American female faculty member, Bass explains how her identity and body function as an instrument of unpaid service used to meet the white institution's diversity needs. Bass, like Krebs and Adolph, insists upon drawing major distinctions between kinds of service. Choosing to mentor African American students and other students of color is Bass's chosen service and emerges from a long legacy of African American women academics, scholars, and activists who see service as transformative activism, as service that "fights the power." In contrast to this kind of service, Bass identifies service that's housework and declares, "I define my service, and I ain't cleaning no institutional houses."

Phyllis van Slyck's essay, "Welcome to the Land of Super-Service: A Survivor's Guide . . . and Some Questions," offers an analysis of service at LaGuardia Community College of the City University of New York. While van Slyck's essay focuses on gendered service at a two-year institution that is unionized and part of a powerful university system, her overall goal is to change the working conditions for all faculty at all community colleges and, like other contributors in this section, to offer insights, observations, and theories that apply to *all* institutions of higher education.

The essays in *"Non Serviam*: Out of Service" make clear that the speedup in academic labor is occurring in some way at all institutions in the United States, and that this speedup is steeped in deeply sexist and racist ideologies. Learning to say "no"—and deciding when "yes" is the best answer—sends a message of immediate practical use and long-lasting theoretical significance.

Part 3, "Service Changes," is the last section of the book, in which authors theorize about the future of service practices by reclaiming, revising, or restructuring them to reflect egalitarian, intelligent, and ethical social justice principles. As our contributors so vividly demonstrate, visions of service as central to intellectual innovation and progressive community collaborations are not impossible dreams but instead dreams that can only become realities by resisting exploitative labor practices. Through developing egalitarian and community-building forms of service, the authors not only reconstruct service in the campus workplace but also the relationship of those workplaces to the rest of the world.

Patricia Meyer Spacks also presents service as a way to foster robust intellectual sociability in "Service and Empowerment." While she is aware that service can involve pointless meetings and/or unpaid tasks unequally distributed along lines of gender and institutional type/classification, Spacks's experience of service is one of significant opportunities for personal development and institutional change. Although she recognizes that service requirements and expectations can be mishandled by administrators and faculty alike, Spacks sees service as an empowering activity and points out that faculty who assist their institutions in achieving their goals are powerful.

Donald E. Hall's argument in "The Hermeneutics of Service" resonates with the collaborative and thoughtful service that Clausen and her colleagues (see text that follows) enact and honor. Although Hans-Georg Gadamer does not address issues of gender or women's marginalized position in universities in particular and intellectual life and culture more generally, Hall nevertheless argues that Gadamer's emphasis on reciprocity, conversation, and dialogue make him a potentially appealing theorist for feminist theorists and practitioners who want to critically examine and transform academic service. Hall calls "dialogue-based communal interactions across and within academic departments" the cornerstone of Gadamer's theory and of his own hermeneutics of service, and one that would help us achieve the change Hall calls for in *The Academic Community: A Manual for Change.*

In "Rewarding Work: Integrating Service into an Institutional Framework on Faculty Roles and Rewards," Jeannette Clausen describes an intriguing project that would accurately reflect what the professional faculty at her institution actually do. Working with the vice chancellor and members of her staff, Clausen contributed to the creation of a document that would offer a framework for integrating service into their university's evaluation of faculty roles and rewards. Consulting current scholarship on the topic, the committee found that the most important source for their research and document was the actual culture of their institution. While the document did not specifically address the gendered aspect of service, by making service visible as labor, their new framework initiated the process of acknowledging all the work that faculty do.

Teresa Mangum sees service as powerful, but she too expresses skepticism about how it is often deployed. Her essay, "Curb Service or Public Scholarship To Go," delineates how service can range from a mundane stint on the parking committee to working with artists, professors, and activists about creating a public art project about the social construction of animals. Mangum, like Adolph, is most enthusiastic about modes of service that are rooted in various kinds of expertise. She too argues that not all service is created equal: public engagement scholarship is not the same as routine "regular" service that one performs on campus. Mangum identifies the "service abyss," that commodious catchall where everything that is not teaching or research is stowed, but she also looks forward to a new generation that will "curb service" and, in so doing, "create educational institutions different from and better than the ones in which they studied."

We close this collection with Valerie Lee's contribution "'Pearl was shittin' worms and I was supposed to play rang-around-the-rosie?: An African American Woman's Response to the Politics of Labor." Lee offers a narrative of one department's thoughtful challenge of institutional politics and restructuring of service policies as well as one model for a more egalitarian future in language and literature workplaces. Weaving in African American folklore and literature, traditions of black women's service both in and out of the academy, and the vexed issue of service done by faculty members of color in U.S. English departments, Lee's essay offers a rich example of service activism and theory. In recounting how her department replaced an all-too-familiar model of inequitable research, teaching, and service with a workload in which everyone has equitable teaching, research, and service expectations, Lee poignantly explains how, on one fateful Friday morning, members of her department "voted ourselves a life." That utopian outcome is one we hope other servants of the servants of the academy will also pursue.

The other authors in this volume also want a more nuanced and fair way to evaluate service. Exposing the blurriness of service and identifying how this nebulous catchall category fails to identify distinctions are only partial, if necessary, aspects of what could help combat exploitation of service labor. If service is the category that accounts for everything we do that is not research and teaching, then we need to show how this work is labor and emphasize that that labor is increasing. Implementing engaged campus projects that are rooted in disciplinary and interdisciplinary methods and perspectives, as well as the personal gifts and talents of faculty, is crucial. Such projects, however, do not necessarily address the stark reality of there being more and more work to be done and fewer and fewer professorial faculty to do it. If the majority of faculty are contingent, then the bulk of service initiatives will fall on the already overextended tenure-track and tenured faculty, or it will be imposed on contingent faculty and part-time instructors who have little choice but to comply.

Over Ten Million Served poses several questions to professorial faculty and faculty in administrative roles who are reading this book:

- What is your own "work"? Have you ever answered the question "How's your work coming?" in terms of a committee? a course?

- Can you say "no" to service at your school without feeling pressured or marked? Can your colleagues, particularly junior and minority members?

- Service is traditionally not "counted" at many schools, not only in terms of merit, tenure, and promotion but in terms of our time. What is your work week? What does your contract say about "service"? Does it divide work between teaching and research? Can you imagine "working to contract"? Working a forty-hour week? Why not?

- Have you advertised for, or encouraged, untenured assistant professors to direct your Women's Studies program? Head your Writing Center? Develop your Cultural Studies concentration? If so, have you supported those colleagues for promotion or tenure on the basis of outstanding service?

- Have you, or your department, developed a rationale for the distribution of service?

- How do you evaluate service in your department? Is there any way to distinguish on annual reports—and in annual raises—between the sometimes-present member of the cookie committee and the chair of your curriculum revision, for example?

- Teaching is increasingly an intensive part of graduate student and junior faculty preparation. Is talking about service also a part of your mentoring and training for graduate students and junior faculty?

- Have you suggested that faculty on your campus address service as part of exploring collective bargaining, Faculty Senate or school task forces, or American Association of University Professors (AAUP) initiatives?

Egregiously unjust policies corrode the profession, higher education more generally, and the spirit of individual faculty most specifically. Many of us have risen to the challenge of resisting them by using our time and scholarship to address pressing issues of labor. By foregrounding service as integral to schools' operations, and by focusing on the gendering of service, this book contributes to a growing body of work and offers fresh perspectives on higher education in the United States as a workplace and not an Ivory Tower. In these theoretical and empirical essays addressing the varied kinds of service work we do in academic workplaces, the contributors to this volume teach us that "service" is a significant object of analysis that helps us understand both what the actual work of academia is and who's doing it.

Notes

1. The body of this essay is largely based upon Michelle's presentation, "Finding Good Help: The Silent Economy of Service in Higher Education," and Katie's presentation, "Superservice as a Threat to Academic Freedom," parts of the 2007 Modern Language Association Presidential Forum, "The Humanities at Work in the World" (Chicago, December 28, 2007).

2. The *Oxford English Dictionary* (OED) defines service as "work done in obedience to and for the benefit of a master" and as "serving (God) by obedience, piety, and good works." We would like to thank Sigrid King for bringing this definition to our attention.

3. See Michelle's interviews "Higher Ed: A Pyramid Scheme" and "Ten Million Served!" in relation to *Over Ten Million Served* at the excellent site Marc Bousquet constructed in relation to *How the University Works* (New York: New York University Press, 2007). See http://www.howtheuniversityworks.com at http://www.youtube.com/watch?v=TXHzzvWyKLQ and http://www.youtube.com/watch?v=ig18SWw-h6g&feature=related.

4. For an interesting reinforcement of this point, see John Lombardi's response to the "Report of the MLA Task Force on Evaluating Scholarship for Tenure and Promotion," in his "Reality Check" series, "Research Competition and the MLA" (January 11, 2007; http://www.insidehighered.com/views/2007/01/11/lombardi).

5. See Dale Bauer's insightful analyses in "Academic Housework: Women's Studies and Second Shifting," in *Women's Studies on Its Own: A Next Wave Reader in Institutional Change*, ed. Robyn Wiegman (Durham, NC, and London: Duke University Press: 2002), 245–57. See also her "The Politics of Housework," in *Women's Review of Books* (February 1998), 19–20.

6. In a Conference of College Composition and Communication presentation, Stuart C. Brown reported upon the data from the third survey he has conducted since 1973 upon the most prestigious site of writing instruction: doctoral rhetoric and composition programs. "Male faculty members were the healthy majority in the 1993 survey and the numbers were relatively equal seven years later. Now, female faculty outnumber male faculty 264 to 224." We would suggest that that trend may mark the field's relative subordination to traditional literature studies and may indeed go hand in glove with the possible decrease in program stability and prestige he mentions. (Scott Jaschik, "What Is a Composition and Rhetoric Doctorate?" See http://www. insidehighered.com/news/2008/04/04/cccc).

Works Cited

Bird, Sharon, Jacquelyn Litt, and Yong Wang. 2004. "Creating Status of Women Reports: Institutional Housekeeping as 'Women's' Work." *NWSA Journal* 16, no. 1: 194–206.

Bousquet, Marc. 2008. *How the University Works: Higher Education and the Low-Wage Nation*. New York: New York University Press.

——, Tony Scott, and Leo Parascondola, eds. 2003. *Tenured Bosses and Disposable Teachers: Writing Instruction in the Managed University*. Carbondale: Southern Illinois University Press.

Boyer, Ernest L. 1996. "The Scholarship of Engagement." *Journal of Public Outreach* 1:1:11–20.

Boyer, Ernest L. 1990 (2d ed. 1997). *Scholarship Reconsidered: Priorities of the Professoriate*. San Francisco, CA: Carnegie Foundation/Jossey-Bass.

Breznau, Anne, Charles Harris, David Laurence, James Papp, and Patricia Meyer Spacks. 2001. "Report of the ADE Ad Hoc Committee on Governance." *ADE Bulletin* 129 (Fall): 1–13. Rpt. in *Profession 2002* (New York: MLA, 2002, 211–28).

Burgan, Mary. 2006. *What Ever Happened to the Faculty?: Drift and Decision in Higher Education*. Baltimore, MD: Johns Hopkins University Press.

Caesar, Terry. 2000. *Traveling through the Boondocks: In and Out of Academic Hierarchy*. Albany: State University of New York Press.

Fogg, Piper. 2003. "So Many Committees, So Little Time." *The Chronicle of Higher Education* 50, no. 17 (November 19); (December 19): A14. See also http://www. chronicle.com/colloquy/2003/collegiality for discussion of the article.

Hogan, Katie J. 2007. "Superservice as a Threat to Academic Freedom." 2007 Modern Language Association Presidential Forum, "The Humanities at Work in the World," MLA. Chicago, IL, December 28.

——. 2005. "Superserviceable Feminism." *The Minnesota Review* 63/64: 95–111. See also http://www.theminnesotareview.org/journal/ns6364/iae_ns6364_superserviceablefeminism.shtml.

Hutcheon, Linda, et al. 2002. "Professionalization in Perspective." MLA Ad Hoc Committee on the Professionalization of PhDs. In *Profession 2002*. New York: MLA, 187–210.

Jaschik, Scott. 2008. "What Is a Composition and Rhetoric Doctorate?" *Inside Higher Ed* (April 4). http://www.insidehighered.com/news/2008/04/04/cccc.

Kerber, Linda K. 2005. "We Must Make the Academic Workplace More Humane and Equitable." *Chronicle of Higher Education* (March 18): B6–9.

Massé, Michelle A. 2007. "Finding Good Help: The Silent Economy of Service in Higher Education." 2007 Modern Language Association Presidential Forum, "The Humanities at Work in the World," MLA. Chicago, IL, December 28.

McCaskill, Barbara, et al. 2000. "Women in the Profession, 2000." Committee on the Status of Women in the Profession. In *Profession 2000*. New York: MLA, 191–215.

MLA Task Force on Evaluating Scholarship for Tenure and Promotion. 2007. "Report of the MLA Task Force on Evaluating Scholarship for Tenure and Promotion." In *Profession 2007*. New York: MLA, 1–84. Members can also access the report online at http://www.mla.org/tenure_promotion.

Nelson, Cary. 2002. "What Hath English Wrought? The Corporate University's Fast Food Discipline." In *Disciplining English: Alternative Histories, Critical Perspectives*, ed. David R. Shumway and Craig Dionne, 195–211. Albany: State University of New York Press.

Porter, Stephen R. 2006. "A Closer Look at Faculty Service: What Affects Participation on Committees?" Copy of uncirculated paper presented at the American Educational Research Association, San Francisco, CA, April 8.

"Rethinking Faculty Work." 2005. Special issue of *Academe: Bulletin of the American Association of University Professors* 91, no. 4 (July–August).

Rich, Adrienne. 1979. "Toward a Woman-Centered University." In *On Lies, Secrets, and Silence: Selected Prose 1966–1978*, 125–55. New York: Norton. (First published in 1975.)

Tokarczyk, Michelle M., and Elizabeth A. Fay, eds. 1993. *Working-Class Women in the Academy: Laborers in the Knowledge Factory*. Amherst: University of Massachusetts Press.

Part 1

Service Stations

1

Careers in Academe

Women in the "Pre-Feminist" Generation in the Academy

Mary Burgan

Like many of the women of my generation who entered the English professoriate in the early 1960s, I had majored in English in college with the intention of teaching high school. That ambition was formed partly from my sense that college teaching would be way out of my reach as a graduate of an obscure liberal arts college for women, and then there were no jobs for women at that level anyhow. As a matter of fact, I went to graduate school only because my undergraduate activism in student governance had precluded taking the student-teaching semester that would have qualified me for a certificate to teach in a secondary school. My undergraduate record was good enough for a tuition scholarship from the University of Illinois in Urbana, but that stipend was not enough to support me for a year's study, there being no money from home for living expenses in graduate school. But at the last minute, a friend at the University of Illinois spotted a flyer that offered room, board, and tuition in return for working as a resident assistant at one of the big women's residence halls on campus. I got one of those assistantships, and so I began my career in higher education as a service worker at one of the basic levels on the contemporary campus—the "student life" area.

I cite this biographical background to emphasize the fact that what I have to say about women and academic service will derive from a focus on the women who were entering the professoriate in the sixties, a decade before the "women's movement" really got under way. Their experience is not of merely passing historical interest, however, for the pattern of women's service to the academy that many of them enacted—willingly or not—has many parallels in the academic life of our own day. Although women professors in today's academy have made spectacular gains in academic administration—becoming departmental chairs, college deans, provosts, and presidents of major universities—much of the "in the trenches" service is still relegated to women in conditions that exploit their idealism and competence. My essay centers on this kind of work—the kind that performs undergraduate "service teaching" in non-major courses, attends to liaison with primary and secondary schools, engages with the accreditation process for regional colleges and universities, and maintains a faculty say in governance at the retail level of department and school committees. Now as in the past, many faculty tend to view such activism as worthy, but leave it for "others" to do.

The women of my pre-feminist generation were among the first to benefit from the sixties' dawning awareness of the need to diversify the professoriate, but they also entered the academy with a sense that their security would be unsteady there. For one thing, they confronted a pattern of gendered service that had been essential for preservation of their departments during the dormancy of the 1940s and early 1950s. In fact, women had come into English and foreign language departments in significant numbers to make up for the absence of male professors during World War II and to meet the instructional needs of GI Bill students who flooded colleges and universities after the war. Some had gained their positions through marriage to a colleague or through some other relation within the institution, a practice that tainted them with accusations of nepotism or privilege, no matter how sterling their credentials and work might have been.[1] Others were teachers who happened to be in the right place to get employment at the local college when there were enrollment crunches. The few who had PhDs were a rarity. Many of these earlier women were viewed as "volunteers." They were not placed on tenure lines, and as the men returned, they had to content themselves with teaching and service in the shadowy corners and closets of their departments. When a new group of highly trained women professors began to arrive in the sixties, these predecessors were eased out gently—or not so gently.

The ambitions of this new generation of faculty women derived in part from the difficulty of gaining entrance to the academy even as it was opening its doors to them. Many of these women came into academe because other fields that required advanced training—science, medicine, law, and businesses—were closed to all but the determined few. As a matter of fact, graduate programs in English and foreign languages at major research universities tended to be almost as difficult to penetrate. Having managed to enter and survive graduate school, however, these gifted women then had to confront a job market that was expanding but was still extremely daunting for women. Once they had succeeded as advanced students, many women in my generation found themselves receiving job offers mainly for marginal positions or in schools that hired them last or at the last minute. And so, like all new PhDs—male or female—at the present time, women in my generation were eager to exhibit the range of talents they could offer a department once they got a hold in a "real" job. In doing so, they may have confirmed expectations that much of the "service" work of departmental life and of introductory teaching could be shifted over to the women faculty. As a matter of fact, the pattern of servitude among the faculty women of the sixties was entwined with the internalized "feminine mystique" of the fifties, and that mystique had been intensified by a post–World War II treatment of women academics that paralleled the domestic social arrangements chronicled by Betty Friedan. And so a significant number of the "new" women faculty in English and language departments embraced the service dimension of faculty work. Their gratitude at having the chance for a job in academia made them enthusiastic, and their experience had taught them how to run things.

The willingness of women of my generation to continue to act as departmental mothers and maiden aunts while competing for tenure in an increasingly research-oriented culture may have also owed much to their backgrounds, varied as those were. A significant contingent of the sixties women had attended women's colleges, assuming there the kinds of leadership roles and status that were frequently denied women in coeducational colleges. And then a number of them came into graduate programs from service arenas in society—public school classrooms, libraries, convents, and, increasingly, domestic kitchens and nurseries. As a result, many had on-the-job training for the kind of executive practice their departments needed. They had worked with adolescents as teachers or stay-at-home parents, for example, and had the kinds of insight into the developmental issues with adolescents that such work brings. They had taught in various school systems and had knowledge of the pedagogies and curricula that prepare students who enroll in college classes. More important, they understood the demands on the teachers who prepared those students in grade school and high school. In the public sphere, they had tended to manage such ventures as the PTA or the League of Women Voters with the fund-raising, small-bore politics, and negotiations with bureaucracies that those organizations encountered. In short, a number of them had held real administrative power and came into the academy ready to react against its time-wasting and dither.

The displaced women instructors of the fifties had left vacancies in service that could be filled only with unease by their new sister colleagues, however. These new women who took their places had to assert a difference from them by committing to the kind of single-minded scholarship that would bring tenure. In my own university, longtime, tenured women faculty from earlier decades had been tricked into teaching heavier course loads than their male colleagues in return for pay raises and respect that never materialized. Teaching undergraduates was "feminized" by such "deals" and thereby devalued. And, of course, since most primary and secondary school teachers were women, it seemed logical that female faculty members would have a "natural" interest in spending their time working with local and regional schools. And then in faculty governance, women had served, but as secretaries rather than policy makers. In replacing these exploited foremothers, faculty women in the sixties found themselves under pressure to emulate their devotion to such service, even though they observed that, in reality, teaching freshman composition or introductory language courses was a distraction from commitment to success in the academy. Nevertheless, many women in this pre-feminist generation took up their careers with a determination to succeed in the game without renouncing the idealism that had led them into the professoriate in the first place.

It should be noted here that there was a sense in the sixties academy as a whole that there was a range in service that simply had to be performed by faculty members. For example, in many English departments, male and female colleagues alike shared in the understanding that faculty had to pay attention to, and actually teach in, its undergraduate courses. That's where we got our majors after all. And this consensus did not exclude the first-year courses; before the pressure of enrollments had overwhelmed departments, many faculty members actually taught at least one freshmen course per school year. This teaching supported the department through the enrollments it generated, but it also validated the importance of basic humanities courses for all students. Indeed, other departments and schools assented to the importance of a liberal base for their own majors by requiring them to take courses in language and literature. In those days it was actually the School of Business that made all of its students take Lit 101 and 102 as well as composition.

Language and literature departments also paid attention to teacher preparation in the sixties. My own English department's children's literature course was required of all elementary education majors, for example, and special senior seminars were arranged for majors who had to spend half a semester student teaching. Although I was active in conducting these courses, so were some of my male colleagues. Thus our students could find at least a few English professors who worked in some kind of liaison with the School of Education and with public schoolteachers.

Finally, in the societal unrest about desegregation and the Vietnam War that enveloped campuses in the sixties, it was clear that the faculty should be active as representatives of informed conscience and as principled moderators between students and campus administrators. Accordingly, election to positions in faculty governance was seen as a duty rather than as a refuge from "real" work. Faculty senates actually made a difference; they protected academic freedom in a time of threat to it, and they validated the ability of the faculty to confront crises in reasoned dialogue. In the process, the practice of faculty governance asserted the competence of the faculty to help in managing the institution's operations. Indeed, the major administrative officers of most institutions tended to be chosen from the ranks of the faculty and with faculty consultation. It was only later that faculty began to delude themselves into thinking that such administrative service demanded business expertise and entrepreneurial success—assenting to the notion that their leaders should be CEOs, anointed by the Board of Trustees to raise money.

I may have painted a glowing picture of service in the sixties academy, but I must point out that there were hierarchies of gender privilege within the practice of faculty service then. My generation of faculty women found that the jobs that displayed the most visible power were most valued, and for a long time they were not assigned to women. Thus, for example, departmental chairs tended to be men, while women managed ancillary centers like the writing or language labs. The senior full professors, predominantly male, engaged in the peer review for tenure and promotion, while experienced women professors visited the high schools or, occasionally, served on review committees for regional accreditation boards. Research-oriented service assignments, like directing graduate studies, had a high profile and tended to be reserved for those with prominent research records. The undergraduate studies and composition programs went either to women or to very junior male faculty.

And it was true then, as it is now, that faculty had to be coaxed into taking on service obligations. Faculty members who had highly developed research programs either escaped such negotiations or demanded so much released time and secretarial help that asking them to perform the slightest chore could initiate a bidding war for additional privilege. Eventually, as tenure became harder and harder to get, senior women of my generation began to warn the new women away from taking on some service assignments—like providing window dressing for a committee that could take up a lot of time to little effect. Indeed, in my experience as a dean in Arts and Sciences and as chair of my department in the 1970s and 1980s, the evaluation of service contributions for tenure and promotion for male and female professors became so contested that departments began to hive such toil off to non-tenure-track faculty, advanced graduate students, or those already tenured faculty who could be threatened or cajoled into taking it on. It was then that composition programs descended into an administrative limbo in English departments. As time passed, however, a cadre of mostly female practitioners formed a field that theorized itself enough to be taken seriously by hiring and tenure committees—theory being preferred to practice in the academy's value system.

Meanwhile, in the seventies and eighties, the diminution of service as a category of value in a faculty member's record became so widespread that the American Association of University Professors (AAUP) felt compelled to comment on it. In 1993, the AAUP's Committee on College and University Teaching, Research, and Publication issued a report titled "The Work of Faculty: Expectations, Priorities, and Rewards," which sought to clarify the relationship between teaching, research, and service. It advised that service should be given recognition and "adequate" reward, even though it also maintained that "dedicated teaching and scholarship" should be the primary concerns in calculating the value of faculty work.[2] Most of the faculty I have talked with in the past fifteen years agree that AAUP's advice has gone unheeded in today's academy, even though it gives only a passing nod to service.

I have given a historical sketch of the way "service" was valued in the academy as I knew it in my work as a professor because the configurations I have outlined in the past continue to be relevant today. For example, much of the nitty-gritty of academic service continues to be gendered feminine. Indeed, a central conundrum in today's academy is why its gendering of academic service recapitulates the patterns of the past. There are several explanations. One is that gender hierarchies are so deeply and mysteriously engrained that their origins in social psychology defy functional analysis. They just go on and on, despite efforts of women—and men—to undermine their power. But other explanations point to trends that are more intentional and possibly more susceptible to change. These derive from the takeover of higher education by a newly regnant managerial ethos that values product over process, individual achievement over collaborative striving, and competition over the cultivation of a mutually supportive community of aspiration.

One of the most significant points of change caused by this ethos is the outsourcing of the kinds of service that used to be done by faculty to a new corps of non-tenure track, frequently part-time, and frequently female faculty.[3] The existence of this body of disenfranchised academics is a major source of the unease that tenured women faculty still experience when they make choices about service in their schools. Most of them are aware that they have sister colleagues who perform much essential but hidden service in managing students and pedagogy for their institutions. These colleagues—like the "volunteers" of the war and postwar period of the 1940s and 50s—perform generously without status or reward. Today, however, they are not "amateur" members of the faculty but fully trained and ambitious members of the "contingent faculty." Thus even though there have been gains in the hiring of women in language and literature departments, the casualization of academic work has ensured that much service in those fields remains gendered. The current generation of tenure-track women faculty may have decided not to make the coffee, type up the notes, or massage the temperaments of demanding colleagues, but they continue to work in the shadow of the realization that much of the important daily business of academic life—its basic teaching, liaison with the schools, and departmental self administration—has been outsourced . . . or ignored altogether.

It is also important to note that under the current managerial regime, the university's departments have been stratified according to their "profitability." The power of liberal arts departments has been enervated by this emphasis on the economic value of higher education, so much so that many struggling liberal arts colleges have redefined themselves—merging English, foreign language, history, and art courses into some kind of "liberal studies" amalgam. Accordingly, college catalogues stress the career opportunities for such studies, noting their intrinsic value only as an afterthought: "The mission of the College of Arts and Sciences is to support the general and specialized core curricular needs of the University at large as well as to field *a select number of academic majors and professional programs in its own right*" (emphasis added).[4] The result of such a service orientation in the humanities is a cadre of women faculty who rarely get a chance to teach in their areas of specialization but toil away in overenrolled introductory classes. In some departments getting to teach a seminar on the Victorian novel can be like winning a spot on *American Idol*. And there is very little awareness of the difficulty in performing the foundational work in language departments by the rest of the vocational university—except when some colleague from Economics wonders aloud, while passing on machine-graded tests to his intern, "What are they teaching in freshman comp these days?"

Faculty in the flourishing non-humanities departments of elite research schools expect a lot from faculty in languages and literature, whom they imagine to be leading relatively cushy lives teaching an occasional course and spending the rest of their time talking to each other in baroque language about obscure textual points—or ideal versions of utopian politics. Such stereotypes are normal, perhaps, but they also denote the extreme stratification in contemporary higher education where roles have become so narrow that faculty rarely know very much about the lives of colleagues outside of their fields. For example, many colleagues outside of the humanities do not realize that although there are many more women in traditional language and literature departments nowadays than there were in the sixties, the total number of faculty available to do the multifarious works of their units has shrunk. Depopulation in humanities departments has left fewer tenured faculty members of either sex to manage them, serve on faculty committees, or lobby for the benefit of their disciplines. And so tenured women faculty members continue to be called to service, not because they are in an exploited minority, but because the humanities faculty as a whole have become undervalued and overstressed.

One of the most critical results of this scarcity of faculty in service work is the loss of vital connections with the secondary and primary school systems. Concerned about this loss in the early nineties, the Modern Language Association (MLA) sponsored a survey of the role of major English departments in teacher preparation. In the report on that survey, department chairs spoke ardently about the need for greater cooperation with primary and secondary education, but most of them admitted a guilty conscience about the minimal contact between their departments and the schools.[5] Few of their departments had specific, active programs for working with prospective teachers.[6] Since that 1994 survey, at least one of the attempts to attend to the preparation of teachers and liaison with teachers has folded: the senior male faculty member from the English Department retired, and the English expert from the School of Education could not afford the time away from her research. The teachers, however, have continued to meet on their own.[7] On the bright side, there has been an uptick in the creation of children's literature programs in a number of schools, and it is no surprise that these programs are staffed mainly by women faculty, pedagogical experts, and librarians in a remarkably open spirit of mutual support across sexes and specialties.[8]

Still, faculty work within the culture of pre-college school systems remains minimal. It is almost defunct in the accreditation of colleges and universities—another service area that cries out for faculty participation. Modern colleges and universities exist in a new era of powerful competition from the for-profit sector today. These new schools—both local and online—tend to consider faculty as contract workers who should have little say on matters of curriculum, governance, or even grading norms. Standards on such aspects of faculty service have in the past been sanctioned by higher education's system of regional accreditation through regular peer visitation and review. Recently, however, regional accreditation bodies have come under pressure by proprietary schools to undo the traditional accreditation process with its emphasis on liberal education and its assumption that fully trained faculty should do the teaching at the college level. Thus the U.S. system of accreditation has become a battleground in recent years—with proprietary schools seeking the kind of validation they can use to attract students and the federal tuition aid they bring. Representatives of the higher education establishment have been active in the fight to insist on the integrity of curricular and instructional values, but most faculty have been unaware of their efforts. Few professors these days serve on accreditation teams. While accreditors claim that they would welcome faculty input (though they are not generally willing to offer any kind of a stipend outside of expenses), they cannot find experienced faculty for this essential peer review of colleges and universities.[9]

Governance is another area of faculty work that has suffered because of the turn against service in today's academy. It is an almost universally acknowledged proposition that faculty governance has died a quiet death on most campuses after a long life of vainly asserting faculty prerogatives.[10] It has been killed by the managerial ethos in higher education that finds advice from amateurs irritating and a waste of time. But the demise of faculty governance has also been aided by the fact that faculty activism cannot find a niche in the current value system of our departments. It may be true that governance activities that bear on the welfare of departments and the disciplines—direction of undergraduate and graduate studies or participation in disciplinary associations such as the MLA, for example—can gain some grudging acceptance because they bring a modicum of publicity to the institution. But standing for election to the faculty senate can be the kiss of death for a faculty member in many departments. There is a sense that faculty who work in governance beyond their departments are either wasting their time or avoiding the "serious" work of research. And if faculty governance is the kiss of death, then leadership in a campus faculty union has often driven a stake through the reputation of a well-meaning faculty member.

Without the informed consents and disagreements of faculty activism in governance, however, faculty teaching and research—those core activities that so depend upon the maintenance of academic freedom—can be sidelined along with the idea of liberal education itself. Indeed, given the erosion of so many foundational values through faculty inertia on our campuses, talk about contemporary service in terms of gender is almost too limiting if it suggests that the problem of service these days is the familiar one of sexual stereotyping. Too often the current degradation of service has been absorbed rather than resisted by too many college and university professors—male and female alike. Working with the MLA and the AAUP in the past two decades, however, I have noticed that this crisis of service has summoned up, once again, the idealism of many academic women. The committees of the MLA and the local chapters of the AAUP are now staffed with a critical mass of women both from the tenured and the contingent faculty. Through them, as always, the academy is benefiting again from the fact that smart and competent academic professionals are willing to ignore inequities in order to meet the needs of their students and colleagues. Many of them have become even more aware of the profound implications of the current managerial ethos than my pre-feminist generation was. They understand that the commercial and vocational emphasis in their schools threatens to transform higher education from a structure of progressive service to American society into an unreflective engine of competition in the global economy.

And so here we are. After many years of subservience, the academy has finally granted women genuine roles in academic leadership, even as that leadership has been weakened by the demise of faculty participation in service. The rise of women in the ranks of presidents and chancellors of major universities testifies to the fact that women have been able to master the multifaceted demands of having careers in the academy—performing well in all of its categories of endeavor. But it continues to be true that for women academics, service involves burdens of low-level administration that are often unrewarded by promotion and pay increases. Further, while many women have been able to do distinguished service, not all women have the desire or the aptitude for such work; the success of their female predecessors has sometimes forced them into identities that don't suit their talents. Finally, and perhaps most importantly, treating ordinary service jobs as essentially woman's work may isolate male colleagues from their own need to contend with the complexities of the academic community.

And so, despite the successes and rewards of my own history, I have to wonder about the unintended consequences of a "service career" like my own. It's not that my professional life has been thwarted by my gender, but rather that enthusiastic participation in service by myself and other activists of my generation may have encouraged some of the men and women who came after to relegate service to those singular souls who are willing to do it. In the sixties, when I was starting out, the McCarthy era was only just ending, and faculty activism by both men and women had helped turn back attacks on their freedom of speech and action. But today, faculty are challenged as my generation never was by more insidious threats to their academic freedom and professional autonomy from inside the academy. Nevertheless, many contemporary faculty consider service an exercise of personal virtue rather than professional duty. But the vitality of higher education depends on the participation of *all* the faculty in service at many levels, including such neglected functions as the articulation of disciplinary understandings with public schools, maintenance of standards throughout the educational spectrum, attention to the conditions of student life and learning, and management of the details of operating a complex organization. Thus in today's crisis, the debate about the value of service is not simply a debate about how faculty work should be defined and rewarded, it is a debate about the necessary conditions for teaching and learning itself. In times when all of the energies of American higher learning need to be concentrated on how well it serves the pursuit of knowledge, the training of its students, and the enlightenment of the general public, we cannot continue to have any sphere of academic citizenship regarded as female and thereby neglected by the rest of the faculty.

Notes

1. The question of nepotism has remained an issue in hiring women in the "feminist" period. For a historical and personal account, see Donna Martin, "The Wives of Academe" (1975), in *Women on Campus: The Unfinished Liberation*, ed. George W. Bonham et al. (Piscataway, NJ: *Transaction*, 2006), 35–43. For spousal

hiring, see Mary Burgan, George Butte, Karen Houck, and David Laurence, "Two Careers/One Relationship: An Interim Report on 'Spousal' Hiring and Retention in English Departments," *ADE Bulletin* 98 (Spring 1991), 40–45 (reprinted in *Profession* 91, [Winter 1991]).

2. B. Robert Kreiser, ed., *AAUP Policy Documents & Reports*, 10th ed. (Washington, DC: American Association of University Professors; Baltimore, MD: Johns Hopkins University Press, 2006), 199.

3. See Elizabeth Ivey, Chin-lang Weng, and Cordelia Vajadji, "Gender Differences among Contingent Faculty: A Literature Review: Final Report," Association of Women in Science, August 12, 2005, http://www.isawos.org/pubs/sloanreport.pdf.

4. This mission statement is from the University of Maryville in St. Louis—a school that underwent considerable faculty unrest under its reorganization in the late 1990s. See the College of Arts & Sciences home page, http://www.maryville.edu/academics/lp/.

5. Phyllis Franklin, David Laurence, and Elizabeth B. Welles, eds., *Preparing a Nation's Teachers: Models for English and Foreign Language Programs* (New York: Modern Language Association, 1999). Although the book was published in 1999, the call for participating departments went out in 1994, and the final report reflects conditions in the mid-1990s.

6. It is probably true that departments in schools with a tradition of teacher training do better than the mainly research departments surveyed by the MLA. See John V. Knapp's critique in "'Wandering between Two Worlds': The MLA and English Department Follies," *Style* (Winter 2000); online at http://www.findarticles.com/p/articles/mi_m2342/is_4_34/ai_74942091.

7. Information from telephone conversation (May 26, 2007) with Donald A. Gray, who wrote the introduction to *Preparing a Nation's Teachers*. He told me about the fate of the informal program he and a colleague had started up at Indiana University-Bloomington in connection with the MLA report.

8. The Children's Literature Association was founded by Francelia Butler, one of the pioneers in making children's literature a respectable field for advanced study. In her day at the University of Connecticut, the field was dominated by women. Today more men are involved, but the association's membership is mainly women, with its committees enlisting less than 15 percent male participation. Information on children's literature programs and teacher preparation in this essay was developed for my unpublished paper "What Ever Happened to the Faculty in Teacher Preparation?" delivered at the Children's Literature Association meeting at Christopher Newport University, Newport News, Virginia, June 15, 2007.

9. The AAUP has published several statements on the accreditation crisis and is preparing a forthcoming document advising faculty on how to become a member of an accrediting team. See *Policy Documents & Reports*, pp. 271–72. For a fuller account of the proprietary school efforts, see my discussion in *What Ever Happened to the Faculty?* (Baltimore, MD: Johns Hopkins University Press, 2006), 86–90.

10. For discussions of the state of academic governance at the present time, see William G. Tierney, ed., *Competing Conceptions of Academic Governance: Negotiating the Perfect Storm* (Baltimore, MD: Johns Hopkins University Press, 2004).

2

Superserviceable Subordinates, Universal Access, and Prestige-Driven Research

Sharon O'Dair

The boy, Leonard Bast, stood at the extreme verge of gentility.
He was not in the abyss, but he could see it, and at times people whom he knew had dropped in, and counted no more.

—E. M. Forster, *Howards End*

In an opinion piece in the *Chronicle of Higher Education*, published in January 2007, a literature professor commented on the Modern Language Association's (MLA) then recently released report on tenure in the profession and wondered why the MLA seeks to aid "a segment of the academic work force that has the least to worry about." As the MLA points out, the odds are very, very good that a scholar on the tenure-track will obtain tenure, 9 in 10, according to Thomas H. Benton.[1] More deserving of attention, thinks Benton, are those who have yet to gain a foothold on the tenure ladder and those who may never do so. Of course, the MLA has attended to those laboring off the tenure track, as I shall note later, but Benton's mild cynicism is understandable, since, as most of us know (even if we do not want to admit it), and as Richard Ohmann pointed out in the introduction to the reissue of *English in America*, published in 1995, the profession's power is focused almost entirely on "regulat[ing] careers and maintain[ing] hierarchies of status among practitioners and institutions."[2] Needless to say, I hope, is that those at the bottom of such status hierarchies have had and continue to have a weak claim on—and in—the profession.

That regulative power, and those weak claims, can be surprising. The most recent report by the MLA's Committee on the Status of Women in the Profession, published in 2000, reveals that "in every category of professional life—from salaries to working conditions to promotion—women's status in the profession has not changed that much since the first CASP report was complied [*sic*] and published in *PMLA* in 1971.... [W]omen are more likely to be located in less prestigious jobs, in lower ranks, and in part-time positions."[3] Oddly, then, although English has become "feminized," a woman's profession, gender equity in the profession has not been achieved. In accounting for the persistence of this regulation of women's careers, Katie Hogan argues that the profession continues to "expect that women, because they are women, will serve their institutions, departments, programs, peers, students, and so on."[4] Even feminist scholarship itself has been relegated to serve, insofar as "ideas about women, gender, and feminism 'service' theoretical arguments" advanced mainly by men. Feminism opens up new areas of inquiry, but feminist scholarship fails to receive credit because "women's status in the university is much lower than men's."[5] Women, and feminism, are, as Hogan claims, "superserviceable."[6]

Women are caught in a double bind, and it might be argued that what women have learned in engaging the academy over the past twenty-five years is that "the master's tools will never dismantle the master's house."[7] Less depressingly, one might also argue that social change simply is slow; such seems to be the inclination of Hogan and, in a different vein, of Ellen Messer-Davidow, each of whom acknowledges that women in the academy have made substantial progress, that the "superserviceability of feminism" and of women has not been entirely negative. Further, Hogan implicitly calls for the profession to recognize the significant implications of the changing, or, perhaps we should say, the changed, nature of higher education in this country: the profession should legitimize and formalize "service" as a part of a professor's workload, and, as importantly, attend to the perspectives of professors working in non-elite institutions—persons who have much to add to the judgments of those working in elite institutions, judgments that dominate our discussions of feminism and of the profession itself. As Hogan tartly observes, "The perspectives of scholars located in doctoral-granting research universities ... are incomplete—although they often do not know they are 'incomplete' and they do not function as 'incomplete.'"[8]

In the rest of this essay, I will make explicit Hogan's calls, but first I would like to make a brief journey into *King Lear*, which the *Oxford English Dictionary* (*OED*) credits with the first use of the word "superserviceable" in 1605.[9] My point, in doing so, will be to suggest that persons and groups holding power will not easily give it up (even if, as arguably is the case today, doing so is the proper course of action). "Superserviceable" occurs in a speech delivered by the Earl of Kent, who has been banished by the old King but has returned in disguise to "serve where [he] dost stand condemned."[10] Kent delivers the speech when, outside the house of Gloucester (another Earl of the kingdom), he meets Oswald, the steward (or head of the household) of Lear's daughter Goneril, who now holds joint power in the kingdom with her sister Regan. Already, tension between Goneril and her father is high: Goneril has instructed Oswald and his subordinates to be insolent toward Lear and his retinue; and, in front of the old King, Kent has already "tripped" up Oswald and beaten him in an attempt to "teach [him] differences."[11] When the two meet, Kent is immediately contemptuous and Oswald wonders:

Why dost thou use me thus? I know thee not.

Kent: Fellow, I know thee.

Oswald: What dost thou know me for?

Kent: A knave, a rascal, an eater of broken meats; a base, proud, shallow, beggarly, three-suited-hundred-pound, filthy, worsted-stocking knave; a lily-livered, action-taking knave, a whoreson, glass-gazing, superserviceable, finical rogue; one trunk-inheriting slave, one that wouldst be a bawd in way of good service and art nothing but the composition of a knave, beggar, coward, pander and the son and heir of a mongrel bitch; one whom I will beat into clamorous whining if thou deniest the least syllable of thy addition.[12]

Shakespeare is famous for invective speech, and Kent's here is a wonderful example of the poet's talent. (Perhaps I should add that Kent does beat Oswald into clamorous whining and is promptly put into the stocks as punishment by Regan's husband Cornwall; this enormous insult to the old King exacerbates tensions between Lear and his daughters, leading to disaster.)

But what interests me here is that superserviceable, which the *OED* defines as "more serviceable than is required or fitting; doing or offering service beyond what is desired; officious," crops up as an adjective between "glass-gazing" and "finical," words suggesting vanity and affectation, and appears in a series with "lily-livered" and "action-taking," both of which suggest cowardice (action-taking means taking legal action rather than fighting). Thus superserviceableness, or officiousness, is gendered here by its association with words indicating femininity; and, by modifying "rogue," it functions as a term of abuse that is used to regulate legitimate status or hierarchy among men, directed in this instance toward a cowardly and foppish male aspirant to higher status, the steward Oswald. *King Lear* is a play much concerned with hierarchy; and its meanings, like those of masculinity, are certainly more complicated than my brief remarks here can suggest. But it is not controversial to assert that in *Lear*, as in others of Shakespeare's plays, emerging norms about hierarchy or masculinity (or the relationship between them) are castigated as feminine in order to defend established norms that are under stress, that seem not to be working in changing social conditions.

I do not mean to suggest here that academe's subordinated are merely officious, that is, superserviceable in Shakespeare's sense, although it is common to see a graduate student's, an adjunct's, or a junior professor's CV filled with markers of service and teaching, as if the subordinated believe that doing more and more and more of that un(der)valued but necessary labor will prove to hiring committees that each is worthy of permanent employment. I do mean to suggest, however, that a form of defense similar to that in *King Lear* is occurring within the prestige-driven and peculiarly aristocratic profession of literary study[13]: emerging norms of institutional life are ignored or derided as the province of women, especially norms related to service and teaching, regardless of whether those duties are performed by men or women (and I wish here to talk of the subordinated, regardless of sex, for in our profession men can fill the role mainly filled by women). Further, the subordination accompanying these emerging norms of academic life is likely to be permanent and thus marks a significant departure from decades past, when subordinate status in the profession was perceived to be temporary, part of a long but terminable academic apprenticeship: one could enter graduate school and hold a reasonable shot at emulating one's professors, confident that if one were plucky, lucky, and smart, one would find oneself teaching graduate students or upper-division undergraduates while pursuing her own research. Today, many newly minted PhDs find that "*the receipt of the PhD is the end and not the beginning of a long teaching career*," that they are not the products of a graduate school but the "'waste product[s]' of a labor system that primarily makes use of graduate schools to maintain a pool of cheap workers."[14] Marc Bousquet is right about this, or partly right, even if, in my opinion, his emphasis on notions like "the managerial faculty" in the "the managed university" misses some of the point. The latter notwithstanding, it indeed is true that institutions ranging from the local community college to New York University educate undergraduates by relying on legions of graduate students, adjuncts, and full-time non-tenure-track instructors—persons the MLA calls "education service workers."[15] The permanence of this change, the reality of it—that lower division undergraduate teaching increasingly is the responsibility of non-tenure-track faculty—demands that we apply more pressure in our interrogations of hierarchy in the profession, of what has become a class system within the profession itself.

This is my goal in this essay, but before proceeding, I would like to suggest that, although important, attempts to address the problem individually, on a case-by-case basis, or through palliative measures—trying to shame star research professors over their selfishness and greed, for example, or encouraging all professors to retire as soon as is possible, regardless of age, or signing an e-mail petition in support of a given year's striking graduate students at NYU—cannot be successful in the long run or with respect to the profession as a whole. In addition, I would like to beg the reader's indulgence by noting that I am working here with a broad definition of service that includes teaching, as is suggested both in the locution "education service worker" to designate those who teach lower-division undergraduates and in the profession's tendency to define real work as one's research and writing—everything else is service of one sort or another. Since this essay is concerned with the structural conditions that create subordination manifested in a two-tier system of professional employment, and thus with the relationship of the education service worker to the research professoriate, it is important to emphasize that *the former serve not only students and the institution but the research professoriate as well*. Furthermore, I assume here that each one of us knows the slipperiness of the term "research professoriate," how working conditions vary considerably among what we commonly refer to as "research schools," such that, for example, the professor at a research school like the University of Alabama makes considerably less money and receives considerably fewer perquisites than the professor at a research school like Vanderbilt University, much less Harvard University or Yale University. That said, I also assume that any professor whose overall service load is reduced and research time increased by the employment of graduate student assistants, adjuncts, or non-tenure-track instructors stands guilty as charged in the following pages, myself included. It is far too easy for us to let ourselves off the hook of responsibility by comparing our own working conditions to those more elite than we, or even those more elite than they. Where those most elite do carry a heavier burden of guilt is in their control of the discourse about the status of graduate education and the profession; one of my hopes is that this essay will further the project of Hogan, noted earlier, to force these elites to realize that their perspectives do not reveal a complete or even compelling picture of the issues at hand.

Two structural conditions are crucial: the development of a prestige-based research culture and the push to make access to higher education universal in the population. Both developed in the postwar period; both, therefore, have a history and are overdetermined and thus difficult to analyze. But both have had deleterious effects on the professoriate, and most particularly on PhD students, because both—democratized access to the dissemination of knowledge and the prestige-driven approach to research or the production of knowledge—require cheap labor.[16] Writing from the position of the most elite, John Guillory has argued that "the modern university is the union of the two social functions of *credentialing*, or the creation of a new social elite of professionals and managers, and *research*, or the production of knowledge."[17] But this is only part of the story, part of the history. At the same time, and for a number of reasons, perhaps the most significant of which was an egalitarian ethos reinvigorated in the 1960s, higher education as a whole was charged with a task more comprehensive and more difficult to achieve than Guillory's credentialing of "a new social elite of professionals and managers."[18] That task was to tackle social problems in the society at large, and like many other groups in society, we embraced that notion and began to see the (public) point of our professional endeavors not as an elitist love of literature or even of the pursuit of truth but as the liberation of the oppressed, the empowerment of the disenfranchised, and the creation of a more just and equal world. Higher education would accomplish these tasks partly through cultural training, urging tolerance, respect for others, and sometimes strenuous political correctness. But mainly it would do so by providing occupational opportunity, under the assumption that, as sociologist Bethany Bryson explains, graduates will be "propel[led] into occupations commensurate with their educational achievements,"[19] occupations, presumably, of upper-middle-class status and remuneration. This assumption was (and is) powerful, but it has proven wrong; the "credential inflation" identified in 1979 by sociologist Randall Collins means that, as Guillory also acknowledges in 2000, "a college degree no longer guarantees a job of the professional or managerial sort."[20] It is not possible, shall we say, to credential (or remunerate) a mass social elite. Nevertheless, in fifty years, this powerful assumption helped double the number of institutions of higher education in this country, as well as the number of bachelor's degrees conferred. The number of students enrolled in higher education sextupled, to around 15 million in recent years, which is a lot, but former President Bush promised to leave no child behind, presumably so that each one could go to college and therefore lead the "middle-class lifestyle" once available to a unionized factory worker and so crucial to America's sense of itself as a classless society. Former President Bill Clinton informed us during his tenure that "every American needs more than a high-school education. . . . A college education is not a luxury."[21] I am inclined to agree: "A college education is not a luxury" if one obtains it in a shopping mall, after a hard day's night of work. Nor is it a luxury if one does not, in the end, obtain a degree in the shopping mall, and here the numbers are worrisome, for a significant gap persists between matriculation to and graduation from college. In 2000, 15 million persons were enrolled in higher education, denoting an enrollment rate of 67 percent of recent high school graduates. But in 2000, the percentage of twenty-five to twenty-nine-year-olds who had completed four or more years of college was just 33 percent.[22] Further, almost all of the increase in the numbers of students obtaining a degree is attributable to a substantial increase in how long it takes to do so, as educational economist Sarah Turner points out:

> Among individuals aged twenty-three in 1970, 23 percent of high school graduates had completed a BA degree, while about 51 percent had enrolled in college for some period since high school graduation. For the same age group in 1999, the share of high school graduates who had enrolled in college at some point rose substantially, to 67 percent, while the share receiving a BA degree rose only slightly, to 24 percent of the cohort. Thus, for college participants measured in their early twenties, completion rates fell by more than 25 percent over this interval. Completion rates at older ages are closer to stagnant, implying an overall increase in the time-to-degree.[23]

Although such data are deeply significant for low-income and minority students, who are most likely to drop out and thus never realize the financial rewards associated with holding a college degree, the data are also significant for those who serve them and those who do not, my topic in this essay: faculties and institutions use graduate students and adjuncts to serve huge numbers of students who will never see a tenure-track professor. Many factors have effected this situation, perhaps especially financial ones at all levels of education, suggesting the accuracy of Clinton's statement, only with a twist: higher education is not a luxury, because no society can afford to provide all of its citizens with luxury, the kind of higher education—small classes, research professors in the classroom, and a curriculum based in the liberal arts only vaguely related to the workplace—that it once provided (and still does provide) to, say, 3 or 4 percent of the college-age population.[24] My point is not that we should pony up, but that institutionalized inequality in the profession is the price we pay for pursuing egalitarian dreams in the society at large. The situation is ironic, to say the least, especially given the weak likelihood of "access" persisting into attainment, as described earlier.

Honest, for the most part, about trends in American higher education, the *Final Report of the MLA Committee on Professional Employment*, presented just over a decade ago, in December 1997, makes for fascinating reading. Much of the *Report*, perhaps as much as half, addresses the effects on employment of higher education's dual "imperatives of access and research." Unlike me, the *Report* does not go so far as to suggest that these imperatives might, in fact, be contradictory, but the *Report* does acknowledge certain "tensions" or conflicts between them, reminding us that the key question in the postwar period was how to reconcile "the student body's escalating need for 'basics' . . . with institutional demands for faculty to engage in 'advanced' research."[25] The answer, of course, was graduate students, growth in established PhD programs and the proliferation of new ones; and the solution worked while resources were expanding. Under such conditions, one's days of teaching composition, of dealing with the "basics," would indeed be numbered. Nowadays, however, with resources flattened or, more likely, reduced, having a reasonable shot at a tenure-track research job seems unduly optimistic, and, as the *Report* acknowledges, the "tensions" between the two imperatives have produced an ambiguity in the professed purpose of graduate education: "Is such education induction into the specialized role of intellectual knowledge worker—a role cultivated by advanced seminars, research papers, and conferences? Or is it training for the more 'basic' job of education service worker—a job implied by the tasks most graduate students actually perform as TAs?"[26]

The answer, clearly, is both, but not necessarily for each graduate student. Some graduate students will take on the former role, and most others will take on the latter. This answer is one the *Report* accepts but also fails to address or assess fully. The *Report* acknowledges, for example, that this "ambiguity" in the purposes of graduate education has its analog in the purposes of professional employment, the end point of graduate education, since more and more institutions now accept that some professors are destined for careers in research and the training of graduate students and advanced undergraduates, while others are destined for careers in lower-division undergraduate teaching and other forms of institutional service, such as administration. But in discussing the prospects of two-tier employment, the *Report* finesses the issue by limiting its discussion to "the university" rather than to tertiary education as a whole: two-tier employment is "the university's intentional or unintentional resolution of the dilemmas associated with its conflicting commitments to broad student access *and* faculty research in a context where resources have for some time been growing more slowly than costs."[27] By so limiting its discussion, and, one should note, by avoiding the question of intentionality and thus responsibility, the *Report* is able to define two-tier employment as a system that "divides the faculty into a decently remunerated tenured portion and a poorly remunerated non-tenure-track portion"[28] rather than as a system that *in addition* divides the nation's faculty in a similar way, into those who primarily engage in research and graduate teaching and those who primarily serve undergraduates or even freshmen and sophomores. By using the former definition, the *Report* is able to offer solutions to perceived inequities—indexing part-time compensation to full-time compensation and, especially, converting part-time positions into full-time ones, even if those positions are not tenure track[29]—without acknowledging that, even if the solutions were enacted, inequity would remain in the form of significant status and pay differentials between those who serve on the tenure track and those who do research on the tenure track. Indeed, the proposed solutions would tend to result in a situation for "the university" commensurate with the latter definition, bringing faculty at "the university" more into line with faculty across the range of institutions of higher learning in this country.

The *Report* falls flat here, I think, partly because it admirably wants to address the most egregious situation first—the exploitation of adjuncts. But the *Report* falls flat, too, because it takes "the university" as its model for tertiary education and because it assumes that graduate education in this country is homogeneous in character, focused upon a prestige-driven approach to the production of knowledge. Like Ohmann over thirty years ago, who claimed "we tend to define [professional] success as holding a post in a PhD-granting department,"[30] the *Report* suggests that all of the approximately 150 PhD programs in English produce graduates who wish to "replicate" the careers of their professors and define success in academia as having "a career in a doctorate-granting institution."[31] Of course, as Guillory pointed out in 1996, this tendency means that "graduate education appears now to be a kind of pyramid scheme": if "to be fully professionalized means to teach graduate students," then "the number of graduate students would have to increase geometrically for this desire to be gratified for all of us."[32] Indeed, a strong motivating factor in discussions of PhD programs by the MLA is the perceived gap between the experience of the PhD apprenticeship and of subsequent professional work in the diverse settings of higher education. Moving accounts of this gap are legion, and much energy is spent offering suggestions to elite institutions to help their students become familiar "with the complex system of postsecondary and secondary education in this country (comprising four-year liberal arts colleges, community colleges, universities, and private as well as public high schools) and the full range of job opportunities available in that system."[33]

In "The System of Graduate Education," published in *PMLA* in 2000, Guillory acknowledges that students from elite institutions "have an advantage in seeking employment at other elite institutions," but "they may . . . be penalized when applying for jobs at nonelite or nonresearch schools."[34] A cynic might read the recommendations in the *Report* and in "Professionalization in Perspective"—for example, to expand the graduate curriculum to include internships and courses in pedagogy[35] or to change the culture of graduate school so that most forms of post-doctoral employment are not seen as "defeat and personal failure"[36]—as ways to minimize the extent to which students from elite PhD programs are penalized in the broader academic job market. A cynic might similarly read the *Report*'s astonishing claim that prestige is "a sort of institutional vanity"[37]; to the contrary and for better or worse, prestige is in fact the principal guarantor of quality within academe. Prestige has long been "the oxygen of higher education," as Dolores Burke concluded in 1988, after replicating research first reported in 1958[38]; it is oxygen that, according to Guillory, has only become richer with "the ongoing democratization of higher education."[39] Certainly, explicit in the *Report* is the notion that all undergraduate students deserve the best education we can provide them, but implicit in it is the notion that, the vanity of prestige notwithstanding, graduates of elite PhD programs are the persons best able to provide that education, if only we can get them to recognize the "rich rewards" that reside, for example, in lower-division service and teaching at unselective institutions.[40] With the latter notion, I respectfully beg to differ. I suggest that the best education for our non-elite students—the ill-prepared and uninterested freshmen and sophomores that the *Report* grudgingly admits we see today, as one result of open access to higher education[41]—is provided by a professor who *wants* to serve these students, indeed, whose primary interest and expertise lies in teaching and service, not in research or writing, and who has spent much energy and time in graduate school learning how to teach and learning how to be a productive colleague. At non-elite PhD programs, students come to graduate school knowing they want to teach a 3-3 load in a liberal arts college or a 5-5 load in a community college rather than emulate Stephen Greenblatt or Judith Butler, or even me, their professor. As a result, they are not disappointed or embittered when they obtain such positions; they do not need to be persuaded of the "rich rewards" in teaching sophomores or being faculty sponsor to the queer students' association or the campus's club rowing team for women. For the graduates of non-elite PhD programs, there is no gap, or at least there is much less of a gap, between the experience of their PhD apprenticeship and their actual professional experience. The MLA so far has failed to see that PhD education is not and should not be homogeneous; the many recommendations offered by the MLA are usually unnecessary for or irrelevant to graduate students in non-elite PhD programs.

What the MLA has also failed to acknowledge (or perhaps even recognize) is that almost all schools are "nonelite or nonresearch" schools. Only about "8 percent of private colleges and universities and 3 percent of public universities are very selective. All the rest, both public and private, are less selective or totally unselective, with the largest percentage concentrated at the bottom."[42] Further, probably only about 3 percent of American professors of English publish at least one paper per year over the course of a career.[43] Increasingly, the work of higher education is service and the teaching of marginally qualified or even unqualified students. When we staff these institutions with faculty who have been trained at elite institutions to produce original scholarship, as we largely do—in 1995, according to the

ADE Bulletin, only "sixteen percent of all tenured faculty members worked in [Carnegie] Research I institutions," that is, in the kinds of "institutions at which most were trained"[44]—we set the stage for mismatches in the classroom and on campus that result in disdain and bitterness, the kinds of frustration one reads about regularly in the opinion section of *The Chronicle of Higher Education* and that the *Report* tries to address. Yet rather than offer the quixotic solution that we become better, less resentful, less disappointed people, I propose that it is time to recognize that PhD programs in general and elite programs in particular are out of sync with the needs of the institutions and the public who will employ them and whom they serve.[45] And further, I ask whether we can put them in sync?

Earlier I suggested that professional inequality is the price we pay for pursuing egalitarian dreams in the larger society. This situation, however, is not one we are powerless to change. We can reduce, perhaps even eliminate, certain forms of professional inequality by getting our graduate education in sync with the realities of tertiary education in the twenty-first century. In a paper from a well-known conference on "The Future of Doctoral Education," held in 1999 at the University of Wisconsin, Walter Cohen observed that although academia depends on "cheap instructors for undergraduate education . . . we are not morally obliged to keep afloat [undergraduate education] through a system of exploitation"; Cohen then repeated the oft-repeated exhortation to reduce the size of PhD programs.[46] In his contribution to the conference, Guillory pointed to several places "in the system where pressure might be applied," including the lower division, where we might separate the task of remediation from that of general education; the system of rewards for professors, which might entail a reduced focus on publication; and the system of graduate education itself, which might be rationalized and centralized, with "some power to accredit or sanction . . . vested in a professional organization, such as the MLA . . . a somewhat different MLA," to be sure.[47] To the suggestions of Cohen and Guillory, one might add the following: increase taxes; increase tuition; eliminate tenure; restructure the division of labor for teaching undergraduates; decrease the demand for instruction by dramatically restricting access to higher education; decrease support for PhD programs that produce professionals focused (almost) exclusively on research and increase support for programs that do not; and be nice to the subordinated—talk to them in the halls, invite them to parties or even to dinner. Another option is to change our egalitarian ideology to fit our hierarchical reality, an option that makes other changes unnecessary.

Even if the public were to acknowledge the hollowness of "access," dramatically reducing access to higher education is politically unfeasible. Among the other proposals, some are more likely than others to be implemented or effective once implemented, but all deserve consideration. Of these proposals, six directly concern the way the profession organizes itself as a research culture, one based on and driven by prestige, the second of the structural conditions that have effected a crisis in professional employment and the institutionalization of subordinate status or two-tier employment among faculty. The prestige-based research culture is, therefore, *the* place in the system where pressure might be applied, the place where we might envision and possibly create a more rational and just system of graduate education and professional life. But should we begin to think about reform of this research culture? Can we reform this research culture but not destroy research? I think the answer to each question is yes. This is not, of course, the general opinion, which in some instances edges toward the apocalyptic and the paranoid. The first lines of Cary Nelson and Stephen Watt's recent book suggest that "within a very few years, higher education as we know it may cease to exist." Already, they claim, external forces and faculty passivity "have led to a serious decline in research that seeks to advance knowledge rather than generate profits."[48] For Nelson and Watt, higher education as we know it *means* research, the kind of research they do and have done, with the sort of material conditions and institutional structure that supports them comfortably. As we have already seen, Cohen admirably insists that reducing the size of PhD programs is essential, but he cannot bring himself to "imagine more than modest progress" for those in the academy who "desire to challenge institutional hierarchy and in particular the subordination of teaching to research."[49] He fears that opting out of the research culture would lead to the "erosion of the research faculty with no gains for others, the conversion of literature departments into cheap service departments."[50]

I find such scenarios unpersuasive. Research professors attempt to silence dissent when they impugn questioning of the status quo, particularly of the amount of resources consumed by the research professoriate, suggesting that such questioning constitutes an attack on research itself. It does not. As Randall Collins puts it to his colleagues in sociology:

> [T]eaching nonintellectual students and indeed undedicated or even alienated students is the price professors pay for the material infrastructure of life on the research frontier. Each professor can pay the price by sharing the burden; or the burden can be shouldered by a lower class of instructors. Structurally either way will work; but the decision has consequences for the ethos of a discipline, especially in an era when ideals of many . . . disciplines are democratic.[51]

We do have choice here, choice that has consequences for the "ethos" of our profession, and we may legitimately ask whether it—or we—has chosen the best way to "pay" for "life on the research frontier." Many have rightfully questioned the recent mutation of the research culture into a celebrity or star culture, which exacerbates an already unequal and demoralizing relationship between research professors and everyone else.[52] But have we ever asked how many research professors there should be, as a proportion of entire faculties, tenured or not? Have we ever asked how privileged they should be in their work and personal lives, coming as that privilege does on the backs of those "education service workers" who teach, as Collins puts it, our "nonintellectual students"?[53] Have we asked to what extent the research professoriate is responsible for relegating these education service workers, these subordinated professionals, to living like the working poor, while they themselves live like the upper middle class? Andrew Hacker points out that at major research universities, full professors' inflation-adjusted salaries have risen as much as 50 percent since 1985,[54] while inflation-adjusted earnings for the U.S. workforce as a whole have risen by just 2 percent in that time period. Are full professors at elite research institutions appropriately privileged when they gobble up between 70 and 80 percent of an institution's instructional budget,[55] and almost all of that institution's undergraduate teaching is performed by adjuncts and graduate students? Or should they consume only 45 percent? Or 90 percent? I do not know, but I do know—if I may invoke *King Lear* once more—that Lear had to fall into madness and Gloucester to lose his eyes before either could acknowledge the injustice of his privilege.[56] I know, too, that I will not be persuaded just by the words of elite research professors or of their institutions' presidents or chancellors. And this is why I admire and respect Cohen's honesty when he says, "I am aware that there is no way for me even to ask these questions [about the research culture] in a disinterested fashion."[57] He is correct.

The same can be said for any research professor at a top-20 PhD-granting institution who talks about these issues. These professors are deeply (in)vested in the status quo; in these conditions, while subordinated professionals suffer, they are doing very well indeed—driving nice cars, playing the stock market, buying second homes in Colorado or North Carolina, sending their children to Stanford and Yale.[58] As a result, if I may appropriate Cohen's words, "It is hard to imagine more than modest progress here." Why? Because, as Collins points out, social conflict theory predicts that mobilization from below cannot by itself "change a system of power; such changes start with breakdown at the top and struggle among competing elites over how to fix it."[59] And the top, as I noted earlier, is focused on "regulat[ing] careers and maintain[ing] hierarchies of status among practitioners and institutions."[60] It truly does seem inconceivable that the MLA and those who dominate discussion about the status of the profession would admit that research, teaching, *and* service are equally professional pursuits; that the principal business of higher education is service, service to students and to institutions; or that most members of the profession, even those thought to be part of the research professoriate, are engaged most of the time in the work of service. It seems inconceivable that the MLA would propose to match the number of PhDs produced annually to the number of tenure-track positions available, which would mean reducing our production by at least 50 percent and possibly as much as 70 percent[61]; or to insist that PhD programs train their PhDs for the tenure-track jobs available, which are almost entirely at schools where teaching and service together constitute more than half of a professor's workload, sometimes vastly more than half.[62] It seems inconceivable that the MLA would recommend instituting systems of reward that credit teaching and service, or restructuring the division of labor for teaching undergraduates and providing service to the institution, so that more professors, or even all professors, would engage in all three areas of professional commitment throughout their lives. We seem incapable of imagining that we might produce knowledge and do research outside a system based on prestige and inequality. And thus, if I may invoke again the words of Collins, cited earlier, it seems we simply do not want to have each professor "pay the price [for research] by sharing the burden"; sadly, it seems, we would rather that the "burden . . . be shouldered by a lower class of instructors," persons who are, as Guillory acknowledges, in almost all instances as qualified, at least at the outset of their careers, as those whose research labors they will support.[63]

Elites in the profession seem incapable of acknowledging the structural conditions creating our professional crisis, much less changing them, especially in the ways suggested here. Rather than a breakdown at the top, the likely scenario, as Collins's argument suggests, is that elites will conclude that hierarchy in our profession is a necessary evil, or even a laudable good, in which case we will continue as we have for decades: challenging hierarchy bit by bit, within individual institutions; encouraging palliative efforts on behalf of the subordinated, getting them health benefits and small research budgets; and hiding our hierarchical reality behind an ideology that promotes the liberation of the oppressed, the empowerment of the disenfranchised, and the creation of a more just and equal world. All that said, however, I would like to conclude this essay with hope, the hope that Collins and I are wrong. Sometimes voices from outside the elite are heard, and perhaps more importantly, some of those voices are resoundingly independent of the ideological hegemony of it. As individual actors, we do have choices, and sometimes powerful people change their minds. In 1999, after reading *Academic Keywords*, in which Cary Nelson and Stephen Watt declare that "*there are no superstars in the humanities*," I would not have thought they might one day condemn some of their fellow elite research professors in English departments.[64] Yet five years later, in *Office Hours*, they ask, "Can we continue to pretend that one group is not living off the exploitation of the other?" Perhaps this change of heart indicates that a breakdown at the top is possible; perhaps someday the research professoriate will become divided enough to wrangle some changes in the profession, changes that might liberate the oppressed and empower the disenfranchised among us. Perhaps.

Notes

Epigraph source: E. M. Forster, *Howards End* (New York: W.W. Norton and Company, 1998), 35.

1. Thomas H. Benton, "A Christmas Present from the MLA." *The Chronicle of Higher Education* (January 19, 2007). http://www.chronicle.com/jobs/news/2007/01/2007011901c/careers.html.

2. Richard Ohmann, *English in America: A Radical View of the Profession* (Hanover, NH: University Press of New England, 1995), xlvi.

3. Cited by Katie Hogan, "Superserviceable Feminism," *the minnesota review* n.s. 63–64 (Spring/Summer 2005), 95.

4. Ibid., 107.

5. Ibid., 98, 108.

6. Ibid., 107.

7. Audre Lorde, "The Master's Tools Will Never Dismantle the Master's House," in *Sister Outsider: Essays and Speeches* (Trumansburg, NY: The Crossing Press, 1984), 112.

8. Hogan, "Superserviceable Feminism," 108.

9. The *OED* lists but four other uses of the word, all between 1815 and 1901.

10. William Shakespeare, *King Lear*, ed. R. A. Foakes (London: Thomson Learning, 1997), 1.4.5.

11. Ibid. 1.3.9–10; 1.4.84–90.

12. Ibid., 2.2.11.23.

13. On the aristocratic nature of the academy, see my *Class, Critics, and Shakespeare: Bottom Lines on the Culture Wars* (Ann Arbor: University of Michigan Press, 2000), 43–66.

14. Marc Bousquet, "Tenured Bosses and Disposable Teachers," *the minnesota review* n.s. 58–60 (2003): 231.

15. *Final Report of the MLA Committee on Professional Employment.* (New York: MLA, 1997), 21.

16. In "Credential Inflation and the Future of Universities," sociologist Randall Collins observes that the causes of "the growing distance between a highly paid elite of noted researchers and a professorial underclass of temporary lecturers ... are in the economic strains of a system whose mass production of educational credentials for employment has become extremely expensive." See *The Future of the City of Intellect: The Changing American University*, ed. Steven G. Brint, 23–46 (Stanford, CA: Stanford University Press, 2002), 23.

17. John Guillory, "The System of Graduate Education," *PMLA* 115 (2000): 1156, emphases in original.

18. Ibid., 1156.

19. Bethany Bryson, *Making Multiculturalism: Boundaries and Meaning in U.S. English Departments* (Stanford, CA: Stanford University Press, 2005), 18.

20. Randall Collins, *The Credential Society: An Historical Sociology of Education and Stratification* (New York: Academic Press, 1979). See also Collins, "Credential Inflation"; Guillory, "System," 1160.

21. Quoted by Erik Lords, "Clinton Uses a Commencement Address to Stress the Value of Attending College," *The Chronicle of Higher Education,* June 23, 2000, sec. A34.

22. P. Michael Timpane and Arthur M. Hauptman, "Improving the Academic Preparation and Performance of Low-Income Students in American Higher Education," in *America's Untapped Resource: Low-Income Students in Higher Education,* ed. Richard D. Kahlenberg (New York: The Century Foundation Press, 2004), 59–100.

23. Sarah Turner, "Going to College and Finishing College: Explaining Different Educational Outcomes," in *College Decisions: The Economics of Where to Go, When to Go, and How to Pay for It,* ed. Caroline Hoxby (Chicago, IL: University of Chicago Press, 2004), 13–56, 13.

24. As Martin Trow observed thirty years ago, "No society, no matter how rich, can afford a system of higher education for 20 or 30% of the age grade [never mind 50% or more] at the cost levels of the elite higher education which it formerly provided for 5% of the population. Insofar as egalitarians insist that there be no major differentials in per capita costs among various sectors of the system of higher education, and at the same time insist on expansion, they force a leveling downward in costs and perhaps also in quality. Insofar as they are committed to a high and common set of standards throughout the system, they are also necessarily urging a restraint on expansion, though they themselves may not recognize this." "Problems in the Transition from Elite to Mass Higher Education." *Policies for Higher Education.* Organization for Economic Co-operation and Development (OECD) (Paris: OECD, 1974), 51–101, 86. See also Collins, "Credential," 30–31, 35–37.

25. *Report,* 20.

26. Ibid., 21.

27. Ibid.

28. Ibid. One wonders why the MLA calls this "multitier" employment, since only two tiers are described.

29. Ibid., 33–34.

30. Ohmann, *English in America,* 238.

31. *Report,* 32.

32. John Guillory, "Preprofessionalism: What Graduate Students Want," *Profession* (1996): 97, 98.

33. *Report,* 32.

34. Guillory, "System," 1155.

35. *Report,* 32.

36. MLA Ad Hoc Committee on the Professionalization of PhDs, "Professionalization in Perspective," *Profession* (2002): 191.

37. *Report*, 18.

38. Dolores L. Burke, *A New Academic Marketplace* (New York: Greenwood Press, 1988), 114. See also Theodore Caplow and Reece J. McGee, *The Academic Marketplace* (New York: Basic Books, 1958).

39. Guillory, "System," 1154–55.

40. *Report*, 32.

41. *Report*, 20.

42. Zelda F. Gamson, "The Stratification of the Academy," in *The Politics of Work in the Managed University*, ed. Randy Martin (Durham, NC: Duke University Press, 1998), 103. See also Anthony P. Carnevale and Stephen J. Rose, who divide the nation's 1,400 accredited four-year institutions into four tiers, and calculate that 65 percent of each graduating high school class enrolls in the bottom two tiers. Only 15 percent of students enroll in the nation's 146 most competitive four-year institutions (103–105). Note that neither Gamson nor Carnevale and Rose include students who enter community colleges. Gamson notes that there are over 3,600 colleges and universities in the tertiary sector; far more than half are community colleges (103). "Socioeconomic Status, Race/Ethnicity, and Selective College Admissions," *America's Untapped Resource: Low-Income Students in Higher Education*, ed. Richard D. Kahlenberg (New York: The Century Foundation Press, 2004), 101–56.

43. I base this estimate on the work of Randall Collins in *The Sociology of Philosophies: A Global Theory of Intellectual Change* (Cambridge, MA: Harvard University Press). Collins points out that "the most thorough data we have on intellectual stratification concern scientific fields" but also that there may be "good reason to believe that the basic structures are similar in philosophy and indeed in most of the humanistic (perhaps also artistic) disciplines" (42). According to Collins, "The shape of the scientific community is a sharply narrowing pyramid: if we look at the population of scientists, the pyramid sits on a wide base of modest producers; if we look at the population of papers produced by those individuals, it is a pyramid with its nose pushed into the ground and its base to the sky. Of those who publish anything at all, the biggest group (75%) produce just one or two papers, adding up to 25 percent of all papers published. About one twentieth of the group [5%] publish half of all papers; they produce 10 or more papers per lifetime. The top two scientists out of 165 (1.2 percent) produce 50 or more papers, and thus produce one quarter of all the papers" (43).

44. Maresi Nerad and Joseph Cerny, "From Rumors to Facts: Career Outcomes of English PhDs," *ADE Bulletin* 124 (2000): 55, 45.

45. Robert Scholes observed a decade ago that the PhD in English is "designed to train graduate students to produce 'original research' (which means research worthy of publication) in some part of the field of English." Yet that research degree is "the primary credential for a teaching position," and this is "such an established part of higher education that we can scarcely see the oddity of it." See Robert Scholes, *The Rise and Fall of English: Reconstructing English as a Discipline* (New Haven, CT: Yale University Press), 1998, 170–71. But this situation is odd, still, and I think, like Kent, admonishing King Lear, that it is time we "see better" (1.1.159). We should see, for example, that Scholes's "we" is a loaded term that excludes colleagues working in non-elite institutions, which, as I have already noted, are most institutions.

Further, and seconding Hogan, whom I cited earlier, we should see the oddity of allowing our assessments of the profession to be produced exclusively by scholars in elite institutions. Consider the conference held in 1999 held at the University of Wisconsin on the Future of Doctoral Education; if the papers published in *PMLA* are representative of the voices heard at that important conference, few if any voices from non-elite PhD programs were heard. For a similar argument about women's studies, See Catherine Orr and Diane Lichtenstein, "The Politics of Feminist Locations: A Materialist Analysis of Women's Studies," *NWSA Journal* 16, 7 (Fall 2004): 1–17. The authors note that commentary about and assessment of the field, not surprisingly, tends to come from scholars affiliated with "what Carnegie would call Doctoral Research Universities—Extensive (formerly called 'Research I') institutions" (2). Yet, the authors note, it is essential to recognize that "academics with high teaching loads, 'high needs' students, or a religious mandate to work around may very well have a unique perspective on the discipline that has been heretofore unknowable to the field's more prominent spokespeople" (4).

46. Walter Cohen, "The Economics of Doctoral Education in Literature," *PMLA* 115 (2000): 1177–78.

47. Guillory, "System," 1162, 1163.

48. Cary Nelson and Stephen Watt, *Academic Keywords: A Devil's Dictionary for Higher Education* (New York: Routledge, 1999), vii.

49. Cohen, "Economics," 1181.

50. Ibid., 1181.

51. Collins, "Credential," 35–36.

52. David Kirp discusses NYU in a chapter called "Star Wars," chronicling the effects on faculties and teaching of the recruitment of stars. He suggests that the "hiring of superstars and the demand for unionization among the teaching underclass . . . are intertwined. The relationship isn't a simple one of cause and effect, for adjuncts are a growing presence at most American universities, but the recruitment of famed scholars hastens the process." See *Shakespeare, Einstein, and the Bottom Line: The Marketing of Higher Education* (Cambridge, MA: Harvard University Press, 2003), 69.

53. Collins, "Credential," 37.

54. Hacker's schools are Harvard, Princeton, Stanford, Columbia, Duke, Amherst, Berkeley, North Carolina, Texas, and Wisconsin. See his "The Truth about the Colleges," *The New York Review of Books* (November 3, 2005): 51–54, 54.

55. See Hacker, "Truth," 54.

56. See Shakespeare, *Lear*, 3.4.28–36, 4.1.67–74.

57. Cohen, "Economics," 1181.

58. Of course I do not have data to support this claim, which shimmers with rhetorical excess, but Peter Schmidt, of *The Chronicle of Higher Education*, does try to document privilege among faculty members by pointing to a 2001 survey of faculty at the University of Illinois, a major research institution, with a top-20 PhD program in English. This study "found that the professors were three times as likely as Illinois residents or the rest of America to have had parents with master's or professional degrees, and were disproportionately likely to be the children of lawyers, civil engineers, and physicians, and people even farther up the social totem pole" (19). See Schmidt's *Color and Money: How Rich White Kids Are Winning the War over College Affirmative Action* (New York: Palgrave Macmillan), 2007.

59. Collins, "Credential," 44.

60. Ohmann, *English in America*, xlvi.

61. "Report of the ADE Ad Hoc Committee on Changes in the Structure and Financing of Higher Education," *ADE Bulletin* 137 (Spring 2005): 89–102. Between 1990 and 2003, the Survey of Earned Doctorates revealed more than 900 recipients in twelve of those years, and more than 1,000 in six. And yet "the direct evidence of all eleven PhD placement surveys . . . conducted [from] 1975–76 to 2000–01, indicates a higher education system that is able to assimilate from between 300 to 500 new doctorate recipients in English each year to tenure-track positions" (97).

62. Such targeting of PhD education would require the elimination of elite programs as well as non-elite programs, and more of the former than of the latter.

63. Guillory, "System," 1161.

64. Cary Nelson and Stephen Watt, *Academic Keywords*, 279; *Office Hours: Activism and Change in the Academy* (New York: Routledge, 2004), 32. Nelson and Watt still manage, I believe, to exempt themselves from responsibility. Their groups are "administrators, academic stars, and the wealthiest disciplines on the one hand, and . . . contingent laborers and marginalized disciplines on the other." I am confident in thinking that, for them, English is a marginalized discipline. I am also, as I said in the body of this text, trying to be hopeful.

3

Superserviceable Feminism

Katie J. Hogan

> Women's lives are spent in service and servitude, learning to be superser-
> viceable, being at the service of others, being serviced. We are a service
> industry, serving husbands, lovers, bosses, children, aged parents, families,
> colleagues. Few of us ever escape this entirely.
>
> —Patricia Duncker

While most human beings, myself included, would not want to escape the
opportunity to serve others—after all, human connection usually deepens
emotional, creative, political, and intellectual development—in the academic
world, an insidious and invisible economy of service has for years exhausted
the energies of women, with women of color being particularly pressed into
service roles. In some instances, this silent economy has cost women their
health, jobs, and professional advancement, and it has tragically prevented
many from expressing their creative, intellectual, and leadership abilities.

The fact is, as the Modern Language Association's Committee on the
Status of Women in the Profession (CSWP) (2000) argued in "Women in
the Profession, 2000," the identification of women with a profession, such
as English, does not translate into gender or racial parity (193). Such status reports support what many women and ethnic-racial minorities already
know from their everyday professional lives. The 2000 CSWP report quotes
a National Endowment for the Humanities (NEH) survey from 1995: "[I]n
English, the largest group of white men were full professors; the largest
group of men of color were associate professors; the largest group of women
of color were assistant professors; and the largest group of white women
were instructors or adjuncts" (Committee 2000, 201). Despite a handful of

female academic stars (whose exceptional prominence is evoked as evidence that women have stormed the academy), in every category of professional life—from salaries to working conditions to promotion—women's status in the profession has not changed that much since the first CSWP report was compiled and published in *PMLA* in 1971. Women and racial/ethnic minorities continue to be overrepresented among tenured faculty in two-year, women's, and non-research/teaching colleges, while these same groups are underrepresented among tenured faculty in elite research institutions and resource-rich public universities (Messer-Davidow 2002; Valian 2004, 1998; Wilson 2004).[1] In short, as Florence Howe noted in 1971, women are more likely to be located in less prestigious jobs, in lower ranks, and in part-time positions (in Messer-Davidow 2002, 17). The neat trajectory of talented women armed with doctorates moving from graduate programs into prestigious, tenured academic positions in the profession has not materialized.

It is crucial for progressive scholars to think about these patterns and trends from a structural and policy perspective. Marc Bousquet (2004), in a 2004 Modern Language Association presentation on the impact of the global economy on the discipline of English, analyzed the political economy of U.S. academic capitalism. Bousquet identified the higher-education system as a site of un-, under-, and semi-regulated employment, an arrangement that makes the university ripe for exploitative labor practices. For example, undergraduate student labor is routinely made invisible under the guise of "service learning." Bousquet cited a list of well-known exploitative culprits: first, the decrease of full-time, tenured-track positions and the increase of part-time and non-tenure-track faculty positions, a policy that has doubled, and, in some cases, tripled workloads for all full-time faculty, at all ranks, compared to the workloads of full-time faculty twenty to thirty years ago; second, the inaction of multiple constituencies—including leaders at prestigious universities—to adequately address the job crisis facing graduate students; third, the refusal of many university and college administrations to support faculty research, and yet the increased expectations for publication and conference attendance in order to receive tenure and promotion, even at institutions labeled "teaching" or "non-research"; and, finally, the anti-family policies that create a second shift for many faculty with daily family responsibilities. These practices are unfortunately familiar, but, as Bousquet underscored, they are particularly harsh on women. In other words, no one, from undergraduate student to endowed professor, is completely spared the effects of downsizing and exploitative, unregulated employment practices. Furthermore, Bousquet shows, "women faculty are the least shielded by this exploitative situation."

In general, the silent economy of gendered service has not garnered much analysis in progressive criticism on the university, even though service is a significant feature of the unregulated economy of academic capitalism. Just as undergraduate student labor is hidden under the mantle of "service learning," and graduate student labor is made invisible under the rubric of "training," much of full-time academic women's labor is occluded by the strategically vague category called "service." And yet, as Michelle Massé (2004) argued in a 2004 MLA talk, "Over Ten Million Served," service is rarely theorized as a key component of the university's political economy, even in progressive, cultural studies of higher education. Cary Nelson's work on academic capitalism, for example, never discusses service, even though omitting the discussion of service is clearly to the university's benefit. In frustration, Massé asks why this form of labor is not acknowledged by administrators, faculty, and scholars—with the exception of a few scholars, who have explored the issue.[1]

Theorizing service reveals an unregulated economy that coexists—and even maintains—a formal, "official" economy, much like women's unrecognized domestic labor props up the formal, official economies of countries throughout the globe. It also exposes how a silent economy of gendered service in the discipline of English has become particularly intense due to decades of systematic conversion of full-time, tenure-track positions to part-time positions, a practice that has led to lower salaries, unattractive jobs, and the "white male flight" from the profession (Committee 2000). For instance, although there are fewer full-time professors to join committees and work closely with students, the paperwork related to service projects and advising has not decreased (Massé 2004). In fact, with the infusion of feminist studies and diversity projects into university programming and course offerings, service work for women faculty has actually increased as administrators pass on this "infusion" work to women's and gender studies faculty (Bird, Litt, and Wang 2004, 194–206). Thus tenure-track and tenured women often take up the slack created by downsized, depleted faculty numbers at the same time they are being asked to improve the climate for women faculty, students, and staff; yet this very work, while immensely meaningful to those who do it, is not counted, acknowledged, or considered prestigious or intellectual. Just as the "care deficit" in a downsized America is being met by the informal care services of women, many of whom are imported from countries ravaged by the imposition of first world structural adjustment programs, the "service" work of higher education is similarly being attended to, in many cases, by women. The silent service economy is a central feature of how the university works.

How the theme of "superserviceable feminism" relates to the unregulated silent economy of service and to the overall gendered labor of the university is also apparent in contemporary theoretical arguments addressing feminism. Feminist texts that chronicle and assess academic feminism today, including *Cool Men and the Second Sex* by Susan Fraiman (2003), *Literature after Feminism* by Rita Felski (2003), and *Disciplining Feminism* by Ellen Messer-Davidow (2002), resonate with the silent economy of service and academic women's status. While none of these authors employs "service" or the gendered labor of the university as a framework for her argument, service is an underlying structure in the creation of theoretical ideas and categories, such as women as emblems of the uncool maternal (Fraiman), the inevitable depoliticization of feminism (Messer-Davidow), and the notion of literary feminism as infusing—or servicing—English departments with an expansive aesthetic (Felski).

Superserviceable feminism is a term that makes visible the various kinds of unacknowledged labor women and feminism perform, in the institutional life of English, in universities overall, and in theoretical arguments. While the CSWP's object of analysis is women's status, Fraiman's, Felski's, and Messer-Davidow's work explores the "status" of academic feminism. Status-of-women-in-the-profession studies rarely function as exemplars of intellectual labor that contribute not only to theoretical arguments on feminism and women's status but to scholarly criticism on the university. This is often the case, even though status studies produce feminist and interdisciplinary knowledge and generate significant insight into the historiography and political economy of the American university. In functioning as a theoretical category, service further operates as a site of unregulated labor, shaping the production and direction of scholarship. Thus there are at least two dimensions comprising superserviceable feminism: the "secret" service labor shaping women's professional lives, and the ways in which ideas about women, gender, and feminism "service" theoretical arguments, including assessments of feminism.

Theorizing Service: The Associate Professor Project

In the downsized service economy of higher education, service in the academy is clearly not the exclusive domain of women. The superserviceable professor is increasingly an expectation for the majority of faculty workers in higher education, regardless of group identity. Formally explicated in Ernest Boyer's 1996 article, "The Scholarship of Engagement," the engaged campus or new service movement seeks to broaden definitions of scholarship, community, and service and has ignited an industry of books, articles, and Web sites devoted to the creation of engaged campuses committed to reviving the university's image as good citizen. But these service-learning courses and university-community "partnerships" are labor-intensive projects largely carried out by women and adjunct faculty. In a 2002 study, Kerry Ann O'Meara found that 90 percent of faculty doing "service scholarship" were women, and 25 percent were identified as racial and ethnic minorities. Meanwhile, faculty members of color and female faculty feel pressed into service labor, and the service ethic that preoccupies many feminist communities and communities of color is cynically tapped and exploited. In other words, not all workers are affected by the service speedup in the same way. Sacrificing one's own intellectual and personal growth for the benefit of others, including the welfare of one's students, colleagues, and institutions, is valuable and meaningful, but it is also particularly expected of women, and the demand is often intensified when racial, ethnic, class, and sexuality dynamics are at play.

Studies on service indicate that women do more service than men, and women at the associate and full professor rank do more service than women at the assistant professor level. According to findings in the "Women in the Profession, 2000" report, in English "the highest rates of service on a scholarly committee were found among full professors (this time women of color at 70%) . . . and the lowest rates of service [were found] among white men at every rank" (Committee 2000, 208–209). In addition, white women at the associate professor rank represented 58 percent of committee members (209). The CSWP became very interested in women's experiences at the associate professor rank after reviewing the 2000 CSWP report, believing that women at this rank are understudied and misunderstood. And although service is not the only issue the CSWP was exploring in relation to the associate professor level, the silent economy of service figured as a central concern of its research focus.

Based on preliminary findings, female associate professors are struggling with increased demands in their professional and personal lives, including the expectation that they mentor junior faculty while also bolstering the efforts of senior (full professor) faculty; engage in more college/university service (both chosen and imposed); and teach and conduct research.[2] At the same time female associate professors experience an increase in workload, they are often encountering an expansion in the demand for unpaid care of family members, such as children, partners, parents, grandparents, and other extended family members. Meanwhile, the requirements for promotion to full professor—albeit sketchy at many institutions—are rooted in the professional and personal experiences of white men whose personal and family lives are often managed by wives. Although there are examples of two-career, same-sex, interracial, transgendered, immigrant, and other forms of relationships and families in colleges and universities, by and large the actual structure and culture of academic work assumes a married, heterosexual male.[3] This model, although it contradicts reality, continues to underscore and affect academic culture, promotional policies and decisions, and academic women's lives.

In addition, the mentoring and institutional resources that are often available to tenure-track female assistant professors tend to evaporate once women reach the associate professor rank. Even at small liberal arts colleges and in regional state university systems, it is customary to shield assistant professors from burdensome service demands and committee work. When I was an assistant professor of English at LaGuardia Community College of the City University of New York, I was assigned a mentor and given opportunities to apply for course reduction that would allow me to join a scholarly writing program as part of my path toward tenure. At research universities, this shielding practice often translates into generous course reductions, research leaves, and fellowships and grants pitched to untenured faculty. However, whatever women's location in the prestige economy of higher education, these supports often vanish once women receive tenure and promotion to associate professor. Instead, women experience an increase in service work that often jeopardizes their candidacy for promotion to full professor. As Bird, Litt, and Wang (2004) contend: "Those who perform service work . . . do so at the risk of losing exchange value in every area of their professional lives" (204).

The CSWP was exploring the existence of a relationship between greater expectations for service at the associate professor rank and a pattern of women spending more time in this rank than men, thus creating a conspicuous gender imbalance at the full professor level. In other words, there is a connection between women being stalled at the associate professor rank and increased demands on women to perform service once they receive tenure and promotion. In the compilation of a Five Question Associate Professor Survey sponsored by the CSWP, one full professor and department chair indicated that the increase in service was the greatest hindrance to women's progressing to full professor.

Karen Lawrence,[5] former CSWP member and former dean of humanities at the University of California, Irvine, and Courtney Santos, Lawrence's research assistant, assembled the responses of participants who completed the Associate Professor Five Question Survey. Respondents included men and women, associate and full professors, and each was asked to answer the same question: "What do you think the five most important questions are that can be asked about the rank of associate professor?" The replies and comments indicate that service is one of many factors involved in women's stalling at the associate professor rank—lack of mentoring; unclear guidelines for promotion; family responsibilities; economic calamities, such as the protracted job market; and heavy teaching loads were also routinely mentioned. But service emerged as a central theme: "Why are female associate minority professors overinvested in service?"; "How are we . . . compensated or rewarded" for our service?; "How many women who are associate professors perform administrative duties, as compared to men, that may prevent them from proceeding to the next rank?"; "I notice that while women make up less than half the faculty at the associate/full rank, they frequently represent two thirds or more of committee members on committees"; "It is obvious that associate professors, particularly women associate professors, are seen as the most likely candidates for departmental administrative jobs that are extremely time consuming"; and "How can women associate professors be spared from being eaten alive by committee work?"

While the respondents' questions indicate an experience of overall gender bias structuring faculty work, the silent economy of service is strikingly audible. In terms of superserviceable feminism, these respondents' questions contribute to the project of theorizing how inequity and the impact of "service" on academic women is a central effect of gendered academic capitalism. These questions also, as I will argue, serve as a fruitful lens for tracing the effects of service on recent scholarship on the status and "uses" of feminism in theoretical arguments.

How Feminism Services Male and Queer Theoretical Texts

Virginia Valian's (2004) research on "gender schemas"—which she defines as deeply ingrained social and psychological suppositions about what it means to be male or female—demonstrates how academic women are consistently underrated, while men are overrated (208). This quiet, ongoing process of undervaluing women rarely erupts into dramatic displays of sexism or gender bias. Instead, it is a subtle course that builds, over time, into a significant advantage for academic men and, unfortunately, a significant disadvantage for academic women. Valian cites a computer simulation study that replicates a "tiny bias in favor of promoting men," which, after several duplications, illustrates how even small amounts of bias "accumulate over time" and create advantages for men (211). Relating gender schemas to the silent economy of service, it becomes clear that women who perform service will be more disadvantaged by this work—since it is gendered female—than men who perform service.

A similar argument about a small scale of bias that occurs repeatedly and builds into a damaging devaluation of women and feminism emerges in Susan Fraiman's (2003) book *Cool Men and the Second Sex*. Fraiman meticulously discerns the practice of subdued bias in the structure and design of theoretical arguments produced by academic stars—those prominent male scholars and queer theorists who populate the pages of mainstream newspapers and scholarly journals, hold prestigious academic posts, and project an aura of coolness, both in their personas and scholarly writing. Similar to Valian's study, Fraiman identifies an underground realm of assumed ideologies about women's intellectual and social inferiority. Fraiman (2003) bluntly asserts, "Much of this discourse is secretly and sometimes quite frankly in love with masculinity" (123).

Fraiman's *Cool Men and the Second Sex* unwittingly works in tandem with the project of theorizing service, illuminating the ways in which women, femininity, emotionality, the maternal, and feminism "service" the advancement of scholarly arguments. In other words, small "textual effects" of bias in male scholarship accumulate to disadvantage women, mothers, and feminism: "What I mean to protest are cumulative textual effects, unexamined and incongruous patterns of sexism just beneath the surface of works purporting to be oppositional (and sometimes feminist)" (2003, xix). In the work of academic stars such as Andrew Ross, Edward Said, and Henry Louis Gates Jr., and in the canon of queer theory, exemplified by Judith Halberstam, Judith Butler, Lee Edelman, and Eve Kosofsky Sedgwick, repression and stasis are coded female as a way to advance the idea that defiance, boldness, creativity, and rebelliousness are working class, anti-corporate, hip, and masculine. A pronounced "preoccupation with masculinity" structures these scholars' arguments, even while they evoke feminism. In this way, arguments that articulate solidarity with women and feminism on one level also mitigate—and in some cases, undermine—solidarity by quietly overrating that which is male and masculine and devaluing that which is female and feminine. A recurring focus in male and queer texts is the motif of a "pejorative maternal" and the tokenization of women and feminism, rhetorical strategies that these well-received and influential texts depend on to create their arguments (Fraiman 2003, 137).

In addition, by focusing on the logic of "coolness," Fraiman suggests that the academic celebrity system rewards style over substance. Men's boldness, even when what they are saying is not truly innovative or politically or theoretically coherent, is rewarded. Because of ingrained habits of gender, we continue to overvalue a bad-boy, masculine, rebellious style rather than reward the substance of a female scholar's arguments. Once again, Valian's research resonates in Fraiman's (2003) observations: "Speaking confidently, for example, is not the same as having something to say. We need to distinguish between someone who expresses a good point tentatively and someone who expresses a bad point confidently, listen to the former more than the latter, and reward the former more than the latter" (214). Although not intended, Fraiman's study captures connections between the silent economy of service and how women and feminism service "cool" male and queer theory scholarship. Emblems of various negative categories such as imperialism and conservative, unattractive conventionality, women, femininity, and the maternal function as the negative ground against which male and queer texts rebel. Fraiman's observations raise important questions about the instrumentality of caricatured visions of women, the maternal, and feminism in Left, progressive cultural studies. In a sense, Fraiman's *Cool Men* approximates the CSWP's theorizing on gender and women's status, because she focuses on how feminist perspectives—in particular, distortions of feminist studies—bolster male and queer texts, just as women often perform the support services that make intellectual work possible for those doing research.

In her final chapter, Fraiman offers her radical vision of social relations that she would like to see imagined and promoted in Left cultural criticism: representations of mothers who engage in sodomy; queer teenagers who thrive instead of commit suicide; and sentimentality that is viewed as liberating instead of restricting. Her creative and thoughtful reading of Leslie Feinberg's *Stone Butch Blues*, for example, develops a model of masculinity that is not, upon closer inspection, about the superiority of masculinity. Fraiman presents Feinberg's character, Jess, as a paradigm for cultural and queer scholars: "I count on the term 'butch' to keep 'the maternal' from being reenshrined as simply domestic, emotional, self-sacrificing, asexual, and necessarily biological" (Fraiman 2003, 147). Fraiman offers Feinberg's Jess as a model for honoring nurturing while resisting oppressive heterosexual domestic femininity.

The character, Jess, is an attractive role model for academic women, because in academic women's lives normative femininity and the maternal are also underlying assumptions linked to the expectation of women's unpaid labor. Not only is service not perceived as intellectual, it is often framed as a labor of love, akin to the work women do for their children, rather than as work for which one should be paid and acknowledged. As Bird, Litt, and Wang (2004) argue:

> Service work currently has no formal reward. Some might argue that service deserves no formal reward because the people who do this work find the satisfaction they receive from doing it reward enough (just as mothering deserves no compensation because women do it "for love"). The satisfaction one receives from the work she or he does, however, is not a reasonable barometer for determining the level of formal rewards (or penalties) for different types of work. Faculty who enjoy work on collaborative research projects or grant proposals also enjoy their work. That they enjoy the work is not why they are being paid for doing it. (203)

Service, like the maternal, is actually a multidimensional and economically layered category. In Patrice DiQuinzio's (1999) *The Impossibility of Motherhood: Feminism, Individualism, and the Problem of Mothering*, she captures the complexity of what motherhood means in a culture that has, historically, constructed this category through discourses of biological sentimentality. Thus until emotion and the maternal are the province of masculinity in the same way they are assumed to be the province of women and femininity, these categories will remain problematic for women. Fraiman convincingly argues that second-wave feminism, a powerful body of intellectual and political work, has not been fully incorporated into cultural studies, critical theory, or U.S. society. She suggests that perhaps cultural studies and queer theory would expand in new directions if the topics of chosen motherhood and expansive emotionality became central theoretical issues. In the meantime, they are often cynically used in the silent economy of service.

How Feminist Studies Services the Discipline

The last sentence of Rita Felski's (2003) assessment of feminist literary criticism, *Literature after Feminism*, elegantly sums up the point of her entire book: "Literature after feminism is an expanded field, not a diminished one" (169). Capaciousness, expansion, new horizons, breakthroughs, innovations—these words are repeatedly associated with what Felski convincingly identifies as the best features of the sprawling, conflicted, contentious, ongoing, creative field called feminist literary scholarship. Unlike Fraiman's assessment, Felski's argument demonstrates how nuanced feminist literary criticism opens up the study of literature—on a large scale, with its own superstars and canonical texts. Rendering stodgy, new critical interpretive practices as rigid and obsolete and overly ideological criticism as grim and narrow, feminist literary criticism creates opportunities for authors and readers to experiment with new literary forms and clarify important human values. In short, the best feminist literary criticism has revolutionized the curriculum of higher education. In this way, Felski's book stands out because it offers the most optimistic interpretation of the state of academic feminism.

Likewise, recent discussions on the gendered labor of the university and the silent economy of service also attend to the "positive" features of feminism's superserviceability. According to Bird, Litt, and Wang (2004), "Ironically, women and minority faculty often find a much needed alternative space within gendered organizations by doing service work because it enables them to connect with each other in mutually beneficial ways" (200–201). Similarly, in "The Politics of Feminist Locations: A Materialist Analysis of Women's Studies," Catherine Orr and Diane Lichtenstein (2004) explain how women's studies is often conflated with "service," but that in some institutions—such as theirs, Beloit College—this collapse is helpful: "[I]n our location, this work is legitimate and valued; indeed, service is indispensable to a tenure case at our college" (7). Service work for academic feminists entails curriculum transformation, innovative programming, and the raising of political awareness; it also can offer opportunities for lifelong friendship and community; in some instances, service is even a professional privilege linked to advancement and recognition. These equally important aspects of service rest alongside the exploitative dimensions I have been identifying, creating a complex and contradictory understanding of service.

For instance, Orr and Lichtenstein (2004) later complicate their own argument about service's value with the realization that, given the structure of work and rewards in academia, they may have been "overly optimistic about the long-term implications of the service work we have been doing" (12). The service work they and other women at their college have been engaged in has led to their being "dubbed by some faculty as the dean's 'fembots,' " characterizing academic women's service work as plodding, unthinking (12). However valuable in the day-to-day life of the average female academic, service work has not revolutionized a theoretical field or the academic workplace. As Bird, Litt and Wang (2004) argue, service has no exchange value. Until the kind of exalted praise that Felski lavishes on feminist literary studies is also formally lavished on service, there remains a disconnect between working conditions and economic issues confronting many female members of the discipline and feminist scholarship such as Felski's.

The impetus for Felski's study was the onslaught of continued attacks on feminist literary studies in higher education by conservative critics. In countering these attacks, Felski highlights the remarkable achievements of feminist literary criticism but also tries to "sort out," as she puts it, the weaker feminist arguments from the stronger. Feminist literary criticism that reduces art to ideology is too narrow and one-dimensional, while criticism that captures the interplay of literary expression and the social world allows for more generous interpretations of both literature and the social world.[6] However, while feminism as a theory and political movement clearly led to the creation of feminist literary studies, their depiction in Felski's text is ambivalent and sometimes unnecessarily disapproving. Similarly, in Felski's assessment of the field, there is little sense of English departments and university campuses as political locations. In fact, in Felski's view, political urgency is located outside the United States.[7]

Yet feminism's impact on academic women's working lives is a topic that has captured the imagination of some well-known feminist literary figures, such as Carolyn Heilbrun. In contrast, Felski (2003) refers only once to the "day-to-day work of feminist scholars" in her book (3). Indeed, her book keeps the politics of the profession and the working lives of women separate from the study of feminist literary criticism (3). This is probably because Felski makes a clear distinction between extraliterary feminist writing and activism and feminist literary studies. In other words, the importance of the daily inequities in the lives of academic women is not Felski's focus, nor should it be, but it is stunning how her argument implies that nonliterary feminist writing and activism should not have much impact on feminist literary criticism. Nevertheless, the category of service as a theoretical lens makes visible a striking contradiction in Felski's book: feminist literary criticism has achieved more prominence than actual academic women. According to an MLA survey, feminist criticism has been more influential than any other form of contemporary scholarship, yet by all recent accounts, the power and influence of most academic women are negligible.

How Feminism Services the Academic System

While Ellen Messer-Davidow's (2002) book *Disciplining Feminism* displays considerable awareness about women's past and recent status in academia, her study holds a different focus: "[H]ow did it happen that a bold venture launched thirty years ago to transform academic and social institutions was itself transformed by them?" (1).[8] Drawing from the work of Michel Foucault and other theorists, Messer-Davidow answers this question by proposing that when feminist activism became intertwined with feminist studies—that is, the moment it became institutionalized in higher education—this was also the moment that feminist studies became "formatted." Feminist insurgent insights and practices were permanently altered by the force and will of academic institutionalization. Once feminism was "disciplined," it lost its rebellious impulse and became disconnected from social change skills, knowledge, and activism. As a result, feminist studies is more successful than the feminist movement, and the word "activist" is more damaging to one's feminist credentials than the word "academic."

One reviewer has argued, however, that Messer-Davidow overstates the disciplining of feminist studies, which results in an insufficient account of the forcefulness, expansiveness, and activism associated with teaching women's studies courses, as well as courses in race, class, sexuality, and gender. Dorothy Helly (2002) writes, "I have no quarrel with [Messer-Davidow's] activist agenda, but it seems to me that she needs to acknowledge that teaching an increasingly inclusive curriculum is a form of activism" (317). In my view, the omission of a more in-depth exploration of the impact of a feminist-inspired curriculum on higher education suggests how Messer-Davidow's argument might itself be "formatted" by her own totalizing framework, one that privileges scholarship and 1960s-style activism to teaching. While the far-reaching influence of the silent economy of service and its impact on academic women's lives is potent, I believe that academic theorizing about this issue is important, and that such theorizing can lead to change—although perhaps in less dramatic ways than we would like. In other words, while we are "formatted" by institutions, institutions can also be "formatted" by us. Helly points out, "Universities may still marginalize feminist programs in their budgets, but they can no longer ignore these programs intellectually" (317).

An equally important argument, while not directly mentioning Messer-Davidow's book, appears in the article by Orr and Lichtenstein (2004), "The Politics of Feminist Locations." Orr and Lichtenstein challenge scholars like Messer-Davidow to develop more awareness of how their own institutional locations affect the kinds of assessments they produce.[9] The authors argue that location is neither neutral nor inconsequential, and that it affects the production of perceptions, theories, and assessments of the field.[10] Feminists located in resource-rich institutions may be unwittingly reproducing their own particular struggles and locations as if these represent the entire field. Orr and Lichtenstein encourage scholars and teachers to question what kinds of insights and knowledge are being left out of recent assessment discourses due to their framing by scholars at similar locations. For example, the debate about whether to label programs women's or gender studies may assume completely different forms and require different kinds of dialogue depending on the institutional location. But because the spokespeople for the discipline are routinely located at similar kinds of institutions, with similar kinds of resources (time to conduct research and write; space; and money), their assessments of the field, while powerful and important, are limited. Institutions that are less focused on research and do not operate within the prestige economy of higher education may actually "have a unique perspective on the discipline" (Orr and Lichtenstein 2004, 4). In these locations, alternative kinds of knowledge and activism may take unusual forms, but such experiments and occurrences are likely to remain unknown if assessments are only published by spokespersons at doctoral-granting institutions.

In a recent interview in the *National Women's Studies Association Journal*, Messer-Davidow qualifies her thesis and explains that she is aware of the material politics of location; she says that women's and gender studies programs at resource-rich institutions, not struggling programs with few resources, are the ones that need to organize social-change collaborations with community-based organizations. Prestigious research universities should take the lead and institute concrete, accessible ways to share the insights and frameworks of feminist knowledge with organizations and individuals committed to equitable public policy and democratic social change. I find this an encouraging insight, but it is not one that appears in her book.

Reading Messer-Davidow's case about the disciplining effects of the academy on rebellious projects such as feminism, I experienced a groundswell of conflicting reactions. *Disciplining Feminism* is a passionate book that takes seriously the politics of disciplines and higher education. The author asks all of us to consider how—or even if—our knowledge-production projects are serving a democratic society committed to resistant social justice. But in her final chapter on the drop in minority applications to colleges and universities, a direct result of the systematic dismantling of affirmative action and the defunding of public education, she evokes a hopeful image of higher education, one that contrasts with the grim "disciplined" world that dominates her study. For instance, she characterizes higher education as "the gateway to employment opportunity, upward economic mobility, and citizen participation" (273). How can she believe in this utopian vision and then say we will all presumably succumb to the institution's disciplinary effects? Helly (2002) provides one answer: "We can agree with Messer-Davidow that there is much to do, that we need to do it right now, and that feminism has to continue to struggle against being 'disciplined' in the traditional exclusionary practices of the academy, but I contend that we have not yet lost that struggle" (318).

Conclusion: Making Superserviceable Feminism Visible

Mogan Spurlock's 2004 film *Super Size Me* exposes how the fast-food marketing and sales concept of "supersize" reflects a systematic effort to increase profit at the expense of people's health; similarly, *superserviceable feminism* is a term that I hope captures the multiple effects—including the positive and the physical—of the silent economy of service on women and on academic feminism.[11] Superserviceable feminism not only illuminates the expectation that women, because they are women, will serve their institutions, departments, programs, peers, students, and so on, but that feminist studies will similarly serve in a multitude of ways as well. Fraiman argues that women, feminism, the maternal, and femininity "serve" progressive, Left, male, or male-identified theoretical arguments by functioning as the Other, as that which male or male-identified arguments resist, renounce, or reject. Felski argues that feminist studies has infused the field with a capacious approach to literature rather than the equally prevalent, though in her view, self-righteous, overly ideological approach. And Messer-Davidow argues that once feminism is inevitably "disciplined," it brilliantly services institutions—by opening up cross-dialogue and new specialisms—but at the expense of its original impulse for social change.

In all of these texts, feminism's service component is its generative function: its potential illumination of political blind spots in progressive criticism; its aesthetic appreciation of women's literature and art; and its infectious political insurgency. However, this fruitfulness is also its downfall, because feminism is itself a form of gendered service, and women's status in the university is still much lower than men's. In women's and gender studies, as Orr and Lichtenstein (2004) point out, the entire field is misunderstood as "service work," so that women in these programs have additional burdens to negotiate. This can also be said of other forms of innovative scholarship. Linh Hua (2003) observes how "black scholarship is thus made invisible by being rendered a service rather than intellectual production worthy of tenure" (13). A response to this paradigm is that formal assessments of feminist studies, literary studies, and critical theory should consider the materiality of the scholar's institutional location and the power of teaching. Again, such a suggestion does not mean assessments produced from the perspectives of scholars located in doctoral-granting research universities are invalid, but that they are incomplete—although they often do not know they are "incomplete," and they do not function as "incomplete."

The need to pay attention to the politics of location is intimately linked to the overall gender and class politics of the silent economy of service. As Michelle Massé has argued, faculty contracts and workload documents should spell out—or, as she puts it, "unbundle"—the tasks related to the amorphous category of service. At my own institution, a private, Catholic, women's university serving largely first-generation, working-class students, I collaborated with a faculty senate committee on inserting service as a category in the official workload document filled out each year by faculty. We asked that faculty on more than one committee be given the opportunity to negotiate between one to six hours of released time a year for committee work. At such an institution, with heavy teaching and service expectations, making service a part of the official workload document could provide some relief. This effort could be one small step toward undermining the tradition of seeing service as "natural," or "just the way things are."

Another suggestion would be to follow the CSWP's lead by seeing "status of women" studies as knowledge production rather than as "get-ahead" schemes devised by privileged women. Women's service becomes a theoretical lens with political implications in the same way that tenure, contingent labor, and the crisis in graduate education are key words for cultural studies and Marxist scholars. The CSWP status reports should be widely disseminated so that deans, provosts, tenure and promotion committees, chairpersons, and the like can begin to "denaturalize" service. In addition to appointing high-level administrators to the CSWP, I recommend appointing men too. In the early years of the CSWP, men were members of the "commission," as it was then called. In my view, contributions from well-connected men in high-prestige English and language departments, as well as men in less prestigious regional, state, and two-year colleges, would augment the CSWP's knowledge production on gender and service.

Finally, I believe the CSWP's studies should be published in *PMLA* instead of *Profession*—the first CSWP reports were published in *PMLA* and *College English* in 197—or *Profession* and *PMLA* should explore cross-dialogue. Scholarship and the institutional politics of the profession are not theoretically or materially separated. Such a change of venue might challenge the false divide between "real scholarship" and cultural analyses of the material conditions of the profession. We need to take seriously the idea of "service," not as silent and unregulated labor but as a nexus of fundamental issues involving gender, class, labor, and the politics of the profession. Most important, we need to change the way we conceive and reward it.Notes

A version of this essay was published in the winter 2005 issue of the *minnesota review*. Originally inspired by the author's 2003–2006 term on the MLA Committee on the Status of Women in the Profession, the essay includes a discussion of that committee's Associate Professor Project.

Notes

1. As Virginia Valian (2004) points out, "Top-tier institutions in particular do not want to hire people from lower-tier institutions. Since women are overrepresented at lower-tier institutions, that reluctance reinforces the status quo" (217).

2. Some examples include, but are not limited to, Dale Bauer (2004), "Academic Housework: Women's Studies and Second Shifting"; Bird et al. (2004), "Creating Status of Women Reports: Institutional Housekeeping as 'Women's Work'"; and Virginia Valian (2004), "Beyond Gender Schemas: Improving the Advancement of Women in Academia."

3. The CSWP's research on the Associate Professor Project has resulted in an Annotated Bibliography, a Funding Proposal to the MLA Executive Council, a Five Questions Survey, and a Pilot Questionnaire.

4. For instance, see Mary Ann Mason and Marc Goulden's (2002) "Do Babies Matter? The Effect of Family Formation on the Lifelong Careers of Academic Men and Women," 21–27. The article recommends "a very different look at the linear career clock that has persisted, almost unchanged, in the face of a radical demographic shift." Also, according to the CSWP's (Committee 2000) "Women in the Profession, 2000," "in both English and foreign languages white men have been significantly more likely to be married or partnered and to have children than any of the other groups under discussion, and least likely to be divorced. Insofar as they outnumber all the other groups, white men also set the dominant pattern for the profession" (211).

5. Karen Lawrence is the president of Sarah Lawrence College in New York State.

6. I am in complete agreement with Felski (2003) that social change, while intimately tied up with women's writing, criticism, and reading, should not result in a fixed, sledgehammer approach to criticism or art. An overly ideological approach to literature, argues Felski, stifles one's ability to experience feelings uniquely stimulated by reading literature. Luckily, "Feminist scholarship, while keeping a firm grip on critical analysis, has clearly overcome its fear of feeling" (56). But what about political feelings, which can also be stimulated by reading literature? What kinds of feelings are acceptable to express when reading literature?

7. Political urgency is constructed in Felski's (2003) text as both outside the United States and as absent from "the study or the seminar room": "And yet it is

also the case that writing from the Third World does sometimes retain an urgency of purpose that it has lost elsewhere. Surely there is a vital role for what is often disparaged as propagandistic art, for writing that sacrifices subtlety for the burning clarity of conviction. In times of extremity, the need to end suffering may simply override all other concerns. Complexity and intricacy, Timothy Brennan reminds us, are much loved by literary intellectuals; their merits are far less obvious to those whose natural habitat is not the study or the seminar room" (162). Based on my research on the gendered economy of service, my experience as a member of the CSWP, and my experiences in academia, I would suggest that political urgency can sometimes erupt in the academy, including in the study and the seminar room.

8. The contradiction between feminist criticism's powerful influence on the study of literature and the still-shaky status of actual academic women is not explicitly addressed in *Disciplining Feminism*. As a former member of the MLA Committee on the Status of Women in the Profession, however, Messer-Davidow (2002) includes in her book important historical accounts of the CSWP's initial creation and the changes it has wrought in the discipline and the MLA.

9. In her opening chapter, Messer-Davidow (2002) locates the impetus of her study in the context of trying to escape her horrendous marriage only to encounter versions of it in the courts, the police, and in the everyday social customs of the 1960s. But the location, as well as the material conditions under which her study is constructed, is a major public research university.

10. Virginia Valian (2004) also argues for the importance of location in analysis and evaluation, particularly when reviewing women's applications for faculty positions: "Institutions could . . . use the knowledge that location creates productivity as much as or more than productivity creates location and use an additional search strategy: identify women who are publishing more than is typical for their locations" (217).

11. I would like to thank Jeff Williams for suggesting the connection between superserviceable feminism and Spurlock's *Super Size Me*.

Works Cited

Bauer, Dale. 2004. "Academic Housework: Women's Studies and Second Shifting." In *Women's Studies on Its Own*, ed. Robyn Wiegman, 245–57. Durham, NC, and London: Duke University Press.

Bird, Sharon, Jacquelyn Litt, and Yong Wang. 2004. "Creating Status of Women Reports: Institutional Housekeeping as 'Women's Work.'" In *NWSAJournal* 16:1:1: 94–206.

Bousquet, Marc. 2004. "The Twenty-Five Year Plan." Reforming the Ph.D. MLA Convention. Marriott Hotel, Philadelphia, Pennsylvania, December.

Boyer, Ernest L. 1996. "The Scholarship of Engagement." *Journal of Public Service and Outreach* 1:1: 1–20.

Committee on the Status of Women in the Profession. 2000. "Women in the Profession, 2000." In *Profession* 2000. New York: MLA, 191–217.

Committee on the Status of Women in the Profession. 2003. Associate Professors, Five Question Survey. Unpublished Survey.

DiQuinzio, Patrice. 1999. *The Impossibility of Motherhood: Feminism, Individualism, and the Problem of Mothering*. New York and London: Routledge.

Duncker, Patricia. 1999. "Post-Gender: Jurassic Feminism Meets Queer Theory" In *Post-Theory: New Directions in Criticism*, ed. Martin McQuillan, Graeme Macdonald, Robin Purves, and Stephen Thomson, 51–62. Edinburgh: Edinburgh University Press.

Felski, Rita. 2003. *Literature after Feminism*. Chicago, IL, and London: University of Chicago Press.

Fraiman, Susan. 2003. *Cool Men and the Second Sex*. New York: Columbia University Press.

Helly, Dorothy O. 2002. Rev. of *Disciplining Feminism: From Social Activism to Academic Discourse,* by Ellen Messer-Davidow. *Women's Studies Quarterly* n.s. 3–4.

Hua, Linh. 2003. Committee on the Status of Women in the Profession. Associate Professors Annotated Bibliography. Unpublished Bibliography.

Mason, Mary Ann, and Marc Goulden. 2002. "Do Babies Matter? The Effect of Family Formation on the Lifelong Careers of Academic Men and Women." *Academe: Bulletin of the American Association of University Professors* 88:6 (November–December).

Massé, Michelle. 2004. "Over Ten Million Served: Service and Activism at Mid-Career." Committee on the Status of Women in the Profession. MLA Convention. Marriott Hotel, Philadelphia, Pennsylvania.

Messer-Davidow, Ellen. 2002. *Disciplining Feminism: From Social Activism to Academic Discourse*. Durham, NC, and London: Duke University Press.

Messer-Davidow, Ellen. 2004. "Women's Studies and Activism: An Interview with Ellen Messer-Davidow." Ed. Brenda Daly. *NWSA Journal* 16:2: 1–17.

O'Meara, Kerry Ann. 2002. "Uncovering the Values in Faculty Evaluation of Service as Scholarship." *Review of Higher Education* 26: 57–80.

Orr, Catherine M., and Diane Lichtenstein. 2004. "The Politics of Feminist Locations: A Materialist Analysis of Women's Studies." *NWSA Journal* 16:3: 1–14.

Valian, Virginia. 1998. *Why So Slow? The Advancement of Women*. Cambridge: MIT Press.

Valian, Virginia. 2004. "Beyond Gender Schemas: Improving the Advancement of Women in Academia." *NWSA Journal* 16:1: 207–20.

Wilson, Robin. 2004. "Where the Elite Teach, It's Still a Man's World." *The Chronicle of Higher Education*. http://www.chronicle.com/free/v51/i15/15a00801.htm.

4

The Invisible Work of the Not-Quite-Administrator, or, Superserviceable Rhetoric and Composition

Donna Strickland

I had accepted a position as an assistant professor . . . after earning my PhD in rhetoric and composition. . . . What I didn't realize until years later . . . was that from the first day in my new job I was an unofficial associate director of composition.

—Mara Holt, "On Coming to Voice"

In her important 2002 essay, "More Than a Feeling: Disappointment and WPA Work," Laura Micciche suggests that writing program administration offers a telling case study of the dilemmas faced by faculty in the current entrepreneurial university. Hired to provide leadership, on the one hand, but frequently positioned without resources or authority, on the other, writing program administrators (WPAs) all too often find themselves caught in a debilitating paradox:

> Invested with the ostensible authority to design curriculum, hire and fire writing instructors, and serve on influential university committees, the WPA seems to occupy a powerful location. . . . [H]owever . . . the WPA's authority and power are challenged, belittled, and seriously compromised nearly every step of the way—a fact compounded by the steady number of WPA positions advertised at the assistant professor level.[1]

By highlighting the continued hiring of junior faculty as WPAs as one way that the authority of the position is compromised, Micciche also reveals a stark reality that faces new PhDs specializing in rhetoric and composition: many of them will be asked to take on administrative work right out of graduate school. And the administrative work may be very overwhelming indeed. Diana George recounts her own near-miss encounter with what Katie Hogan has called "superserviceable" expectations when interviewing for a position at a large state university:

> They needed someone who could direct the first-year composition program, train teaching assistants, teach undergraduate writing courses and graduate courses in rhetoric, administer the technical writing courses, correct problems in the writing center, design and run a new writing across the curriculum program that had yet to be funded or approved, create and administer an outcomes assessment exam that had been mandated by a faculty senate not at all sold on writing across the curriculum, *and, I found myself thinking, coach the volleyball team?*"[2]

As I have argued elsewhere, this alignment with managerial duties distinguishes specialists in rhetoric and composition from most other assistant professors in English departments.[3] What I want to argue here is that even when not hired as administrators, specialists in rhetoric and composition are nonetheless affectively *aligned* with these duties.[4] Even when not asked to take on an administrative title before tenure, assistant professors can see administrative work looming on the horizon. In preparation for that inevitability, rhet/comp assistant professors may find themselves performing service work that amounts to administration. Mara Holt, for example, in a soul-baring essay, recounts the professional toll taken by the "invisible WPA work" that she was asked to do as an "unofficial associate director of composition":

> Within a week of my move . . . , I was teaching the TA training course, a five-credit hour theory/practice course with a hefty set of responsibilities. After that, I was on rotation, teaching the course every other year. This means that for half the TAs at any given time, I was a teaching advisor, often attempting to explain and justify policies that I had had no voice in creating. The WPA, who also held the WAC position, had me do workshops for campus-wide and regional campus faculty, supervise a faculty mentoring program for TAs, select textbooks, revise the curriculum, defend the writing program, and fulfill a relentless series of other tasks, a situation no doubt familiar to many untenured rhetoric/composition faculty members.[5]

Holt, in other words, was asked to carry out a host of administrative duties *while wearing no official administrative hat.* While Holt did manage to get tenure despite this heavy load of not-quite-administrative service, she found herself "exhausted," with "a kind of deadness" toward her scholarship at the end of six years. She had gained tenure, but she felt that the burden of her local service work had deprived her of a professional presence.

The "good job market" in rhet/comp, which Marc Bousquet (2004) critically examines in his introduction to the collection *Tenured Bosses and Disposable Teachers*, does not in fact guarantee that the "boss" will be tenured, nor that the "boss" will be rewarded for the work she or he does. The unacceptable working conditions for most non-tenure-track faculty who teach composition is one consequence of the managed university, a consequence that both Bousquet and I (along with others, most notably Eileen Schell) have worked to expose and transform. Another consequence, however, one that has received scant attention outside of journals and books directed at WPAs, is the negative consequence that the expectation of administrative work may have on the careers of faculty in rhetoric and composition, especially assistant professors and women.

In this chapter, I want to give voice to my fellow faculty in rhetoric and composition, especially those without tenure who are routinely expected to perform service that often goes unremarked. I argue that rhetoric and composition professionals, by virtue of their association with a service course (first year composition) and to a certain kind of administrative service (directing writing programs), inhabit a "superserviceable" position in departments of English, and that this position poses unique problems for assistant professors in the field. Katie Hogan recently introduced the term *superserviceable* to describe the heavy service expectations faced by women faculty in the academy. The term seems appropriate as well for rhetoric and composition faculty, especially given that the vast majority of specialists in the field are women. Although the numbers that Theresa Enos provides in her book are outdated, they are nonetheless telling: in the period 1987–1988, "70 percent of all job candidates holding degrees in rhetoric and composition were female."[6] Moreover, extending Micciche's claim that "our profession inculcates affective positions," I maintain that what Eileen Schell has called a "femininist" ethic of care also dominates work in rhetoric and composition and helps perpetuate the invisibility of the not-quite-administrator of composition's service work.[7]

Like Hogan, however, I am not trying to denigrate service nor to cast aspersions on my fellow rhetoric and composition faculty who find themselves consumed by it. Neither of us "would want to 'escape' the opportunity to serve others—after all, human connection usually deepens intellectual, creative, political, and emotional development," yet "an insidious and invisible economy of service has for years exhausted the energies of women."[8] Hogan

notes that female associate professors, in particular, often find themselves
exhausted by service, with their research stagnating. In rhetoric and composition, a field dominated by women, however, that exhaustion may come
on long before tenure.

Are You Directing the Program?

Over fifteen years ago, Charles Schuster made a cogent point that I often
repeat: "No department I know of would hire a beginning assistant professor
of literature to chair the department. . . . Yet these same departments choose
freshly minted PhDs to direct writing centers and composition programs."[9] In
recounting his own experience of being denied tenure in 1984 after serving
as the WPA at a large research university, Schuster writes that his former
dean asked, "If we granted Charles Schuster tenure, what would he do in the
English department once he no longer directed the composition program?
What in the world *could* he do?"[10] To be in rhetoric and composition, at
least in 1984, was to be wedded to a writing program. Once a person was
no longer attached to the program, the person lost all value.

While things have surely changed in the more than twenty years since
Schuster was denied tenure, including the visibility and continued expansion of PhD programs in rhetoric and composition, the identification of
rhet/comp faculty with writing programs has not. It may be less popular to
hire new PhDs as writing program directors, but it still certainly happens,
as the recently published *Untenured Faculty as Writing Program Administrators: Institutional Practices and Politics* (see Dew and Horning 2007) makes
clear. Early on in two of my tenure-track jobs, literature colleagues wondered
aloud what kind of administrative work "they" were giving me. When I
told them, more or less accurately, that I wasn't currently doing any administrative work, they seemed surprised. More recently, a colleague at a party
asked me how directing the program was going, even though I wasn't (nor
had I been) directing. Apparently, it isn't clear what I do if I'm not doing
administrative work.

So while it may look as if departments are now more often hiring
"assistant professors in rhetoric and composition as colleagues and specialists, not as administrators and not as temporary staff members," as Schuster
called for in 1991, the inevitability of administrative work tends to loop
back and color their experiences all the same.[11] Even in departments where
the junior compositionist may be forbidden to do administrative work, that
same faculty member may be expected or feel compelled to do service for
the writing program, service that may not be rewarded insofar as it is almost
a-consciously considered part of one's job as a compositionist.

My first job out of graduate school, for example, had me developing a computer-assisted writing program from scratch (by which I mean: no infrastructure, no precedent, and no funding). The institution was a small private comprehensive university that employed only one other specialist in rhetoric and composition, while hiring numerous adjunct faculty to teach writing. The presence of the tenured rhet/comp faculty member, however, helped me believe I would be spared administrative work. Schuster tells job candidates in rhetoric and composition to "go where a senior colleague will protect you."[12] I thought I was doing that: I thought that I was avoiding early administrative work by going where a tenured faculty member was leading the composition program.

However, although the job ad merely mentioned the need for some expertise in technology, when I was offered the job it became clear to me that I was expected to create a program. The person who hired me indicated that a dedicated computer classroom for English was in the works, but no such space materialized. When that same person wondered mid-year why the program was taking off so slowly, I pointed to the lack of computers. Besides having no dedicated classroom for computer-assisted English courses, the non-tenure-track faculty who taught many of the first-year writing courses had no reliable access to updated computers in their own offices. In an effort to be able to do the job I found myself expected to do, I spent many hours researching computer-assisted programs at peer institutions and writing pro- posals for funding. To be fair, I had been given one course release during my first semester to give me time to build the program, but I still had courses to teach, including an upper-level course I had never taught before.

But my contributions didn't stop there: within the first few weeks of my first semester, I had been tapped by the dean to be on a committee dealing with technology, and by the end of the year the dean of academic affairs had asked me to serve on an electronic portfolio committee (in exchange, I was promised money for a laptop computer classroom). Although I had never promoted myself in my CV or in interviews as a "technology" expert, I was expected to play that role. It bothered me that my actual research (on the economic history of the field and on labor conditions in writing programs) was ignored, and that I was being interpellated into a completely new profes- sional identity, connected to the kind of service I was being asked to do.

In addition to working to find ways to introduce technology into composition courses without any resources during that first year, and in addition to the other four committees (at the departmental, college, and university levels) I served on, I also collaborated with the director of writ- ing to address the needs of the largely non-tenure-track faculty who taught first-year writing. I attended and led sessions at a pre-semester workshop for non-tenure-track faculty before the year began and continued to serve on the Composition Committee throughout the year. And the Composition Committee had volatile issues to deal with, as a proposed salary increase for non-tenure-track faculty was denied by upper administration. In the middle of my second semester, the director of writing was removed from her position after taking a strong stand against the administration's decision. I was expected to take over her duties the following year. I began furiously to try to define the position in such a way that it wouldn't mean the end of my research. That meant more investigation and more proposal writing, pulling together information on WPA duties at other institutions. My department chair was sympathetic to my plight, but need I explain why I became desperate to leave before my second year began?

At the time, I assumed the "problem" came from being at a smaller school. The English Department consisted of about fifteen tenured and tenure-line faculty (compared to thirty to fifty when I moved to larger schools), so I believed that the reason I found myself being asked to take on a heavy service and administrative load had to do with the size of the department and the institution itself, which certainly cultivated an ethic of service among faculty. When I moved to a research university, then, I hoped and believed its larger size and research mission would save me from so much service. And, in a sense, it did: I was on only one departmental committee in my first year of my second tenure-track job. Even so, I happily helped out with the pre-semester workshop for graduate teaching assistants before the first semester began. And, before I knew it, I had an invitation from the provost's office to join a Communication across the Curriculum committee. Based on my experience of feeling obliged to take on committee work in my previous job, I panicked. I feared I would be asked to direct this leaderless program, just as I had been expected to serve as the director of composition before. Luckily, I trusted my chair and asked him if, in fact, I had reason to be afraid. He thought not, and so I joined the committee.

But a couple of years later, under a new chair, I found myself serving as the interim director of the department's writing program. Despite the fact that I was the only junior rhet/comp faculty member in a department that employed five tenured rhet/comp faculty, none of them was approached to serve. No one, moreover, officially asked *me* to take on this role. Rather, it was assumed that I would do it. To some extent, the assumption made a kind of sense. Even before I began serving as interim director of the program, I was steeped in service work connected to it. I regularly taught the course for new graduate student teaching assistants. I taught it out of a great desire to teach it, but, like the first-year composition course itself, this course is considered a service course. Both first-year composition and the course in composition teaching are required courses and so serve to prepare students for a range of future activities (writing or teaching in other disciplines).

Even if the assumption that I would move into the position of interim director made a kind of sense, I felt, all the same, taken for granted. It had simply been expected. And so there I was, an untenured assistant professor, directing a composition program as our faculty union (of which I was an active member) threatened to go on strike. Graduate teaching assistants in my department were told to report for duty or otherwise account for themselves in the case of a strike. Worried, many of them came to me to ask what they should do. It was not the most comfortable position I've ever found myself in.

For various reasons, not the least of which was yet another abrupt removal of a director of writing, I decided to leave that position too. When an associate dean at my new institution—a flagship state research university—wondered why I hadn't yet finished my book, I explained that I had a heavy service load at my former university. He assured me that wouldn't be the case in my new position.

And yet . . .

At my new institution, I found myself tapped to represent my field on one standing departmental committee. I also willingly joined the Composition Committee, since I was hired with the understanding that I would in the near future be asked to direct the program. So I prepared myself, serving on various subcommittees, including one to revise the curriculum of the first-year course. I again regularly taught the service course for new graduate teaching assistants. I worked with the composition staff to mentor and supervise teachers of composition. I met regularly with the acting director of composition to keep me informed of reports from the chair and dean. Together we developed a plan to help keep the leadership of the composition program more stable.

And yet, gentle reader, that was not administrative work. I was granted a one-course release for some of my work with the composition staff. But most semesters, it has been simply service work that I did on my own time. Moreover, because much of it is difficult to account for and quantify (how to list "e-mailed worried graduate student" or "planned with interim director" on my CV?), much of it goes unnoticed, undocumented. And even if I could document it, it would count little toward my tenure case. As one (tenured) colleague told me, "No one cares about service. They just want to know that you've done some."

All the same, I must admit that part of me *wanted* to do this work, even as I recognized that it was taking up a great deal of my time and that it wouldn't help me gain tenure (and might even distract me from what would). I had been rather well prepared to take on a good bit of quasi-administrative work even before I took my first job. While completing my PhD with a specialization in rhetoric and composition, I served two years as a writing-across-the-curriculum consultant and another two years as a course director (and a year as something like a Writing Center director, although both my duties and my pay were unclear). These experiences were enriching, providing me with broad knowledge of academic writing and administrative procedures. They also made me a very popular candidate when I fully entered the job market, in my sixth year of doctoral work. (Despite the course releases, it could be that all that "administrivia" slowed me down a bit.) After all, I found myself meeting with faculty across campus, addressing other instructors' students' complaints. It was indeed excellent experience. But it also inculcated in me an undeniable *feeling* that going above and beyond teaching and research was part of my job as a rhetoric and composition specialist, whether I was tenured or not. I was affectively linked to the service of rhetoric and composition.

Service, Administration, and Intellectual Work

As my narrative suggests, service and administrative work are closely allied with and for rhetoric and composition faculty. The required first-year composition course, at most institutions, services all departments. All students, no matter their major, take the course. Writing-across-the-curriculum programs, too, by their very nature, are service-driven. Writing centers, which also need directors, typically serve the entire university. And even at the graduate level, the required course in the teaching of composition services all students in English (or, at a few institutions, inside and outside of English). In fact, unless a person is doing graduate work in rhetoric and composition, or possibly undergraduate work at a smaller school, it would be unusual to interact with a faculty member in rhetoric and composition outside of the context of service.[13] It's little wonder, then, that faculty outside of the field associate rhetoric and composition faculty with service, even if they are not conscious of making that association.

Recognizing how little service work tends to be rewarded in the academy, the Council of Writing Program Administrators, a professional association founded in 1976, has sought to redefine WPA work as primarily intellectual. Theresa Enos, a former president of this organization, notes that in her survey of WPAs, "71 percent said that their administrative work (*in the form of service only*) did count."[14] While she seems pleased that the majority of respondents were rewarded for their administrative work, her italics indicate dismay that WPA work is associated with service alone.

To work to counter this association, the WPA Council has developed a position statement on "Evaluating the Intellectual Work of Writing Administration." The purpose of this statement is to make WPA work visible and quantifiable, on par with teaching and research: "By refiguring writing administration as scholarly and intellectual work, we argue that it is worthy of tenure and promotion when it advances and enacts disciplinary knowledge within the field of Rhetoric and Composition." It notes that service is "a category distinguished by its lack of clear definition," and that both research and teaching tend to be defined with "detailed subcategories" such as those "under 'Research' (books, articles, chapters, reviews, presentations, and grants) and 'Teaching' (student evaluations, supervisory reports, curriculum development, presentations and publications)." Drawing from the MLA Commission on Professional Service's 1996 report, "Making Faculty Work Visible: Reinterpreting Professional Service, Teaching, and Research in the Fields of Language and Literature," along with Ernest Boyer's 1990 *Scholarship Reconsidered*, the WPA document offers guidelines for understanding writing administration "as a form of inquiry which advances knowledge and which has formalized outcomes that are subject to peer review and disciplinary evaluation." The document also defines five categories of intellectual work: program-related textual production, program creation, curricular design, faculty development, and program assessment.

As a not-quite-administrator while completing my graduate work and subsequently in a series of three assistant professor positions, I have been involved in all five kinds of work. The problem, for non-quite-administrators like Mara Holt, myself, and countless others, is that we have no title to begin with. So while we may be developing programs, revising curricula, and working with writing instructors both in and outside classrooms, we have no official title to validate this work. This intellectually rich work will be relegated to what the WPA document calls the "ill-defined and seldom-rewarded category of 'service.'"

So while I concur with the belief that writing program administration is intellectual work, work that requires research, planning, and writing if done well, my own experience has led me to question what is left invisible if administrative work is elevated above service work. And my conclusion is that what is left invisible is all the service work done by those composition specialists who are not officially administrators.

Don't get me wrong: I'm not hung up on titles. And even the compensation that I might get as the official WPA isn't so appealing that I'm desperate for it. What does seem curious, as I've previously suggested, is that as a specialist in rhetoric and composition, I seem to be addicted to doing service work, work that will benefit the composition program and teachers within the program. At the same time, as a specialist in rhetoric and composition, I seem to be *expected* to be involved in some sort of administrative work. The situation seems classically dysfunctional: I want to do service that may harm me, and my employers seem to want me to do it. They may not wish me harm, but they seem unaware of the service expectations that come my way.

It's true that my experience as a not-quite-administrator has led to a good bit of success in the job market (I recognize that I am fortunate to have found three tenure-track positions in succession) and some knowledge of university hierarchies (it isn't every assistant professor who has worked directly with deans and provosts). At the same time, I can't shake the feeling I have that my experience as an "assistant professor of English" is different from many of my cohorts' and that that difference is also hard to generalize. Something is always calling, even if it isn't rhet/comp related. Because of my status as a rhet/comp professional, I get called on to do extra service too. Rhet/comp, like feminism, is superserviceable in the academy.

As I argued earlier, this superserviceability stems in part from the affiliation with what is commonly considered a "service" course, making my very presence in the academy seem fully service oriented. Some rhetoric and composition scholars, most notably John Trimbur, have argued that the first-year writing course should be an introduction to "writing studies," an introductory course akin to a survey of literature. Doing so, some argue, would remove first-year writing from the service expectation of effectively preparing students for all writing they will do in college (an impossible task, given the diversity of writing conventions across the curriculum and even within English departments). Even if I might endorse such a view, however, that hardly changes the current reality that for most faculty in the university, including faculty in English, the required first-year course in composition is understood to be a service course. Indeed, when scanning English department Web sites, I've noticed that first-year composition is often not even listed as an undergraduate course in English (even when upper-division courses in writing may be). It is programmatically and affectively separate from the rest of English. It services.

Anyone who identifies herself (or, in fewer cases, himself) with rhetoric and composition, then, immediately takes on an affective affiliation with service, even if that person is not involved in the administration of the composition program. It's as if a PhD in rhetoric and composition identifies a person as a good service worker. Otherwise, what would explain the reason I was asked to join committees at a rate unlike any other new faculty member in my first job (unless it might be a colleague in history, one of the very few African American women faculty in the whole institution)? In short, I argue that making the case for the intellectual work of writing program administration, while an important step, does not go far enough. Even when not doing administrative work, faculty in rhetoric and composition, like women faculty more generally, are superserviceable. The problem faced by rhetoric and composition faculty, then, is a problem they share with all women faculty.

The Quandary of Caring

It should come as no surprise that a field so strongly identified with service as rhetoric and composition is also dominated by women, as are the feminist fields of women's and gender studies. Hogan, borrowing from the work of Catherine Orr and Diane Lichtenstein, among others, notes that "women's studies is often conflated with 'service.'" As I have been arguing, a similar conflation occurs with rhetoric and composition.[15]

Hogan (2005) goes on to call the association between women and service a "silent economy of gendered service," one that "has not garnered much analysis in progressive criticism on the university, even though service is a significant feature of the unregulated economy of academic capitalism." She continues:

> Just as undergraduate student labor under academic capitalism is hidden under the mantle of "service learning" and graduate student labor is made invisible under the rubric of "training," much of full-time academic women's labor is occluded by the strategically vague category called "service."

In fact, missing the "significant feature" of service is to miss part of the reason that many rhetoric and composition scholars were defensive in response to Marc Bousquet's critique of the managerialism in the field.[16] Writing program administrators *already* feel overburdened with service. To be accused of complicity with academic capitalism seems like too much to bear.

As a rhetoric and composition scholar, however, I tend to resist the defensive reflex. Moreover, my own work has offered an assessment of the field that similarly exposes the managerial imperative. All the same, I can understand the defensiveness, particularly as a woman who has performed a great deal of not-quite-administrative service but has never felt empowered as a "boss." Enos suggests that women in the field of rhetoric and composition have in fact more often been called upon to do "service" rather than to lead programs:

> What came out in the survey and narratives was that within rhet/comp programs, male faculty tend to hold the "real" positions with the "real" titles while women faculty tend to handle the many details of day-to-day committee work and the nitty-gritty work with students that does *not* get recognized because it is less organized, less associated with a "position." More than any other topic, administrative responsibilities elicited more stories about the heavy burden that "comes with the job in composition," and the disciplinary and gender bias that operates within English

departments and writing programs because of writing program ("service") work.[17]

In fact, even when tenured women hold the official position of director, they may continue to find themselves "servicing" their institutions. This situation is described vividly in Alice Gillam's "Collaboration, Ethics, and the Emotional Labor of WPAs." Gillam recounts her realization that she had become more of a caretaking "minister" of a writing program than the "kind of masculine [agent] described by Ed White in 'Use It or Lose It: Power and the WPA': aggressive and decisive . . . [with] tough talk, and strategic, preemptive moves."[18] In taking over a program with a writing proficiency requirement (demonstrated through testing or portfolio), Gillam states:

> My role was primarily that of caretaker, the "minister" of proficiency, in the sense that the OED defines *minister* as "one who acts under the authority of another, who carries out executive duties as the agent or representative of another." After all, I was appointed not to make policy but to manage and "care for" an already-formulated policy, one deeply imbricated in the local cultural ideal of certifiable writing proficiency for all. I was acting under its authority and executing my duties through its agency.[19]

As a caretaker, Gillam is motivated by what Eileen Schell (borrowing from Elizabeth Flynn) has identified as a "femininist" ethic of care. According to Schell, early feminist approaches to writing pedagogy advocated "maternal thinking" and called for an "ethic of care" that would strive for "a nonhierarchical and noncompetitive classroom."[20] Schell argues that an ethic of care makes "it difficult for feminists in composition to address gender inequities in academic work," including the inequities associated with non-tenure-track faculty. An ethic of care may reinforce feminine gender socialization, "in which women work hard but appropriate few professional rewards for themselves."[21]

As Gillam found, the costs of caring exact a price from all faculty associated with first-year writing, from the mostly non-tenured faculty who teach it to the tenured faculty who supervise their work. Drawing from Sandra Bartky's phenomenological epistemology, Gillam describes the emotional toll her care took on her as a kind of "epistemic and ethical 'lean,'" in which she took on the perspective of those above her and had difficulty finding her own stance toward the program she was charged with directing.[22] Gillam concludes that her caretaking left her with no place to stand, so that she had difficulty seeing the real problems with the program she found herself defending: "Caretaking of even noble principles," she explains, "can be blinding and can work against self-critique."[23] And although she does not draw the connection between service work and the caretaking she felt compelled to do, she does offer an excellent anecdote that speaks to the work's invisibility. At a meeting to plan orientation for new freshman, after the program she had been hired to defend had been dismantled, a recruitment director approached her to say, "I hope you will think this is funny but when I told someone who all was coming to this meeting and I mentioned your name, he said, 'Oh, I heard she died.' "[24]

Conclusion

Women should not have to die, literally or figuratively, in service to writing programs or to any other institutional work. In fact, Gillam, in an earlier essay on administration, makes this plea:

> [I]t is crucial that we talk about the convergence of our personal and professional lives and that we redefine our work in a way that does not exclude or denigrate the personal. For our own sakes and for the sake of those who follow us, we must insist not only on professionally acceptable terms of employment but also on a concept of professional work that does not require us to sacrifice our personal lives, our personal relationships, and our health.[25]

Service hinges on our personal affective commitments, commitments that we may be shy to examine in public, or that may lie too closely to our sense of ourselves. For over twenty years, writing program administrators have been talking about their work in isolation. It's time that they talk to all faculty in rhetoric and composition, all women faculty, all superserviceable faculty. This book provides a context in which to talk. Beyond this, we need to join together for action.

Notes

1. See Micciche 2002, 434.
2. See George 1999, 23, emphasis in original.
3. See Strickland 2004.
4. Here I use *affect* in the Deleuzian sense of potential to act, as explained by Brian Massumi (1987, xvi): "*L'affect* . . . is an ability to affect and be affected. It is a prepersonal intensity corresponding to the passage from one experiential state of the body to another and implying an augmentation or diminution of the body's capacity to act." Rhetoric and composition professionals carry the potential to move into administration, a potential that is not personal to them yet affects their actions.
5. See Holt 1999, 28.

6. See Enos 1996, 9.

7. See Micciche 2002, 434.

8. See Hogan 2005.

9. See Schuster 1991, 94.

10. Ibid., 89, emphasis in original.

11. Ibid.

12. Ibid., 94.

13. In fact, I recently met a graduate student in literature whose undergraduate advisor at a prominent liberal arts college happens to be a nationally known scholar in rhetoric and composition. This scholar has been president of professional organizations in rhetoric and composition and has won national awards. The student had no idea. To the student, the person was simply an advisor.

14. See Enos 1996, 72, emphasis in original.

15. Hogan (2005) adds that in some institutions—"such as [Orr's and Lichtenstein's], Beloit College—this collapse is helpful," given that a successful tenure case at their college depends upon the successful demonstration of service work. I suspect that the case may be the same for some rhetoric and composition faculty at certain institutions. My own experience, as I've mentioned, is limited to small comprehensive and large research universities.

16. See, for instance, Grabill et al. 2003; Harris 2002; and the archives of the WPA-L.

17. See Enos 1996, 66.

18. See Gillam 2003, 116.

19. Ibid., 116–17, emphasis in original.

20. See Schell 1998, 77.

21. Ibid., 88.

22. See Gillam 2003, 113.

23. Ibid., 119.

24. Ibid., 120.

25. See Gillam 1999, 71.

Works Cited

Bousquet, Marc. 2004. "Introduction: Does a 'Good Job Market in Composition' Help Composition Labor?" In *Tenured Bosses and Disposable Teachers: Writing Instruction in the Managed University*, ed. Marc Bousquet, Tony Scott, and Leo Parascondola, 1–10. Carbondale: Southern Illinois University Press.

Council of Writing Program Administrators. 1998. "Evaluating the Intellectual Work of Writing Administration." October 17, 2007. http://www.wpacouncil.org/positions/intellectualwork.html.

Dew, Debra Frank, and Alice Horning, eds. 2007. *Untenured Faculty as Writing Program Administrators: Institutional Practices and Politics*. West Lafayette, IN: Parlor.

Enos, Theresa. 1996. *Gender Roles and Faculty Lives in Rhetoric and Composition*. Carbondale: Southern Illinois University Press.

George, Diana, ed. 1999. *Kitchen Cooks, Plate Twirlers, & Troubadours: Writing Program Administrators Tell Their Stories*. Portsmouth, NH: Boynton/Cook.

Gillam, Alice. 1999. "Taking It Personally: Redefining the Role and Work of the WPA." In *Kitchen Cooks, Plate Twirlers, & Troubadours: Writing Program Administrators Tell Their Stories*, ed. Diana George, 65–72. Portsmouth, NH: Boynton/Cook.

Gillam, Alice. 2003. "Collaboration, Ethics, and the Emotional Labor of WPAs." In *A Way to Move: Rhetorics of Emotion and Composition Studies*, ed. Dale Jacobs and Laura R. Micciche, 113–23. Portsmouth, NH: Boynton/Cook.

Grabill, Jeffrey T., James E. Porter, Stuart Blythe, and Libby Miles. 2003. "Institutional Critique Revisited." *Works and Days* 41/42: 21: 119–237.

Harris, Joseph. 2002. "Behind Blue Eyes: A Response to Marc Bousquet." *JAC* 22: 891–99.

Hogan, Katie. 2005. "Superserviceable Feminism." *minnesota review* 63/64 (Winter): http://www.theminnesotareview.org/journal/ns6364/iae_ns6364_superservice-ablefeminism.shtml (accessed June 22, 2007).

Holt, Mara. 1999. "On Coming to Voice." In *Kitchen Cooks . . .*, ed. Diana George, 26–43. Portsmouth, NH: Boynton/Cook.

Massumi, Brian. 1987. Notes on the Translation and Acknowledgments. In *A Thousand Plateaus: Capitalism and Schizophrenia*, ed. Gilles Deleuze and Félix Guattari, xvi–xix. Minneapolis: University of Minnesota Press.

Micciche, Laura R. 2002. "More Than a Feeling: Disappointment and WPA Work." *College English* 64: 432–58.

Schell, Eileen E. 1998. "The Costs of Caring: 'Feminism' and Contingent Women Workers in Composition Studies." In *Feminism and Composition Studies: In Other Words*, ed. Susan C. Jarratt and Lynn Worsham, 74–93. New York: MLA.

Schuster, Charles I. 1991. "The Politics of Promotion." In *The Politics of Writing Instruction: Postsecondary*, ed. Richard Bullock and John Trimbur, 85–95. Portsmouth, NH: Boynton/Cook.

Strickland, Donna. 2004. "The Managerial Unconscious of Composition Studies." In *Tenured Bosses, Disposable Teachers: Writing Instruction in the Managed University*, ed. Marc Bousquet, Tony Scott, and Leo Parascondola, 46–56. Carbondale: Southern Illinois University Press.

5

Foreign Language Program Direction

Reflections on Workload, Service, and Feminization of the Profession

Colleen Ryan–Scheutz

For many faculty members, days are long and the appointments, deadlines, and responsibilities are many. In most cases, distinctions among activities involving research, teaching, and service are quite clear. Different, however, is the reality of the language program director (LPD), whose innumerable duties frequently blur the distinctions between the three categories. Several of these duties are not only hard to categorize, but they also require personality traits or professional abilities that go unspoken or unwritten, but are nonetheless beneficial to the position. These invisible aspects of the job comprise unique, important, and relatively unexplored dimensions of the LPD's role, particularly for those who have never occupied it.

While the invisible dimension incorporates and influences different aspects of the LPD's research and teaching, many of its key tasks remain difficult to categorize in terms of academic workload, and many even exceed normal expectations for program, departmental, or university-level service. How can we better define the concepts of service versus administration in the case of foreign language program directors? What kind of professional and personal profiles can we attribute to these roles? Is the LPD position gendered in some way? If yes, then what are the costs, alternatives, and benefits of this reality? When everything is spelled out in terms of quantity and diversity of responsibilities, language program direction demands the research and teaching abilities and willing disposition vis-à-vis service that all academics must demonstrate. In addition, it involves a sizable and challenging administrative component as well as great variation and frequent shifts in task within each of these professional categories. Furthermore, whether filled by a man or a woman, the LPD role is quite possibly a feminized one. This means the position has taken on qualities more often associated with women, which constitutes a problem and needs our attention.

Background

Over the past twenty years, several issues and challenges have come to light. Among the most prominent are those regarding status, qualifications, and workload. There have been calls not only to recognize the business of LPDs as "academic," but also to hire them with the same research expectations as for literature or linguistics faculty, because by lightening their research load, one risks reducing the regard that administrators and faculty might have for the colleague and his contribution.[1] There have also been calls to recognize the advantages of hiring an applied linguist in this role, as opposed to methodologists, historical linguists, literature faculty, and so on.[2] For Katz and Watzinger-Tharp (2005), the applied linguist's research agenda informs teaching methods and curriculum design in ways that can have a positive impact on the quality of language teaching in general. And while some scholars strive to articulate the quantity and quality of a methodologist's or director's work in a consciousness-raising fashion (Guthrie 2001; Sadow 1989; Teschner 1987), others go so far as to suggest that the LPD should be considered the equivalent of a deputy chair (Harris-Schenz 1993; Huber 1994).

In 2005, Renate Schulz published the results of a nationwide survey called "The Role of Basic Language Program Director: Result of a Survey," which explored several aspects of advertised job descriptions and real-life LPD roles. Schulz used the information provided by 99 (of 218) respondents across several languages to compile and discuss an important set of data about the position. One of the most interesting facts was that 75 percent of all 116 LPD respondents in 2002 were women. Her study revealed also that 90 percent of the 99 surveys included in her data analysis held a PhD, and that 72 percent of PhD holders specialized in applied linguistics or associated fields such as foreign language pedagogy and educational technology. This means that 28 percent of the PhD holders (approximately twenty-five individuals) specialized in literature, cultural studies, or fields other than linguistics.

Schulz's study also disclosed that although 79 percent of all respondents claimed to be satisfied with the support of their department chairs, 69 percent perceived their workload to be higher than that of the other faculty members in the department. Finally, among many other interesting facts, Schulz discovered that almost half (46%) of LPDs were junior faculty with one to five years of experience, and that another 25 percent were junior faculty with six to ten years of experience, indicating that the majority of directors had a pretenure or prepromotion status with regular research and publication expectations.[3] Consequently, Schulz concludes that workload is a continuing problem, since it continues to increase rather than decrease. Even job descriptions in the MLA List indicate that "[...]departments are becoming more demanding with regard to the LPD's background, expertise, and responsibilities."[4]

Schulz's main recommendations include the establishment of: (1) professional organizations that define the position, develop models, and make recommendations about workload and (2) high-ranking members of institutions and departments that mentor, support, and raise awareness about the contributions of the LPD to the department.[5] In her view, many colleagues are still uninformed about the need to fully integrate or the steps required to fully integrate LPD colleagues in the intellectual life of the department.[6] Equally persistent is the problem of perception. Though not directly measured, it seems LPDs are often considered administrators of inferior scholarly status.[7] According to Schulz, it appears that "the LPD's position has become the catchall for all those duties required by the university administration that other faculty members find tedious or do not wish to perform."[8]

Guthrie confronts the subjects of both perception and isolation by suggesting the LPD be a key player in establishing an integrated curriculum, "where intellectual content is included from the beginning and language development continues through all levels." This "calls into question the LPD's role as administrator of a service program and suggests ways in which the LPD can fruitfully contribute to the department beyond the language program."[9] The problem, as Guthrie sees it, is that the LPD's responsibilities are "overwhelmingly administrative,"[10] to the extent that an LPD might not be considered a faculty member involved in "developing intellectually coherent programs from the beginning courses through the completion of the major."[11] "When an LPD is to be hired," Guthrie says, "departments have the opportunity to reflect on their curricular vision, the language program's place in it, their expectations of the LPD, and their commitment to supporting the intellectual and professional growth that is crucial to an LPD's effectiveness."[12]

Along with Guthrie, several other scholars emphasize the importance of the LPD's research. For example, Lee and Van Patten claim that language program direction is an *academic* matter and maintain that decreasing research expectations is the same as decreasing the seriousness and/or prestige of the role.[13] For this reason, they suggest a three-year plan for slowly integrating the LPD scholar into the program. This plan includes the systematic delegation of secondary duties to qualified TAs and clerical staff to increase time and energy for research.[14]

LaFollette Miller agrees that the LPDs' many tasks can easily distract him from research and makes the case for the "sustained creation of meaningful scholarship."[15] At most institutions, faculty who do not publish "will, in the long run, be at a disadvantage in comparison with their more productive counterparts."[16] According to LaFollette Miller, published research not only represents a priority for academics seeking promotion, but also job satisfaction. Furthermore, "If we want to challenge our students to reach their highest intellectual potential," she says, "we should serve as role models, engaged in the process of constant intellectual growth ourselves."[17]

So where does this leave the language program director in terms of workload and the general direction of the profession? Since Schulz's survey showed that 75 percent of LPDs in and around 2002 were women, it might be interesting to consider the language program director role in light of the MLA's report on "Women in the Profession, 2000." In brief, the MLA study suggests that English and foreign language departments have begun to lose earning power and prestige because of an increase in the proportion of women in these fields and an increase in part-time faculty. As a result, salaries remain low, and research productivity can be affected: "Women working in so-called feminized areas may experience discrimination from within their fields as well as from outside them. When women who are trying to manage multiple roles are also faced with low salaries, finding the time and energy to maintain a research agenda can become extremely difficult."[18]

Workload and Service for the LPD

Having acknowledged the LPD's innumerable responsibilities and the importance of maintaining a research agenda that is on a par with those of literary colleagues, we now turn our attention to the notions of academic workload and service to articulate the issues of quantity, quality, and interrelatedness that characterize these concepts for the LPD.

The portion of workload designated as "service" can be a very slippery slope for LPDs, because so many of their duties lie outside of the realm of official scholarship and classroom teaching, while they are also intricately connected to it. On the subject of workload theory and practice, Howard Mancing looks at service in the academy, stating that it falls into the two main categories of "institutional" and "professional." "Institutional service includes administrative duties, committee work, and student advising," while professional service "usually refers to work done in support of one's academic discipline" and involves serving on committees for professional organizations, organizing or chairing conference sessions, refereeing or editing for journals, and so on.[19] Balancing these activities alongside teaching and research requires "frequent and substantial mental shifts," which can, in turn, "produce frustration and inefficiency."[20] However, in the case of the LPD, such frustration, and, in particular, inefficiency cannot factor into the job—at least not openly and visibly. The "frequent and substantial mental shifts" are thus to be expected and accepted, because directorship, much like departmental chairpersonship, requires it.

The similarities between language program directorship and departmental chairpersonship, says Harris Schenz, make the LPD position unique. Since both figures must interact with and address the needs and concerns of such a variety of people—undergraduates, graduates, faculty, staff, deans, and administrator—they are "high-visibility" figures both within the department and beyond. Yet no matter how comparable the two positions may be, "a large gulf exists between them not only in such day-to-day matters as the staff support they receive (e.g., photocopying, typing, filing) but also in the less tangible issue of departmental and institutional support and recognition for the work they do."[21]

Returning to the specific portion of academic workload called "service," the question of what constitutes service can vary among institutions, departments, and even languages within a department. At its best, it is unclear. The following section outlines some common responsibilities of the LPD to demonstrate how many are ill defined with respect to the traditional categories of teaching, research, and service and, thus, how the value attributed to them may be either reduced or nonexistent.

TA Training and Professional Development

If LPDs receive a course reduction or summer salary for planning and conducting new teacher orientation each August, then this major responsibility can count toward teaching. If not, then it constitutes a ten-to-fifty-hour, highly concentrated service commitment. And if weekly meetings throughout each term for TAs and faculty teaching multisection courses count as teaching practicum hours, then they fold into the teaching workload. If not, then the weekly meetings comprise a multihour service commitment for the creation of quality teaching and assessment materials.

If conducting classroom observations, writing reports, and holding follow-up meetings is an extension of teacher training, then it might belong to "teaching." If not, then these activities constitute more hours of service—anywhere between two and 100, depending on the size of the program and how much help assistant coordinators might give.[22] On the average, the LPD spends two to three hours per instructor observation each semester.

Course Supervision

Drawing up a teaching schedule that accommodates the needs (wishes, conflicts, etc.) of all instructors (ranging from five to fifty or more people) counts neither as teaching nor research because it is administrative work. But for lack of a fully established "administrative" workload category for faculty, this time-consuming task falls into the ambiguous category of "extras" or service. Although departments might assign the first steps of scheduling to an administrative assistant (the call for preferences, organization of information received, compilation of a preliminary schedule), only LPDs know the target language proficiency and teaching abilities of each instructor. Ultimately, they must make decisions that will benefit the individual, the working group, and the overall quality of undergraduate education.

Similarly, certain aspects of the organization, creation, revision, copying, and distribution of assessment materials (exams, quizzes, guidelines for oral exams, compositions, portfolios, etc.) for the different courses comprising a four- or six-semester language program can be delegated to assistants in the program and in the office. But LPDs nonetheless participate in each stage behind the scenes, giving their advice and approval on most steps. And if reviewing lesson plans for new instructors and organizing the sharing of written and visual teaching materials for each week is perceived as an extension or integral part of the LPD's teaching, then we can broaden that category further. If not, the gathering, organization, and centralization of pedagogical materials comprise another aspect of service.

Research, Mentorship, Professional Development

Mentoring graduate students who aspire to teaching careers and helping them prepare application materials and teaching dossiers is another important responsibility of the LPD. Is this part of their teaching, or do such advisory hours fall into the category of service? The same question pertains to theses and research. While most professors accept theses and independent study commitments, the LPD is often the only person qualified to guide research in pedagogy and/or linguistics.[23] Furthermore, since the primary field of research of approximately one fourth of LPDs is neither pedagogy nor linguistics, research direction does not necessarily work favorably as an extension or application of their own research. Thus, these collaborative hours become service.

Curriculum Design

Examples of central curricular decisions that LPDs commonly face are where and how to integrate authentic literature into the program (with what materials and methods) and what proficiency levels constitute the "common minimum" versus "aspirational goals" for the end of the foreign language requirement. Admittedly, these questions might be an extension of the LPD's research, but if not, this expertise-based responsibility becomes service. Likewise, hours spent collaborating with university centers for writing, for curriculum development, or for excellence in teaching might benefit the LPD's own research or teaching, but when such work becomes an expectation, with the goal of improving teaching and learning throughout the program, it is more aptly categorized as service. And what about department- or college-wide committees that involve the study of language (redesigning the language resource center, hiring a new director for the center, revamping online placement tests, or creating a department-wide assessment plan)? Does the LPD's leadership or participation in these efforts count for official workload purposes?

Cocurricular Program

A lesser-considered but equally important aspect of language program direction is the conceptualization, organization, and implementation of an engaging cocurricular program, which runs the gamut of clerical work (booking rooms, creating and copying publicity), to volunteer work (purchasing, making food), to community-building efforts (motivating students and faculty to attend). Though it is usually a very satisfying part of the job, how does it fit into the academic workload? The same problem arises for work conducted with overseas studies programs to publicize, encourage participation, and establish official equivalents for course offerings and credits at the home institution.

This list is not intended to be exhaustive, but it does aim to span a vast and diverse range of roles and responsibilities that we cannot neatly categorize as research or teaching. Nor does this list even begin to describe the second category of "external service," which Mancing describes generally as service to the profession. Let it suffice to say that LPDs are usually active members of several national organizations for their language and/or fields of specialization (applied linguistics, supervisors and coordinators, etc.). They also organize and chair conferences, edit and referee for journals, and serve on task forces and advisory councils and review external tenure, accreditation, and assessment committees.[24]

Recommendations

At first glance one might say "just delegate" many of the jobs. As Lee maintains, certain clerical tasks such as reserving rooms, ordering books, and copying and distributing exams may easily be delegated, but most of the aforementioned tasks are curricular decisions with potential for great impact.[25] So it simply makes professional sense that the director attend to these tasks. It is also true that LPDs who are too visibly detached (even if justifiably protective of their research time) or who assume a strictly managerial approach might lose the respect and collaborative spirit of teaching staff and other colleagues. But even in the best-case scenario, in which all willingly meet, constructively discuss, and efficiently agree, the diplomacy skills and background organization work constitute time-consuming forms of service.

Whatever the primary reason for not delegating as much of the workload as possible to others (quality control, not wanting to overburden students or colleagues, not having official staff support for certain jobs), the LPD is ultimately responsible for the results or quantity/quality of the work achieved. Thus even if, in the case of exam creation, the LPD might cut down "service" hours by having a TA proofread and assemble exam sections and by having a staff member photocopy and distribute exams, the LPD must still oversee the different phases of exam creation and ensure that the whole reflects the program's criteria and best practices in teaching and learning. My recommendation, therefore, is twofold: first, distribute all tasks that are indeed appropriate for the staff, and, second, make a concerted effort to build infrastructural support among language-teaching colleagues to create a program directing team that can make informed decisions together. The latter might necessitate making a formal case for funds or other forms of compensation (course release) for those to whom you entrust more course- or program-wide responsibilities.

Another recommendation resonates with Guthrie's, Harris-Schenz's, and Lee and Van Patten's calls for consciousness raising and equity in the department: dialogue regularly with your colleagues, chair, and other appropriate faculty or administrators about workload, and identify and address the inequities between the LPD and literary faculty, particularly those involving service. Beyond addressing issues of equity, efficiency, and job satisfaction for the LPD, bringing LPDs into the mainstream of the department culture will help "to give language programs the centrality they deserve, and thus to raise the overall teaching effectiveness of the departments."[26]

Finally, I strongly recommend creating a fourth professional category that factors into overall workload (that is, in addition to teaching, research, and service): administration." It is high time that we articulate for the LPD the distinction between regular committee service (type of committee work and quantity of committee work assigned to the faculty member on the average) and the seemingly endless executive service responsibilities, which do not fall neatly into the three traditional categories. For purposes of annual review, promotion, and tenure, the LPD (much like the chair) would submit a separate statement on program direction and administration rather than embedding the mention of these invaluable contributions in discussions of teaching and service and, potentially, diminishing the importance of her or his work this way.

The LPD as a Gendered Profession

At first glance there is nothing that seems particularly feminine about the LPD position. All of the aforementioned tasks are not only perfectly achievable but also regularly and successfully accomplished by men. Nevertheless, in addition to Schulz's 2005 finding that the majority of LPDs are women, and in addition to the MLA-stated trend toward feminization (and, consequently, devalorization) in the fields of English and foreign languages, language program directorship strikes me as a distinctly gendered position, regardless of the sex of the person filling it.

We have already seen that many of the LPD's daily or weekly tasks fall into the "secretarial" or "clerical" category, which remains a predominantly female sector. Other responsibilities of the LPD are, I venture to say, maternal. Although many of today's fathers render the patriarchal family framework weak or invalid, there remains something feminine about the program director's role. Let me explain. The LPD who enjoys the respect and willing collaboration of his or her team of teachers is not, generally speaking, merely a supervisor, director, or manager. Even the most efficient and gregarious of managers will be called upon in this work to be empathetic listeners, caretakers, or nurturers in the profession. In addition to the fact that this person truly "keeps house" for a large number of people (reminding them of *their* responsibilities, deadlines, and even dress code), she or he must foster, support, praise, and reprove all in a day's work. So in addition to setting a good example, always thinking with the "group" in mind, tracking the different personalities, talents, and progress of individual teachers in and out of the classroom, and creating a positive work environment so that motivation may rise, the LPD can easily be considered a professional den mother of sorts. Alternatively, the metaphor of sports coach works too—the central figure who must practice what she or he preaches, keep spirits high, and lead the team steadily toward a common goal.

The point I would like to make is that this caretaking function is structurally and functionally built into the job. And because it is generally more acceptable for women to do clerical work and to take interest in the reflective or emotional aspects of colleagues' work experience, this might be a contributing factor. If LPDs are mostly women, then perhaps subtle assumptions about what women are good at actually work toward keeping the LPD's role the multidimensional and multitasking position that it is. In other words, if the majority of LPDs were men, then it would be hard to imagine that greater demands would not be made to change the structure and function of the job—changes that would make the job consonant with the kind of work either that our culture feels men are good at or, at least, consonant with the total workload of faculty in related fields.

Even if some research suggests that there is biological evidence for women's ability to multitask, the purpose of this discussion is not to draw conclusions about gendered behavior or different brain functions in women and men.[27] Each of these paths of analysis is problematic at best. However, what is potentially central to the discussion at hand is the fact that women have "gravitated toward jobs that require multitasking."[28] That is, women often choose professions that require the ability to work with divided attention and/or jobs in which the time, skills, and effort to keep things rolling behind the scenes can easily go unnoticed. Ellen Galinsky, executive director of the Families and Work Institute in New York, calls this work "invisible" and "focused on the process of maintaining relationships." It is work to make work work."[29] But if women are attracted to and/or accepting of this invisible work, then are they not partly responsible for the devaloriziation of their roles in the workplace? And in light of the Profession 2000 findings, would this not indicate a double feminization for the LPD profession?

Conclusion

The multitasking, secretarial, and nurturing responsibilities of most LPDs raise the question of whether this particular aspect of the foreign language academic profession can rightfully be considered "gendered." Given the tendency for the field to be occupied by more women, the trend for these positions to warrant fewer tenure-track slots, and the inclination of chairs and hiring committees to decrease research expectations as a way of recognizing the LPDs service work, the answer is decisively "yes." Without the glorified clerical work, the LPD would be something far more on a par with that of a department or deputy chair. This is how the LPD is asked to function all along, yet without the standard perks and recognition given as a matter of course to a chair in a "nonfeminized" discipline such as philosophy or history.

At the same time, even though the LPD's behind-the-scenes work may escape the attention of many faculty and students, that work can easily "make" or "break" a language program. It is precisely for this reason that the tremendous amount of service and administration work that the LPD undertakes merits greater attention. And it seems that there are two viable and equally respectable ways of conceiving and approaching the complex position. One approach to awareness and equity entails covering the basic supervisory necessities of the program and delegating other tasks to eligible and capable department staff persons. This does not mean that the director completely renounces the quality of the program—all of the characteristics that might invigorate a working group or curriculum. Rather, it means that this person makes a conscious decision to limit his or her hours of administrative and service work to an amount and a kind that is comparable to that performed by other department members of similar rank. The colleague opting for this approach will be selective in undertaking projects and incorporating "extras" and will prioritize the tasks for a given week, month, or semester.

The second approach to awareness and equity calls for reconceptualizing the role of LPD as a hybrid faculty/administration position and is recommended for those involved in building programs, revitalizing curricula, increasing enrollments, or breaking new ground in the profession. This option permits colleagues (and students) to acknowledge and accredit the LPD's creative and entrepreneurial spirit, and it gives demonstrable value to top-quality organization, communication, and collaboration. This formulation openly recognizes the many important crossroads that exist among teaching, research, service, and administration, but it also emphasizes the notion of holistic (year one to four) or integrated (language-literature) curriculum. Moreover, this approach not only prioritizes up-to-date, top-quality education (undergraduate and graduate through the accompanying methods course and teaching practicum) but also fosters an ongoing commitment to professional development. And although this approach ups the ante in terms of "cost," it does so equally in terms of "benefit," as it instills in instructors a self-reflective mode of operation, and the will to follow and expand upon best practices and to partake in a community of engaged and developing teacher-scholars.

Whether a male or female, and whether an applied linguist or literature, educational technology, or contemporary literature expert holds this position, let us not lose sight of the fact that language program directors have a common identity as master teachers and methodologists—practical philosophers, writes Sadow, "who identify problems and concoct solutions that must work for other people."[30] Unlike many departmental peers,

> they must be able to filter their institutions of what might work through a lens of empirically obtained findings. They must be able to absorb material from many different sources and then decide what is possible in any foreign language classroom, not just their own. Moreover, they belong to a field that is international in scope, highly organized, and constantly reassessing itself.[31]

LPDs have a finger on the pulse of department life in almost every sense. They are pivotal figures whose work needs to be valued not only as wholly academic but also as vital to the progress and flow of the most fundamental program components and new initiatives. The LPD's ongoing commitment to reflection, problem solving, and innovation should alone suffice to merit sizable recognition and equitable compensation.

Notes

1. See Lee 1987, 22. See also Katz and Watzinger-Tharp 2005, 490–502; Lalande 1991, 15–18; Lee and Van Patten 1990, 113–28; Teschner 1987, 28–35.

2. See Katz and Watzinger-Tharp 2005, 490. The following numbers are also of interest for our discussion: of 155 surveys, 45 were completed and returned, with a participation rate of 29 percent, with representation from German, French, Spanish, Slavic, Arabic, Chinese, Italian, and multiple languages. Fifteen LPDs (33%) had dissertations in literary fields or in cultural studies and 20 (45%) in applied linguistics, theoretical linguistics, or sociolinguistics. It is important to note that many of the individuals with backgrounds that are not particularly "applied" in nature had shifted to more interdisciplinary research agendas: 79.1 percent reported that their research was linked to pedagogy, or 72.1 percent interdisciplinary in nature. Almost 60 percent were originally hired to be a methodologist, while 21.4 percent moved into that position (p. 494).

3. See Schulz 2005, 33.

4. Ibid., 37.

5. Ibid., 38.

6. See Lalande 1991, 17. "Many departments and colleges have been stung by the experience of having hired faculty members who performed well in their supervisory and coordination responsibilities, yet who, as a result of being overburdened by these duties, failed to realize their potential for research in their linguistic or literary fields of specialization and who were subsequently denied tenure." See also Sadow 1989, 27.

7. See Schulz 2005, 37. See also LeBlanc 1999, 45.

8. See also Schulz 2005, 37; Lee 1987, 22; Harris-Schenz 1993, 49.

9. See Guthrie 2001, 41. "Until departments devise ways for the language program coordinator's knowledge and experience to be shared and appreciated by teachers of upper-level courses, the college curriculum will continue to be profoundly disconnected."

10. Ibid., 44.

11. Ibid. Guthrie provides a comprehensive overview of the activities of the LPD under the following primary categories: "Teaching and Program Direction," "Training and Supervision of Instructors," and "Professional Engagement and Service." Her list, although not exhaustive, raises awareness of the many areas of work and responsibility.

12. Ibid.

13. Lee and Van Patten 1990, 123. The writers use Dvorak's expression the "ivory ghetto" to create the sense of marginalization that the LPD has often experienced. See Dvorak 1986, 217–22.

14. Ibid., 123.

15. See LaFollette Miller 2002, 49.

16. Ibid.

17. Ibid.

18. See "Women in the Profession, 2000. MLA Committee on the Status of Women in the Profession," 2000, 193.

19. Mancing 1991, 32.

20. Ibid.

21. Ibid., 48.

22. A set of ten language faculty would require ten in-class hours for observation, at least a half hour for the preparation of each report, and anywhere from a half to a full hour for follow-up and discussion. It is reasonable to assume that ten observations would require some twenty-five hours of time. In larger programs (generally with ten-plus instructors), the LPD will have assistant directors or coordinators with whom to share such duties. But the question of perception/categorization vis-à-vis the workload pertains to them as well.

23. Often these subjects require more consultation, guidance, and even signatures (preparation of pedagogical materials suitable for classroom experiments, university permissions for human subjects, orchestration of experimental treatments with the regular course syllabi, etc.).

24. See Mancing 1991, 32–33.

25. See Lee 1987, 24.

26. See Harris-Schenz 1993, 48.

27. See Criss 2009. In a study at University of Western Michigan, Criss explored whether women naturally possess multitasking skills (a question of nature), perhaps due to the fact that they possess a wider corpus callosum, or if women acquire these skills through "routine exposure to their environment" (a question of nurture). And in her article, "In Multi-Tasking, Women Take Lead But Men Do It Too," Healy (2006) asks several experts how each of the sexes copes with competing mental demands. Gur responds in general terms, stating that "women cope with multiple demands on their brainpower with greater deliberation, while men respond with faster action."

28. See Healy 2006.

29. Ibid.

30. For a complete description of the methodologist's role, see Sadow 1989, 27–28.

31. Ibid.

Works Cited

Criss, Brandy. 2009. "Gender Differences in Multitasking." Department of Psychology. Missouri Western State University. http://www.clearinghouse.missouriwestern.edu/manuscripts/815.asp.

Dvorak, Trisha R. 1986. "The Ivory Ghetto: The Place of the Language Program Coordinator in a Research Institution." *Hispania* 69: 217–22.

Guthrie, Elizabeth. 2001. "The Language Program Director and the Curriculum: Setting the Stage for Effective Programs." *ADFL* 32:3 (Spring): 41–47.

Hagiwara, Michio P. 1970. "Training and Supervision of Graduate Teaching Assistants." *ADFL* 1:3 (March): 37–50.

Hagiwara, Michio P. 1976. "The Training of Graduate Teaching Assistants: Past, Present, and Future." *ADFL* 7:3 (March): 7–12.

Halpern, David. 2000. *Sex Differences in Cognitive Abilities*. Mahway, NJ: Lawrence Erlbaum Associates.

Harris-Schenz, Beverly. 1990. "Helping with the Bootstraps: The Mentor's Task." *ADFL* 21:3: 18–21.

Harris-Schenz, Beverly. 1993. "Between a Rock and a Hard Place: The Position of the Language Program Coordinator." *ADFL* 24:2 (Winter): 45–50.

Healy, Melissa. 2006. "In Multi-Tasking, Women Take Lead But Men Do It Too." *Los Angeles Times*, July 23.

Huber, Bettina J. 1994. "The Responsibilities of and Compensations for Being a Department Chair: Findings from the MLA's 1989–90 Survey of Foreign Language Programs." *ADFL* 25:3 (Spring): 107–18.

Katz, Stacy, and Johanna Watzinger-Tharp. 2005. "Toward an Understanding of the Role of Applied Linguists in Foreign Language Departments." *The Modern Language Journal* 89:4: 490–502.

LaFollette Miller, Martha. 2002. "A Department Chair's Challenge: Dealing with Impediments to Research." *ADFL* 33:3 (Spring): 47–51.

Lalande, John F. 1991. "Redefinition of the TA Supervisor-Language Program Coordinator Position into the Lecturer Series: A Sensible Idea?" *ADFL* 22:2 (Winter): 15–18.

LeBlanc, Leona. 1999. "Research Opportunities, Research Cautions: The Case for College Foreign Language Supervisors and Coordinators." *ADFL* 30:3: 45–48.

Lee, James. 1987. "Toward a Professional Model of Language Program Direction." *ADFL* 19:1 (September): 22–25.

Lee, James F., and Bill VanPatten. 1990. "The Question of Language Program Direction Is Academic." In *Challenges in the 1990s for College Foreign Language Programs*, ed. Sally Seloff Magnan, 113–28. Boston, MA: Heinle.

Mancing, Howard. 1991. "Teaching, Research, Service: The Concept of Faculty Workload." *ADFL* 22:3 (Spring): 44–50.

Mancing, Howard. 1994. "A Theory of Faculty Workload." *ADFL* 25:3 (Spring): 31–37.

Sadow, Stephen. 1989. "Methodologists: A Brief Guide for Their Colleagues." *ADFL* 21:1 (Fall): 27–28.

Schulz, Renate. 2005. "The Role of Basic Language Program Director: Result of a Survey." *ADFL* 36:2: 32–39.

Teschner, Richard. 1987. "A Profile of the Specialization and Expertise of Lower Division Foreign Language Program Directors in American Universities." *Modern Language Journal* 71:1: 28–35.

"Women in the Profession, 2000. MLA Committee on the Status of Women in the Profession." 2000. *Profession 2000*. New York: Modern Language Association, 191–217.

6

Ten Million Serving

Undergraduate Labor, the Final Frontier[1]

Marc Bousquet

The alarm sounds at 2 a.m. Together with a half dozen of her colleagues, the workday has begun for Susan Erdmann, a tenure-track assistant professor of English at Jefferson Community College in Louisville, Kentucky. She rises carefully to avoid waking her infant son and husband, as her husband commutes forty miles each way to his own tenure-track community college job in the neighboring rural county. She makes coffee, showers, and dresses for work. With their combined income of around $60,000 and substantial education debt, they have a thirty-year mortgage on a tiny home of about 1,000-square feet: a galley kitchen, a dining alcove, and one bedroom for them and another for their two sons to share. The front door opens onto a "living room" of 100 square feet; entering or leaving the house means passing in between the couch and the television. They feel fortunate to be able to afford any mortgage at all in this historically Catholic neighborhood originally populated by Louisville factory workers. It is winter: the sun will not rise for hours. She drives to the airport. Overhead, air-freight 747s barrel into the sky, about one plane every minute or so. Surrounded by the empty school buildings, boarded storefronts and dilapidated, underclass homes of "south central" Louisville, the jets launch in post-midnight salvos. Their engines lack the sophisticated noise-abatement technology required of air traffic in middle-class communities. Every twelve or eighteen months, the city agrees to buy a handful of the valueless residences within earshot.

Turning into the airport complex, Erdmann never comes near the shuttered passenger terminals. She follows a four-lane private roadway toward the rising jets. After parking, a shuttle bus weaves among blindingly lit aircraft hangars and drops her by the immense corrugated sorting facility that is the

103

United Parcel Service main air hub, where she will begin her faculty duties at 3 a.m., greeting UPS's undergraduate workforce directly as they come off the sort. "You would have a sense that you were there, lifting packages," she recalls. "They would come off sweaty, and hot, directly off the line into the class. It was very immediate, and sort of awkward. They'd had no moment of downtime. They hadn't had their cigarette. They had no time to pull themselves together as student-person rather than package-thrower." Unlike her students, Erdmann and other faculty teaching and advising at the hub are not issued a plastic ID card/door pass. Erdmann waits on the windy tarmac for one of her students or colleagues to hear her knocking at the door. Inside, the noise of the sorting facility is, literally, deafening: the shouts, forklift alarms, whistles, and rumble of the sort machinery actually drown out the noise of the jets rising overhead. "Teaching in the hub was horrible," recalled one of Erdmann's colleagues. "Being in the hub was just hell. I'd work at McDonald's before I'd teach there again. The noise level was just incredible. The classroom was just as noisy as if it didn't have any walls." In addition to the sort machinery, UPS floor supervisors were constantly "screaming, yelling back and forth, 'Get this done, get that done, where's so and so.'"

Erdmann is just one of a dozen faculty arriving at the hub after midnight. Some are colleagues from Jefferson Community College and the associated technical institution; others are from the University of Louisville. Their task tonight is to provide on-site advising and registration for some of the nearly 6,000 undergraduate students working for UPS at this facility. About 3,000 of those students work a midnight shift that ends at UPS's convenience—typically 3 a.m. or 4 a.m., although longer during the holiday and other peak shipping seasons.

Nearly all of the third-shift workers are undergraduate students who have signed employment contracts with something called the "Metropolitan College." The name is misleading, since it's not a college at all. An "enterprise" partnership between UPS, the city of Louisville, and the campuses that employ Erdmann and her colleagues, Metropolitan College is in fact little more than a labor contractor. Supported by public funds, this "college" offers no degrees and does no educating. Its sole function is to entice students to sign contracts that commit them to provide cheap labor in exchange for education benefits at the partner institutions. The arrangement has provided UPS with over 10,000 ultra-low-cost student workers since 1997, the same year that the Teamsters launched a crippling strike against the carrier. The Louisville arrangement is the vanguard of UPS's efforts to convert its part-time payroll, as far as possible, to a "financial aid" package for student workers in partnership with campuses near its sorting and loading facilities.

The material web of connection between Erdmann's extraordinary 3 a.m. service obligations as a faculty member and the situation of her students is the rapidly evolving role of higher education in the global service economy. As a result of carefully planned corporate strategy, between 1997 and 2003, UPS hired undergraduate students to staff more than half of its 130,000 part-time positions (Hammer 2003). Students are currently the majority of all part timers, and the overwhelming majority on the least desirable shifts. Part of UPS's strategy is that only some student employees receive education benefits. By reserving the education benefits of its "Earn and Learn" programs to workers willing to work undesirable hours, UPS has, over the past decade, recruited approximately 50,000 part-time workers to its least desirable shifts without raising the pay (in fact, while pushing them to work harder for continually lower pay against inflation; see "Earn and Learn Factsheet" 2007). The largest benefit promises are reserved for students who think they can handle working after midnight every night of the school week.

UPS is possibly the most prominent example of the wholesale conversion of the U.S. undergraduate population to a cheap workforce for the service economy. This represents a profound intensification of higher education's role in capital accumulation: no longer merely a training ground and "warehouse" for future workers, higher ed has become a workhouse through which millions are put to work in low-wage jobs that they supplement with debt, family gifts, and government aid. Their low wages are essentially subsidized by the students themselves, their families, and other taxpayers, representing a pervasive form of corporate welfare.

Some modest critical attention about the situation of undergraduates has focused on debt and the direct donation of labor in unpaid internships and service learning. As with faculty service, the unpaid internship and a reasonable degree of student debt can for some individuals be understood as a canny investment in an individual's future. A number of elite schools, for instance, have adopted policies that provide additional financial aid for students who would like to take unpaid internships that they feel would be advantageous to their careers. This is in some ways similar to the way that some individuals experience faculty service—as an opportunity to make contacts, get noticed, exercise power, and enjoy rewards otherwise unavailable to them (Spacks 2010). Indeed, for certain faculty, the gifts of service can lead to substantial economic rewards, as when they lead to administrative appointments.

But there are vast inequities between the lucrative "service" of an administrator and the demands for unpaid service increasingly placed on contingent faculty by those same administrators. Gender is just one way of understanding the inequity, but it is an important one. The ranks of upper administration in higher education remain predominantly male, while the ranks of the superexploited contingent faculty are primarily female. Indeed, at just the period when women began entering the ranks of higher education faculty in larger numbers, administrative "service" masculinized under the rubric of "education leadership," while faculty "service" increasingly feminized, as in Erdmann's dispiriting experience of 3 a.m. advisement. Administrative service increasingly represented high compensation (such as the payment of a "family wage" sufficient to support a family with one working parent), while faculty service, especially in majority female disciplines, increasingly became identified with gifts of devotion and dedication, as if proceeding naturally from the needs of the contingent faculty to be of use to others. There are few campuses today where the majority of individuals holding advanced degrees and earning a "family wage" for their service are not male, and where the majority of individuals holding advanced degrees and earning wages lower than bartenders are not female.

Similarly, there are vast differences in the ways undergraduates experience service. For example, 20 percent of undergraduates do not work at all during their undergraduate career. Many of the nonworking minority can afford to make the gamble of debt and unpaid service in internships, often reaping the rewards of lucrative careers. In contrast, many of the 80 percent working majority experience service as ill-paid wage labor, with potentially disastrous consequences for their efforts to frame a better future. In ways that need a great deal of further study, it is hardly accidental that just as women have grown to comprise the majority of the undergraduate population undergraduate life has become instrumentally tied to accumulation in the service sector. Women outnumber men in higher education generally, but they outnumber men in the exploitative UPS program by more than 2 to 1.

The largest and earliest of the earn and learn programs is the "Metropolitan College," which exists for the sole purpose of recruiting night-shift workers at the Louisville main hub. Between 1998 and 2005, UPS claims to have "assisted" 10,000 students through the Metropolitan College arrangement (Conway 2005). Of the 7,500 part-time employees at UPS's Louisville hub in May 2006, some are welfare-to-work recipients who are picked up in company buses from the city and even surrounding rural counties. A few hundred are Louisville area high school students in school-to-work programs. Three-quarters of the part-timers—5,600—are college students (Howington 2006). More than half of the students—about 3,000—are enrolled in the Metropolitan College, which, with few exceptions, enrolls only those willing to work the night shift.

Metropolitan College's "enrollment" and "recruitment" activities are entirely driven by UPS's staffing needs. Ditto for scheduling: all of the benefits enjoyed by the Metro College students are contingent upon showing up at the facility every weeknight of the school year at midnight and performing physically strenuous labor for as long as they are needed.

The consequences of night-shift work are well documented, and the preponderance of available evidence suggests markedly negative effects for the Louisville students. Every instructor to whom I spoke reported excessive fatigue and absenteeism (due to fatigue, but also to an extraordinarily high physical injury rate: "They all got hurt," Erdmann reports.) Students who signed employment contracts with Metro College showed substantial failure to persist academically. "I would lose students midterm, or they would never complete final assignments," Erdmann said. "They would just stop coming at some point." Erdmann served as chair of a faculty committee that attempted to improve the academic success of students employed by UPS at her institution. The group scheduled special UPS-only sections between 5 p.m. and 11 p.m., both on campus and at the hub, and began the ritual of 3 a.m. advising. Since nearly all of the faculty involved taught and served on committees five days a week, their efforts to keep students from dropping out by teaching evenings and advising before dawn resulted in a bizarre twenty-four-hour cycle of work for themselves.

"I Dread Work Every Day"

UPS has long pioneered low-cost benefitless employment, abetted by the Teamsters themselves, who in 1962, under Jimmy Hoffa Sr., signed one of the first contracts in American industry to permit the regular use of part-time employees. This second tier of employment was massively expanded after the Teamsters agreed to 1982 protocols that raised the wages of full-time workers while freezing those of part-time workers. In that year, part-time UPS employees started at $8 per hour, the equivalent in 2007 of about $17 per hour ($34,000 per year). Similarly, in 1982, part-time employees averaged about $10 per hour, the equivalent in 2007 of $22 per hour ($44,000 per year).

Not incidentally, at the 1982 wages, a UPS part-time worker could indeed successfully fund a college education. One employee from the 1970s recalls:

> At the old full and fair rate prior to the 1982 UPS wage reduction despite soaring volume and profits a pt worker in exchange for back breaking work could afford to rent a room, pay tuition, buy food and clothing, and afford to own and operate a used car. This was a good deal that was profitable to the student and society as well as profitable to UPS. I went through six years of college that way and am very grateful to the Teamsters for the good pay. I find it a national disgrace that UPS has effectively reduced the pay by nearly 65% adjusted for inflation since 1982 and destroyed a positive job for over a hundred thousand workers

and for society as well. There are [UPS] pt workers living in
homeless shelters in Richmond, California, and other parts of
the country. [punctuation regularized]

As with Wal-Mart and other predatory super low-wage employers, many of
UPS's student workers are homeless. At the Louisville hub, Erdmann recalled,
"I knew people [who were] sleeping in their cars."

After the union's concession to a radically cheaper second tier of
employment, 80 percent of all new UPS jobs were created in the "permanent
part-time" category. While the pay between part time and full time diverged
slowly between 1962 and 1982, the differential accelerated rapidly in the 1980s
and 1990s. Serving as a UPS driver is still a coveted blue-collar position.
From the Reagan years to the present, these full-time Teamsters continued
to enjoy raises, job security, and due process with respect to their grievances
and substantial benefits, including a pension. But over the same period of
time, these and other full-time positions became the minority of employees
covered by the contract. The highly compensated drivers, commonly earning more than faculty in the "feminized" academic disciplines, are male by
a substantial majority. As in higher education, the poorly paid contingent
workers are far more likely to be women.

In less than fifteen years, permanent part-time workers became the
majority of the UPS workforce in the United States. The ratio of permanent
part-time workers was particularly pronounced at the Louisville main hub,
where a high-speed, high-pressure night sort was conducted. As the wages
of the part-time majority steadily shrank against inflation, opportunities to
join the full-time tier all but disappeared. Today, even the company's human
resources recruiters admit that while full-time positions "still exist," it can
take "six to seven years or even longer" to get on full time. A single-digit
percentage of the company's part-time employees lasts that long. Few of
those who do persist are actually offered full-time work. During the long
night of Reagan-Bush-Clinton reaction, according to employees, the company
unilaterally abrogated work rules, including safety limits on package size
and weight. Injuries soared to two and a half times the industry average, in
especial disproportion among part-time employees in the first year.

As jointly bargained by UPS and the Teamsters, the part-time positions
devolved into one of the least desirable forms of work in the country, with
one of the highest turnover rates in history. Featuring poor wages, limited
benefits, a high injury rate, and unreasonable scheduling, the Teamster-UPS
agreement created compensation and working conditions for the part-time
majority so abysmal that most rational persons preferred virtually any other
form of employment, or preferred not working at all.

Most part-time workers departed within weeks of being hired. According to George Poling, director of the Louisville Metropolitan College, the

average term of employment for part-time workers on the night sort was just eight weeks. At the Louisville facility, 90 percent of part-time hires quit before serving a year. Across the country in 1996 UPS hired 180,000 part-time workers on all shifts, but only 40,000 of them were still with the company at year's end. In part as a result of steadily accelerating turnover, UPS agreed in just sixteen days to the most-publicized core demand of the 1997 Teamsters strike, the creation of 10,000 new full-time jobs out of some of the new part-time positions.

Overlooked during the press coverage of the Teamsters' apparent victory was the fact that these new "full-time" positions were paid well below the scale of existing full-time workers, and these workers would earn just 75 percent of the rate of regular full-time workers by the end of the contract. This introduced a new, lower-wage tier in the ranks of full-time workers. The lower wages of this group would continue to support the wage increases and benefits of the union's powerful minority constituency, the shrinking core of long-term full-time workers. (Readers employed in academic circumstances will recognize this strategy as having been pioneered in their own workplaces, with the institution of nontenurable, full-time lectureships as one of the "solutions" that the long-term tenured faculty have accepted to management's expansion of part-time faculty.) It would take three years of foot-dragging through arbitration and federal court before UPS delivered even these watered-down full-time jobs.

Despite credulous ballyhoo about the strike as the decade's exemplar of labor militance and solidarity between full- and part-time workers, the part-time majority of UPS workers benefited little from the Teamster "victory."

The starting wage for part-time workers, which had remained at $8 per hour for fifteen years (since 1982) was raised in the 1997 contract a grand total of 50 cents. Ten years later, the Teamster-negotiated starting wage for UPS part-time package handlers working between 11 p.m. and 4 a.m. remains at just $8.50, or exactly one raise in a quarter century. This is a loss against inflation of more than half. In 1982, the $8 per hour starting wage for part-time workers was more than twice the minimum wage ($3.35) and slightly above the national hourly average wage ($7.72). In 2006, the UPS starting wage was about half of the national average hourly wage of $16.46 for nonsupervisory workers. With the "minimum" wage so low that only a half million Americans earn it, the $8.50 per hour UPS starting wage in 2006 was equal to or lower than what most traditionally "minimum wage" occupations actually earn and lower than the statutory metropolitan living wage established in many major cities. This is not $8 or $9 per hour for eight hours a day, 9 a.m. to 5 p.m., but $8 or $9 per hour for *showing up five nights a week at midnight and working three and a half to five hours, depending on the flow of packages for physically demanding, dangerous night-shift work at the company's convenience.* The pay starts at midnight and ends three hours later, but there is at least a half hour, often more, of unpaid commuting around airport security on either side of the paid three hours.

The total commute each way can total as much as an hour, even for students living just a mile or two from the facility: "When I was there, you'd have to be in the parking lot by 11:30 at the latest if you wanted the shuttle bus to get you to the gate by 11:40, where you'd then wait to have your ID checked, and then walk through the maze of hub buildings for 500 yards before finding your workspace and clocking in," one worker recalled. "The point being if I got parked at 11:45, I'd be late and get bawled out. The traffic outside UPS leading into the shift is nightmarish, so you'd really need to leave the house an hour before work to have a shot at getting to the sort station on time." That's five hours of third-shift time, being paid close to the minimum wage for just three hours.

In the past twenty-five years, working conditions at UPS have eroded even faster than the wage. With the union's lack of interest in part-time workers, UPS has increasingly introduced ultra-short shifts, technology-driven speedup, and managerial surveillance of every aspect of the work process, including real-time tracking of errors. Employing constant surveillance by a battalion of "part-time supes," themselves generally students, UPS deploys cameras and manned watchtowers throughout the multilayer sort. "They're always watching you work from tall perches that exist nearly everywhere in the plant," one former student worker recalls, "The perches are ostensibly ladders to other layers of the sort, but the consistent presence of management at the stair landings creates the feeling of almost total surveillance. Even when you can't see them, you know they're in hidden rooms watching you on camera." Nearly all student workers are repeatedly tested by "salting" the presorted containers with bad address labels; employees decry the practice as a "particularly nasty" form of continuous stressing of their work environment.

Several current or former UPS employees have begun Weblogs to chronicle the high-speed, high-stress nature of their employment. One, writing as "Brown Blood," explained that he had begun the Weblog for "the employees of UPS to express [their] true feelings about [their] job in all aspects," noting, "I must apologize now for any fowl language that may . . . *will* occur in this community, because most of these jobs not only test the limitations of your physical capacity it also shatters all anger management." On the JobVent blog, UPS workers' ratings of the workplace were consistently *below zero*:

> Little did I know that I would spend 4 hours a day in a dark, oven-hot dungeon being screamed at by idiotic powertrippers who having givin' up beleiving [*sic*] life has some kind of meaning

and now want to make themselves feel better by humiliating the
only people in their lives that they have any sort of advantage
over. All this while you are sweating liters and giving your back
life-long injuries. I couldn't help but laugh in disbelief when I
received my first paycheck for $120. IF YOU EVEN THINK OF
WORKING AT UPS realize that if you don't want to spend the
next ten years of your life being treated like toilet paper just to
become a lousy driver then go work for FedEx, the benefits are
as good, the pay is better and you get just a little respect . . . a
friend of mine worked there for 5 days and became a driver.
UPS is no less than 7–10 years. Bottom line, UPS SUCKS A
BIG ONE!!!!!!!!! I dread work every day.

According to at least one long-term Teamster full-time worker, the part-time
students working the night sort are driven particularly hard: "They cram eight
hours' work into five." Agreeing with this characterization of the workload
for undergraduate employees, one student worker said, "Around finals time,
I'd go for days without sleep. The scary thing is, I'd see the sleepless period
coming, know there was nothing I could do about it other than quit school
or quit work, and then learn to psyche myself up for it."

Most bloggers complained of the pay ("pathetic"), schedule ("random,
terrible hours"), injuries ("I was killing myself physically"; "constant muscle
pulls/strains, a lot of safety hazards;" "horrible; you'll sweat like a dog in
the summer and freeze in the winter—unsafe—watch out for sharp objects
and falling boxes"), and supervisory harassment. Holistically, the evaluations
were resoundingly negative: "This was the worst job I ever had"; "You can
imagine it's bad when the highest UPS scores with me in any category is a
-2"; "If [you're] thinking of working here, DON'T DO IT!" Many of the
bloggers give a vivid portrait of the stressful nature of the work. Every error
is tracked, and a minimum standard for error-free sorting is one error in
2,500. How often do you make an error while typing? If you're like me, you
make several typing errors per page, for an error rate per word of 1/60 or
so. At UPS, an error of 1 in 500 is considered extremely poor. The student
workers are particularly likely to be placed in these high-stress positions. If
younger, they are commonly inexperienced at work generally. If older, they
have typically suffered substantial economic and/or personal distress. Either
way, those who don't express rage and disappointment, or vote with their
feet by quitting, appear likely to internalize management's construction of
them as slow-moving failures. Students sometimes contribute to Weblogs
like "Brown Blood" less to complain than to get coping advice ("Is there a
better way of doing this without going miserably slowly? . . . I want to show
that I can be competent in some form of employment.").

The work of the loaders intensifies during the holiday rush:

> I hate how UPS is always fucking you over. On a normal day I load 3 trucks and lately it's been a total of about 800–900 packages. . . . They told me I would only have the 4th car one day per week. Well guess what? They gave me 4 cars 3 days this week. Today I had a total of over 1,600 packages with no help, the bastards. My loads were shit and my drivers were bitching, but what the hell can I do about it?
>
> I suppose the fact that I've slept less than 5 of the past 55 hours had something to do with my despising work today, but Red Bull helps with that.
>
> I'm so f-ing glad it's a long weekend. ("hitchhiker42")

These notes of stress, fatigue, and powerlessness on the job are nearly uniform among the UPS permanent part-time workers.

Employee of the Month

Seventy percent of the workers in the main UPS hub in Louisville are women. The average age is thirty-four, and many workers are parents. Some of the women work in data entry, but most of the work involves package handling. For every teenage worker, there's another part-time worker who is well into her forties.

The reality of the undergraduate workforce is very different from the representation of teen partyers on a perpetual spring break, as popularized by television ("Girls Gone Wild"), UPS propaganda ("They're staying up until dawn anyway"), and *Time* magazine ("Meet the 'twixters,' [twenty-somethings] who live off their parents, bounce from job to job and hop from mate to mate. They're not lazy—they just won't grow up" [Grossman 2005]).

More than 15 million students are currently enrolled in higher ed (with the average age being approximately twenty-six). Tens of millions of persons have recently left higher education, nearly as many without degrees as with them. Like graduate employees, undergraduates now work longer hours in school, spend more years in school, and can take several years to find stable employment after obtaining their degrees. Undergraduates and recent school leavers, whether degree holders or not, now commonly live with their parents well beyond the age of legal adulthood, often into their late twenties. Like graduate employees, undergraduates increasingly find that their period of "study" is in fact a period of employment as cheap labor. The production of cheap workers is facilitated by an ever-expanding notion of "youth." A University of Chicago survey conducted in 2003 found that the majority of Americans now think that adulthood begins around twenty-six, an age not coincidentally identical with the average age of the undergraduate student population.

The popular conception of student life as "delayed adulthood" is reflected in such notions as "30 is the new 20," and "40 is the new 30" (Irvine 2003). The fatuousness of these representations is confounded by looking at the other end of one's employment life. Few people are finding that in terms of employability after downsizing that "50 is the new 40." Persons who lose their jobs in their fifties often find themselves unemployable. What are the economic consequences for a person whose productive career can begin in their mid-thirties or later and end at age fifty or sooner? This pattern presents real obstacles for both women and men wishing to raise a family. Yet mass-media representations of extended schooling and the associated period of insecure employment are often cheery, suggesting that it's a stroke of good fortune, an extended youth free of such unwelcome responsibilities as home ownership, child-rearing, and visits to health-care providers. In this idealistic media fantasy, more time in higher education means more time to party—construing an extended youth as a prolonged stretch of otherwise empty time unmarked by the accountabilities of adulthood.

But, concretely, the apparently empty time of involuntarily extended youth associated with higher education is really quite full. It's full of feelings—the feelings of desperation, betrayal, and anxiety, the sense that Cary Nelson has captured for graduate employees under the heading *Will Teach for Food*. Writers such as Anya Kamenetz (2005) and Tamara Draut (2007) have captured the similar feelings of upper-middle-class college graduates in books such as *Generation Debt* and *Strapped*, respectively. Most of the persons Kamenetz and Draut describe will have added graduate school to successful bachelor's degrees at first- or second-tier institutions. But little attention has been paid to the role of higher education in organizing the vast majority of the lives it touches—those who don't graduate, or those who graduate with community college, vocational, or technical degrees.

"Employee of the Month" is typical of the more successful students employed by UPS. As related on her Weblog ("The Dance That Is My Life" 2006), this "mom/stylist," age thirty and the mother of two children, ages three and five, is a fan of Christian apocalyptic fiction and a part-time student who hopes to become a teacher. She has an "A" average. Her Weblog portrays her husband as a substance abuser who provides no contribution to the household finances. During the months covered in her Weblog, he moves in and out of the house. Like most students who find a job with UPS, she was already working hard before signing on with Big Brown. While parenting and starting school, she was working three jobs, including office work and hair styling. In the first few weeks, she enjoys the work: "I am digging this job! I get to work out for 4–5 hours a night," plus collect education benefits. Anticipating the 50-cent raise, she writes, "The pay sucks at first, but within 90 days I should be okay." She plans to continue working as a stylist but feels that she can quit her other two part-time jobs: "With doing hair three days a week I will be making just as much as I have been making [with three jobs] and only working about 35–37 hours a week total. Woo Hoo!"

Rather than a partying teen, this far more typical working undergraduate is a devout thirty-year-old woman who is thrilled simply to be able to work a mere full-time equivalent at two different jobs, in addition to schoolwork and the solo parenting of two small children.

After the Christmas rush, and still in her first two months of employment, the upbeat blogger notes: "I am getting muscles in my arms and shoulders, my legs are getting a little toned. I do need to lose about 25 lbs., so the more muscle thing is a good start. . . . I am getting better at my job now that I am a little stronger and can lift the boxes up to the top shelf."

Within six months, that is, by March 2006, she makes "Employee of the Month" at her facility.

In the same month, she has her first work-related injury: a strained ligament from working with heavy packages. Per her physician's orders, she is placed on "light duty," dealing with packages weighing one to seven pounds (seven pounds is approximately the weight of a gallon of milk).

This blogger has become discouraged about her prospects of continuing her education and considers dropping out.

She finds that her family life is increasingly stressed by the UPS job. In order to collect less than $30 a night, she has to leave her children to sleep at her mother's house five nights a week.

Now that the holiday rush is past, she finds that, on her UPS salary and even with a second job, she is unable to afford such everyday staples as Easter baskets for her children, which her sister provided.

"A guy at work told me about a job at a private school. I applied and had an interview. I hope I get the job. I need to pay bills, and the UPS job isn't enough." She concludes:

> My kids did have a good Easter, thank-you to my sister. We went down to her house and she bought my kids candy, toys, and each kid a movie!! I thought that was above the call of duty. I can't tell you how much I appreciate my family for coming to my aid in my time of need this past year. I know I could get another job and put my kids in daycare all day again and

be able to support them better, but I wouldn't be able to go to school. It's hard right now, but I am already a year into school and I will be a teacher in a few years. I can't stop now. Even with this drama going on in my life, I have still kept a 3.6 grade point average. I want to finish it. My son still wants me to be a teacher, so I have to show him that with work and perseverance you can accomplish anything despite your circumstances. Facts don't count when it comes to reaching a goal. ("The Dance That Is My Life" 2006)

In other words, for UPS to receive one super-cheap worker, that worker's parents have to donate free child care, and other family members have to donate cash, time, and goods. Like the vast majority of her coworkers in a UPS earn-and-learn arrangement, this "A" student and employee of the month is so sapped by the experience, physically injured, undercompensated, and domestically disarranged that she's on the verge of quitting school.

Despite her qualifications, energy, and commitment, the only thing keeping this UPS worker going is the desire to shore up achievement ideology for her children ("I have to show him that with work and perseverance you can accomplish anything despite your circumstances"), to create a Disney narrative out of their lives when she drops them off to sleep at their grandparents' house five nights a week, one that will prove that "facts don't count when it comes to reaching a goal."

Supergirl: "My Back Hurts So Fricken' Bad"

This 5'2", 110-pound twenty-three-year-old undergraduate woman writing under the moniker "supergirl" has a charming sardonic flair: "America needs no more cheese, ham, huge-ass boxes of summer sausage, holiday popcorn tins, or kringles . . . I think I've moved enough of these that every man, woman, and child should already have one by default. No wonder obesity is an epidemic" (Supergirl 2005).

As with most, her daily UPS shift is a second job. After a year, she's ready to quit. She's had one work-related arm surgery: "I really don't want to have another, or, worse, risk permanently damaging the nerves in both arms," she writes, "and I sincerely don't think I'm being paid enough to stay there two years and blow out both arms unfixably . . . I know pain and can tolerate it, but I can't even fucking sleep because every position somehow puts pressure on a nerve in my arm that's already got problems and is being pushed to the limits." When I asked another Louisville student employee to comment on "supergirl's" representation of the injury rate, he called the physical toll exacted by the workplace a "key point," adding, "The physical harm this work does will long outlast the span of the job."

She complains of the culture of UPS—of speedup, the pressure to deny injuries and work through them, and the pressure to continue employment through the milestones that dictate education benefits such as loan and tuition remission.

Under the rubric "Don't make UPS yours," she warns away other prospective student employees:

> My back hurts . . . so fricken' bad. It doesn't benefit me to say I hurt because I've noticed that if you hurt of any kind the sort super just asks you to quit (in not so many eloquently and legal to say to an employee words). I lift tons of shit that's got 20–30 pounds on me, but as I stand, a girl of 5'2" and a buck ten . . . I can't do that kinda shit everyday . . . I guess I can be supergirl fast or supergirl strong or a normal mix of either, but I can't be both every fucking day. Who can, anyway? (Supergirl 2005)

What disturbs her most is the pressure (from family, coworkers, supervisors) to work through her injuries to benefit-earning milestones. She understands the pressures driving everyone else to push her to continue, "but shit why can't I just say I'd like to not be at a job like that?" In any event, she writes, "Everyone should know I'll probably just stay there anyhow . . . cause I'm too damn busy to find anything else anyway."

10,000 Students and 300 Degrees

There is little mystery regarding UPS's motivation for the "earn-and-learn" programs—not benevolence, but the cheapness and docility of the student workforce. In addition to the ultra-low wage, students' dependency on UPS includes loan guarantees and tuition remissions that are lost or reduced if the student resigns "prematurely" from the program. As a result of its campaign to hire undergraduates, UPS's retention of part-time package handlers has improved markedly, despite speedup and continued stagnation of the wage between 1997 and 2007. Average time of employment for part-time workers grew by almost 50 percent, and retention improved by 20 percent, with some of the most dramatic improvements in the Louisville main hub. This tuition benefit is tax deductible and taxpayer subsidized. It's a good deal for UPS, which shares the cost of the tuition benefit with partner schools and communities and saves millions in payroll tax (by providing "tuition benefits" instead of higher wages) while holding down the part-time wage overall.

All "earn-and-learn" students must apply for federal and state financial aid. Many attend community colleges, where tuition is often just a few hundred dollars. Many students are subjected to a bait-and-switch tactic: attracted to the program by the promise of tuition benefits at the University of Louisville (currently over $6,000 a year), program participants are instead steered toward enrollment in the community colleges—a decision that doesn't reflect their academic needs, but as Metropolitan College director Poling admits, it is exclusively the desire of the state and UPS to contain costs. Studying on a part-time basis, as most in the program do, a student seeking a bachelor's degree can therefore remain in a community college for three or four years before earning the credits enabling transfer to a four-year school. One student pointed out that trying to schedule around the UPS job was a "lot harder than it sounds," and for many it was "downright impossible to do this and get the degree in any reasonable period of years." Students that attend inexpensive schools, or those who qualify for high levels of tuition relief (as is often the case in the economically disadvantaged groups targeted by UPS recruiters), substantially reduce UPS's costs. Undergraduate students also represent lower group health insurance costs.

Another way in which students reduce UPS's cost is by quitting before they become eligible for benefits, by taking an incomplete, or by failing a class. No benefits are paid for failed or incomplete classes. Students who drop out of school but continue to work for UPS also significantly lower UPS's costs.

To put UPS's costs in perspective, in a decade, it has spent no more than $80 million on tuition and student loan redemption in over fifty hubs. In contrast, its 2006 deal with the state of Kentucky for a 5,000-job *expansion of just one hub*, involved $50 million in state support over ten years. Company officials are fairly frank about UPS's dependency on cheap student labor, supported by massive taxpayer giveaways. "It would have been nearly impossible to find an additional 5,000 workers [for the expansion] without the resources of Metropolitan College," a public-relations VP told the Louisville business press (Karman and Adams 2006). It has expanded "earn-and-learn" programs to fifty other metropolitan centers, to Canada, and to for-profit education vendors such as DeVry.

It's a lot less clear whether this is a good deal for students. "We've solved employee retention," Poling admits, "but we've got to work more on academic retention."

It's hard to estimate the size of Poling's understatement, since UPS and Metropolitan College refuse to supply standard academic persistence data on its huge population of undergraduate workers. But it's a whopper.

Of the 10,000 students Poling's program claims to have "assisted" with their higher education since 1997, Poling is able to produce evidence of just

300 degrees earned, 111 associate's and 181 bachelor's degrees. Since both UPS and Metropolitan College refuse to provide public accountability for the academic persistence of undergraduate workers, it's hard to estimate what these numbers mean by comparison to more responsible and conventional education and financial aid circumstances. However, the most favorable construction of the evidence available for Metropolitan College shows an average entry of slightly more than 1,000 student workers annually. Based on two and a half years of data after six years of program operation, according to Poling, the program between 2003 and 2006 showed an approximate annual degree production of about forty associate's and seventy-five bachelor's degrees.

This approximates a 12 percent rate of persistence to any kind of degree.

UPS's student employees in the Metropolitan College program are more likely to be retained as UPS employees than they are to be retained as college students. In May 2006, of the 3,000 or so Metropolitan College "students" working at UPS, only 1,263 were actually taking classes that semester. This means that during the spring term, almost 60 percent of the student workers in UPS's employ were not in school: "Another 1,700 or so," in Poling's words, "took the semester off" (Howington 2006).

Of the minority actually taking classes, at least a quarter failed to complete the semester. UPS pays a bonus for completing semesters "unsuccessfully" (with withdrawals or failing grades) as well as "successfully." Counting the bonuses paid in recent years for "unsuccessful" semesters, along with the successful ones, Poling suggested that during terms in which between 1,200 and 1,700 student workers were enrolled, between 900 and 1,100 students would complete at least one class, or a ratio of perhaps 3 to 4.

These numbers appear to hang roughly together. If in any given year the majority of UPS night-shift workers are "taking the semester off," and 25 percent or more of those actually enrolled fail to complete even one class during the semester, then this seems consistent with an eventual overall persistence to degree of 12 percent.

In plain fact, it would seem that *UPS counts on its student workers failing or dropping out*. Because of the high rate of failed classes, withdrawals, and dropping out, UPS ends up paying only a modest fraction of the education benefits it offers. If each of the 48,000 students who has passed through its "Earn-and-Learn Program" had collected the full UPS share of tuition benefits over a five-year period, then it would have cost the company over $720 million. In fact, it has so far had to spend just *10 percent* of that total—$72 million—on tuition remission, or an average of only $1,500 per student (the equivalent of just one semester's maximum tuition benefit per participant). Similarly, the loan remission benefit (theoretically as much as $8,000 after four years' employment) would total almost $384 million. But as of 2005, UPS had paid only $21 million, an average of just $438 per student worker, well under 10 percent of its liability if all of its student workers actually completed a four-year degree.

The labor time of the low-wage student worker creates an inevitable, embodied awareness that the whole system of our cheap wages is really a gift to the employer. Throwing cartons at 3 a.m. every night of one's college education, it becomes impossible not to see that UPS is the beneficiary of our financial aid, and not the other way around.

Higher education has been transformed into an industry, like others in the service economy, that is "structurally and substantially" reliant on youth labor (Tannock 2001). Campuses of all kinds are critically dependent on a vast undergraduate workforce that is, as in the fast-food industry, desirable not just because workers are poorly paid but because they are disposable and "more easily controlled" (Schlosser 2001). This can hardly be separated from the fact that women are, on most campuses, the majority of undergraduate students, just as women are the majority in many of the sectors of higher education employment where the extraction of donated or partially donated labor is most prominent.

Note

1. This contribution is adapted from chapter 1 of the author's *How the University Works: Higher Education and the Low-Wage Nation* (NYU, 2008).

Works Cited

Bok, Derek. 2004. *Universities in the Marketplace: The Commercialization of Higher Education*. Princeton, NJ: Princeton University Press.

Conway, Charnley. 2005. "Metropolitan College Develops Skilled Workers." *Business First of Louisville* (April 15).

"The Dance That Is My Life" (Weblog). 2006. http://www.walkingingrace.spaces.live.com (accessed December 2006).

Draut, Tamara. 2007. *Strapped: Why America's 20- and 30-Somethings Cannot Get Ahead*. New York: Anchor.

"Earn and Learn Factsheet." 2007. http://www.pressroom.ups.com/mediakits/factsheet/0,2305,777,00. html (accessed March 2007).

Grossman, Lev. 2005. "They Just Won't Grow Up." Time (January 24).

Hammer, Maryann. 2003. "Wanted: Part-timers With Class; UPS Launches Earn and Learn." *Workforce* (June). New York: Crain Communications.

Howington, Patrick. 2006. "Students May Fill Many New Jobs." *Louisville Courier-Journal*, May 18.

Irvine, Martha. 2003. "Americans Find Themselves in 'Delayed Adulthood.'" *Louisville Courier Journal,* October 27, p. A4.

Kamenetz, Anya. 2005. *Generation Debt: Why Now Is a Terrible Time To Be Young.* New York: Riverhead.

Karman, John. 2000. "Delivering an Education: UPS Boosts Its Recruiting Effort Outside Jefferson County for Metropolitan College." *Business First of Louisville* (March 24). http://www.louisville.bizjournals.com/louisville/stories/2000/03/27/story3.html.

Karman, John, and and Brent Adams. 2006. "Close Ties among UPS, Government and Development Officials Helped Package Come Together Quickly." *Business First of Louisville* (May 19). http://www.louisville.bizjournals.com/louisville/stories/2006/05/22/story1.html.

Kirp, David. 2004. *Shakespeare, Einstein, and the Bottom Line: The Marketing of Higher Education.* Cambridge, MA: Harvard University Press.

"Kody" (pseud). Weblog post. 2005. (April 28). http://www.basildangerdoo.blogspot.com (accessed December 2006).

Schlosser, Eric. 2001. *Fast Food Nation.* New York: Harper Perennial.

Slaughter, Sheila, and Gary Rhoades. 2004. *Academic Capitalism and the New Economy: Markets, State, and Higher Education.* Baltimore, MD: Johns Hopkins University Press.

Spacks, Patricia Meyer. 2010. "Service and Empowerment." In *Over Ten Million Served,* ed. Michelle A. Massé and Katie J. Hogan, ch. 14. Albany: State University of New York Press.

Stack, Carol. Forthcoming. *Coming of Age at the Minimum Wage.*

"Supergirl" (pseud.) Weblog post. 2005. (March 1). http://www.jealousthendead.livejournal.com (accessed December 2006).

Tannock, Stuart. 2001. *Youth at Work: The Unionized Fast-food and Grocery Workplace.* Philadelphia, PA: Temple University Press.

Washburn, Jennifer. 2005. *University, Inc.: The Corporate Corruption of American Higher Education.* New York: Basic Books.

Part 2

Non Serviam: Out of Service

7

The Value of Desire

On Claiming Professional Service

Kirsten M. Christensen

> I feel as though I have fallen into a spinning vortex that has
> nearly consumed me. I am at a small school, so I am always
> busy in the way one has to be at a place like this. For the past
> two years I have also been running a program on my own that
> is intended to be run by two tenure-track people, so that's made
> me extra busy. But this semester's workload, with me chairing a
> tenure-track search with 150+ candidates and newly elected to
> a major university-wide committee, is beyond what is normal,
> even for here, I think. I have actually had days where I was
> never even in my office, running from class to meeting to class.
> I have never felt so overwhelmed and scattered, with so many
> individual irons in the fire on some days that I can't even keep
> my to-do list up to date.[1]

This description of my workload one recent semester likely feels very
familiar to colleagues at a vast array of institutions. It highlights a central
feature—overload—of the service life many of us face. Too much service is
problematic in its own right because of its tendency to exhaust and embitter.
More troubling than what it causes, though, is what it obscures—namely,
desire. Many of us genuinely *like* to serve, but that emotion is smothered
most days by the sheer volume of the service load before us, and certainly
also at times by the sense that we are not able to choose how and when
we serve. Acknowledging and making space for desire in our professional
service, though, can surely not only preserve individuals but also strengthen
and invigorate institutions.

It is probably often in the tricky intersections between personal contribution and institutional demands, between expectation and reality, that desire most often ends up languishing, even disappearing. Those intersections are often muddied from the outset, since preparation in graduate programs rarely includes overt discussion of or preparation for the role that service plays in the day-to-day life of a faculty member, especially the impact that institution type and size might have on the nature and volume of service. Graduate students in our profession are often given opportunities to teach, and in the best programs they are trained in pedagogical theories and teaching methods. But the predominant focus, of course, is on development as a scholar. Such a myopic focus can easily set new faculty members up for a rude awakening. In a powerful essay on the frequent disconnect between hiring committees and candidates at nonelite colleges, for example, Nona Fienberg suggests that "after having dedicated . . . years to the language of yearning and desire, [candidates] will have to learn a second language," which, she argues, will be "the language of accommodation . . . of teaching, of pedagogy . . . of intellectual self-preservation," an "essential tongue" that we must acquire or risk "sink[ing] into embitterment."[2]

David R. Evans similarly articulates the conflicted reality of many academics who have spent years nurturing a set of ambitions inculcated in us by the dominant discourse of the profession, even though it is a frustrating certainty that many of these ambitions simply cannot be achieved in the circumstances our colleges present to us.[3] The "dominant discourse" that Evans describes is what John Guillory calls the "phantasmic mode of professional desire," in which "every professor is accountable as a research scholar,"[4] in spite of the reality that the vast majority of available positions in our profession are not at Research I institutions. With this reality in mind, it seems counterproductive, even destructive, to use the vocabulary of acquiescence and defense to define the teaching and service activities that comprise the bulk of our professional endeavors, since doing so establishes a depressing dichotomy between desire (research) and everything else we do.

Such a dichotomy posits professional service, in all its forms, as the part of our work to which we are simply doomed.[5] But a more hopeful approach would be one in which we craft and articulate our service in a way that will allow us—and our institutions—to see its value clearly. In short, we should resist acquiring a second language of accommodation and self-preservation and instead seek to foster a culture that allows us to use our first language—the language of desire—when we speak of service.

Having grown up in a religious tradition that emphasized charitable service, I had, before entering the profession, always associated the word "service" with activities that helped others and usually produced in me a feeling of value and satisfaction as well. It was thus something I almost always viewed as desirable. Since entering the profession, and after having taught at three institutions, I have developed numerous other associations—both positive and negative—with the term *service*. These associations have largely been determined by the atmosphere or ethos of service I experienced and perceived at my institution. I have encountered wide variation in the way institutions value service, both in the activities they identify as service and how they "count" it for renewal, tenure, and promotion. What I have been slower to recognize is the extent to which my desire to engage in particular service activities has been obscured or overridden by the value of that service and my status within the institution. Yet it is clear that when desire and value are closely aligned, both worker and institution benefit.[6] This essay thus seeks to untangle the often knotty relationship between institutional value systems (both expressed and implied) and personal desire in professional service for full-time faculty. It also considers ways in which workers can fruitfully and confidently claim desire as an important and a justified factor in their service choices, as well as ways in which administrators might acknowledge and build on desire for the good of the institutional community.

Personal desire and institutional value intersect in the academic workplace in the following predominant scenarios. No ranking is implied in the ordering.

For particular services that are inherent in a position (e.g., program administration),

- the faculty member does not want to perform a particular service or aspect of a larger service load but is unable to refuse because it is an essential part of a position;

- the faculty member desires to do the service, but even though it is inherent in her position, it is not valued by the institution for promotion and tenure and thus, paradoxically, impedes her progress.

For service that is *not* an inherent part of a faculty member's position,

- the faculty member does not want to perform a particular service but does it anyway out of concern or fear that refusing will be perceived negatively at her institution and will thus negatively impact her professional progress;

- the faculty member wants to perform a particular service but chooses *not* to do so out of concern or fear that the service will be perceived negatively at her institution and will thus negatively impact her professional progress;

- the faculty member wants to perform a particular service but chooses *not* to do so out of concern or fear that the service will negatively impact her professional progress by taking time away from other activities that would be acknowledged at her institution;

- the faculty member wants to perform a certain service opportunity that is valued by the institution but chooses *not* to take it on out of concern that the additional workload could impede her progress overall.

- the faculty member wants to perform a particular service that is valued by the institution and chooses to do so even though she knows it will add significantly to her workload and could impede her progress in other areas that are also valued.

- the faculty member's desire to perform a particular service is matched or nearly matched by the institution's value of that service, allowing her to choose it as a distinct part of her overall profile—so that worker and institution are equally satisfied and rewarded.

In all but the last instance, the benefit of service is unequally distributed between faculty member and institution, which results in a range of reactions from both sides, including disappointment, frustration, anger, disenchantment, disenfranchisement, disciplinary action, or, in extreme cases, dismissal or resignation.

Tellingly, in most of these scenarios, not desire but rather a faculty member's perception of the value attached to a particular service opportunity by the institution is the deciding factor in the acceptance or rejection of that service. Whether or not that *perceived value* accords with the *actual value* the institution gives to that service, however, is a crucial, but often unasked, question. The disconnect between perception and reality, usually manifested in faculty member fears or worries, could probably often be remedied by improved communication. Documents that contain institutional expectations for tenure and promotion are a major form of such communication. Many institutions, however, are unwilling to be too specific in the materials they provide (if they provide any at all), partly to protect themselves from potential lawsuits, but certainly also, more positively, to allow for the necessary and fruitful variety that must exist across individuals and disciplines. Whatever the reasons for lack of specificity, the resulting guidelines many faculty members have before them as they make decisions and choose commitments often feel vague at best, confusing or contradictory at worst.

Other forms of communication can also be crucial in establishing clarity on institutional values. Advertisements for new faculty hires, for example, are probably often written with an ideal scenario, rather than the reality on the ground, in mind. Since that job ad, however, may be the only job description the successful candidate ever sees, if it does not jibe with the actual conditions or expectations of the position, then she will be set up for extreme frustration. Any other cases in which expectations made of faculty are never stated but are fundamental to their evaluation, or where coherence between the goals of individual units and the larger institution is lacking or weak, will set up faculty members for frustration, if not failure.

In many of these instances, personal communication with trusted senior colleagues can be greatly reassuring. A wise mentor might be able to explain, for example, that a perception that certain activities are not valued by the institution is not borne out by the record of other colleagues. Or perhaps the perception is accurate, but the individual faculty member might nonetheless, in a frank conversation, be able to articulate the importance of and her desire to engage in a particular "unvalued" activity to her chair, dean, or provost early on and garner support that will be crucial later on.

Like perception, categorization also has an enormous impact on the decisions faculty members make about the service obligations or opportunities they accept. Each of the aforementioned scenarios, for example, assumes that the service obligation or opportunity is categorizable *as* service at the faculty member's institution. Yet the personal desire/institutional value relationship is significantly complicated by the fact that there are many activities we perform routinely—both those we desire and those we do not—for which no institution, no CV or tenure review file, has a category, let alone a reward. The important report of the MLA Commission on Professional Service (1996) concluded that "the traditional triad of research, teaching, and service has increasingly become a hierarchy, ranked in order of esteem,"[7] a model that "hinders appreciation of the range and diversity of faculty work because much is excluded or trivialized by the categories in use."[8] The MLA Commission's report thus strives to change the terms of the conversation about service by acknowledging that the scope of the service we perform encompasses not only "intellectual work" but also "academic and professional citizenship," both of which deserve to be rewarded.[9]

Unfortunately, though, many discussions of academic service still focus only on those activities that have a formal, familiar label, notably committee work. John Lemuel's tellingly titled essay "Death by Committee" describes what happens when a faculty member's strengths and desires are exploited in committees rather than valued.[10] Stephen Porter's analysis of committee service "reveals few differences in committee participation between females and faculty of color and white male faculty." Porter calmly summarizes that "this is [in general] good news; while females and faculty of color may share a disproportionate burden in terms of institutional service, it appears that this is not taking place in departmental and university committee member- ships."[11] While it is certainly useful to have this data, and while other forms of service were not within the purview of Porter's study, his summary may nonetheless inadvertently highlight a core gendered issue of professional service—that since women are apparently not shouldering a disproportion- ate burden of committee work, the majority of it is likely happening in less visible, less measurable, less categorizable arenas.

Some studies add nuance to our understanding of service by addressing the mislabeling of certain activities (for example, certain intellectual work that, while closely aligned with scholarly undertakings, is considered service and thus undervalued),[12] but the many services we perform each day that are largely invisible to our institutions have remained mostly invisible in scholarship as well. Katie Hogan's cogent analysis of the silent economy of service at play in academia is a recent and an important exception.[13]

This silent economy of increasing service burdens stems from many insidious factors, including the wide-scale erosion of tenure-track positions, which ramps up the workload of all full-time faculty.[14] At most schools, not only faculty lines but also administrative and staff positions have fallen victim to corporate-model downsizing, yet there has been little if any discussion of the powerful ripple effects of inadequate administrative support on the work life of faculty. At a school with adequate staffing, for example, faculty would ideally be able to turn to a staff member for support for everything from receipts processing to travel reservations to purchasing refreshments for events. At less well-funded institutions of any size, these and many other uncategorizable tasks will never be made visible on CVs or annual reports. Even though a stated purpose of the MLA's Commission on Professional Service was to "make faculty work visible,"[15] its categories nonetheless utterly obscure many of the small yet enormously time-consuming administrative or clerical tasks that we routinely perform.

In a recent article in the *Chronicle of Higher Education*, Lynne Murphy identifies what she calls "the service trap" for junior faculty, that is, agreeing to a personally meaningful but burdensome service load (in her case, program administration) that is not valued by the institution when it comes time for tenure or promotion. "[S]ervice obligations weigh heavily in the critical first few years of a tenure-track job, when a neophyte faculty member ought to be establishing and carrying out a research agenda," she describes. Murphy's use of the term *ought* is somewhat indistinct, since, while it obviously reflects the institution's (or at least some institutions') point of view, it also seems to imply that she has accepted it. Crucially, though, she later makes clear that she is troubled by the institution's priorities and gets at the heart of her dilemma by bringing desire into the picture:

> What gets lost in all of this is that I love my work, my university, my students, and even some of my colleagues. . . . I am very proud of the program I have helped to put in place here. I know that I have given something enduring and positive to the university and to its students.[16]

As Murphy describes, program administration can be a particularly egregious example of the double standard evident so often in the service arena—a sort of "Little Red Hen" mentality in which administrators want or even expect someone else to grind the institutional grain and bake its proverbial bread, which they then eat with satisfaction, without rewarding or at times even acknowledging the work required to produce it. Worse, some institutions ultimately punish those who perform such work by not renewing, tenuring, or promoting them, since they have not also published sufficient "traditional" scholarship. Murphy's essay thus articulates a profound irony: that the very conditions of our work often obscure our desire for it. Or, more accurately, when institutions do not value what we do, disenchantment replaces desire. No one wins when that is the case.

Unlabeled and unrewarded administrative tasks are only one side of the silent and often gendered economy of service; what we might call emotional labor, in particular counseling or supporting students or colleagues on non-academic issues, is another side. The Commonwealth Partnership's "Open Letter" sketches the broad outlines of this type of service:

> Our faculty members shape students' educational experiences as much by who they are as by what they teach. They share an interest in the personal as well as intellectual development of young adults. At different times and with different students they must be nurturing and demanding, supportive and critical. The personal interaction . . . is essential to the education we offer.[17]

For any number of reasons, this aspect of service may well be highly gendered. It is also clear from several studies that the demands for this kind of service to students are far greater on faculty of color than on white faculty.

Such emotional service is extremely difficult to define or discuss. While some colleagues and administrators may well have sympathy for and support our attempts to lessen our administrative burdens, those same administrators may tell us that the time we spend counseling students or colleagues is our own problem or even our fault, rather than understanding that this kind of service, which supports and may even help retain students, is not just a personal preference but has real value to the institution. Articulating that value can help combat the mind-set that holds that our "job[s] as professor[s] ha[ve] more to do with writing books than with the students assigned to read them."[18] Those who hold that view would assume that one would always want to reduce "emotional" encounters with students, so advice they offer, if any, would likely be to make oneself less available, to refer students elsewhere. If one continues such service in such an unsupportive environment, then the clear message is that it will have to be on one's own time, on the "second shift" that Dale Bauer so adroitly identifies, while our "real" workday is spent doing what the institution values.[19]

In an attempt both to concretize the desire/value correlation and to make visible the complicating effect of some of the uncategorized service we perform, I will describe the culture of service as I experienced it at the three institutions at which I have served since completing my PhD. Each institution raised distinct issues about the value of service and the room left for expressing personal desire through that service. These experiences can provide, I hope, a framework for a broader understanding of the challenges of service in the language and literature workplace.

I taught first at a small women's college in New England, on a one-year appointment as a visiting assistant professor. The colleagues who hired me made it clear to me from the outset that the small size of the program demanded that visitors assume at least some of the service obligations of the tenure-track faculty members they replaced. The workload in general was frequently close to overwhelming, as I believe it often is at smaller schools, and as it surely usually feels in anyone's first year on the job. The service obligations were not a huge portion of the overall workload and were mostly quite pleasant experiences with students (such as German Club, Conversation Hour, theater excursions). However, because nearly all of them were evening or weekend responsibilities, the time slot often loomed larger than the time commitment, since it so blatantly cut into what I had always considered personal time.

The value of service with which I grappled in this first job was not merely (or perhaps not really) connected to the institution that hired me. Indeed, I could likely have shirked some or even all of the service obligations I was given with few or no repercussions from the institution itself, since I was going to be leaving after a year anyway. But I understood the service to be part of my job description, so my sense of duty was strong, in spite of my frustrations with the schedule, frustrations that were also occasionally assuaged by the benefit of meeting with other colleagues. I was also, of course, very concerned about the ways in which my service at that institution would be valued by other institutions that might consider hiring me the following year, so I overlooked desire in favor of professional survival.

My next job was a tenure-track position at a mid-size, church-affiliated research university in the Midwest. Because of the high value the institution placed on research, untenured faculty members were routinely "protected" (the institution's word) from service obligations it felt would impede research progress. This protection was always presented as an enlightened policy, and I often felt very grateful for the acknowledgment inherent in it that the institution had the obligation to create conditions for faculty that supported the high research output it demanded. And since my research as a medievalist was then and continues to be the most deeply intellectually sustaining part of my work, I also simply appreciated the time to focus on it.

Still, I came to see the culture of "protection" from service as problematic, since it implies both that service is something negative, even dangerous, to be sheltered from (at least while one is developing one's scholarly profile), and that once one is tenured, one suddenly no longer needs or deserves protection.[20] It is also patronizing, in that it assumes that the most important contribution every new professor can make will or must be in her scholarship. Moreover, it renders nearly inaudible the voices of junior faculty on important university bodies, and it diminishes the agency of junior faculty who might want to be more involved in service and who have the experience or foresight to choose their own commitments wisely. Worst of all, this approach denies the fact that even at major research institutions it is both unrealistic and even detrimental to have a system of faculty development in place that does nothing but teach its member to speak "the monolithic discourse of the research institution."[21] Such a discourse creates "the fiction . . . that every other institutional or professional demand is a distraction from . . . "real work,"[22] but faculty members will speak it to the exclusion of all other discourses if it is the only one to which the host institution will respond. The alienation and lost opportunities of such an exclusionary discourse are manifold and profound, not least because even the most elite institutions need their faculty members to be excellent teachers and citizens, yet they assume that faculty will develop those strengths even though institutions attach little real value to them, that is, toward renewal, tenure, and promotion.

"Protecting" new faculty from service can also isolate them from some of the very people who could most effectively mentor them. There were many afternoons when I sat in my office, feeling grateful, on the one hand, for the "protected" time to write, but on the other hand feeling confined and cut off from the larger community outside my door. Moreover, and ironically, the college- and university-wide committees from which the university "protected" me would likely have been far less time consuming than the departmental committees that I considered both important and meaningful but that I was neither protected from nor felt free to say no to.

I also regret that I chose not to engage in certain service opportunities that ranked high on my personal desire scale but that had negative value on the institution's scale. These included choices not to engage in public actions undertaken by an independent faculty women's organization to which I belonged and choosing not to use my union organizing experience to advocate with university administrators for frustrated adjunct faculty and staff workers. Knowing some of the history of adversarial relationships between the administration and campus activists, I avoided these activities out of fear that they might keep me from tenure. I am not proud of these choices, even though I understand why I made them.

After five years at that institution, I moved for family reasons to my current institution, a small, regional, church-affiliated teaching university in the Northwest. I was initially hired in a one-year visiting position and then after that year onto the tenure track. The culture of service between these two schools could not differ more. The expectation and high pressure of a near-cloistered scholarly existence have been replaced by a highly communal atmosphere where service to the department, the college, and the university is not only expected but, indeed, required and highly valued for tenure and promotion. The sense of shared mission and cooperation among faculty and often between faculty and administration is usually palpable here and remains one of my favorite features of this job. Many of the frustrations I felt at my previous institution have been relieved here and many of my strengths have been validated because I have the sense, as Paul Handstedt articulates of his and other small schools, that "very little service goes to waste from a professional perspective—it is seen, it is recognized, and it is valued."[23] Indeed, in my tenure process, I submitted my file with a great deal of confidence that "the ways in which [I've] added to the day-to-day life of the college [would be] what's most salient in the minds of the committee members."[24] At the same time, the sheer volume and breadth of service obligations and opportunities continue to nearly take my breath away, not to mention to take away almost any time I might ever hope to devote to my research, which I must also continue if I hope for further promotion. The need for an approach that balances the attitude of my current school with that of my previous one seems clear.

The variety of types of service my colleagues and I perform here (as countless others surely also do at other schools across the country) has caused me to consider more deeply the cost of the uncategorizable activities I raised earlier, and these considerations beg several questions. What is the definition of service, and who has the right to formulate that definition? If we cede that right solely to our institutions, will the resulting definition continue to obscure much of the work many of us do? And to what extent is service gendered? It may not necessarily be that service burdens always or predominantly fall on women faculty, although that is certainly the case in many programs and departments but, rather, that the model of service in practice at most institutions is patriarchal and patronizing and thus disenfranchises faculty of both genders by largely denying room for desire or agency. And certainly as long as the corporate model rules the organizational structure of our institutions, the exhaustion from the sheer volume of required work will continue to obscure, if not obliterate, desire and the enriching role it could play.[25]

One way to begin to make visible the service we perform and to make room for the service we most highly desire is simply to begin to document what we do on a daily or hourly basis. Chances are, both we and our administrators would be surprised to discover how many vital yet unrecognized activities we perform each day, which ones we desire and which ones we do not. As an experiment in making my own work visible, I decided to log the activities of a single day. My log includes not only the tasks I performed but also my notes and questions about how to categorize them:

- one committee meeting

- began review of a manuscript for a journal (service or scholarship?)

- met with one student who wants to drop the major, one class shy of completion (This is academic advising, but he's not an official advisee of mine, so he is "invisible.")

- met with another student who was upset about what she saw as the university's dismissive response to a recent hate crime against a homosexual student and the overall less-than-supportive environment for gay and queer students (emotional service? mentoring? just listening?)

- had two conversations with Dean of Residential Life and two students to discuss information a student had passed on to me about an as-yet unreported off-campus rape of another student (???)

- met with a first-year student who came into the program in advanced standing and wanted to craft an internship for independent study (This is clearly academic advising, but she's not an official advisee of mine, so she's "invisible" too.)

- had a long phone conversation with a colleague on leave about problems with a study abroad program she was to lead that had recently moved sites. Our discussion included consideration of a short-notice plan B if the on-site organization didn't come through with the details they had promised. (Is this teaching [since it's related to a course—but someone else's]? Program development?)

The details of my day matter less than the bigger issues they raise. I was immediately struck by the many fluid boundaries and blurry demarcations I discovered between the traditional "big three" areas of teaching, research, and service in my day, even within the "new model" that includes "gray areas" that the MLA Commission on Professional Service attempted to develop over a decade ago. It is not that every individual task we perform must be listed somewhere, but that such cloudiness, alas, usually leads to invisibility of the task performed, and if it is a task a faculty member performs regularly, then an entire category and certainly many hours, even weeks, of valuable contributions end up lost, a fact that can profoundly impact her future and security.

The discoveries we can make from the simple act of documentation could lead to important conversations about creating categories or at least finding support for the activities that have traditionally been the most invisible and have thus left faculty vulnerable and institutions running less than efficiently. But describing and documenting will do us little good if it is one-sided. What is most likely needed is an expanded paradigm, embraced by faculty and administration alike and similar to Ernest Boyer's influential model for scholarship, that makes visible—and thus meaningful and valuable—the varieties of service we perform, and from which our institutions and students benefit.[26] Such an expanded rubric would, at least at some institutions, make clear how many strictly clerical functions we perform that perhaps few of us desire to do for their own merits (even though we do them because we desire for our programs to run smoothly), and that are probably, in most instances, not the most efficient use of our knowledge or skills. This, in turn, may make it easier to argue for increased administrative support.

Boyer's redefining paradigm includes:

- scholarship of discovery, the most closely aligned with traditional understandings of scholarship;

- scholarship of integration (interdisciplinary, or disciplinary work in a wider context, as well as reviews of others' work);

- scholarship of application (related to service, in that it uses professional skills for the development of the wider academic community); and

- scholarship of teaching, which incorporates one's research or other professional development into the classroom and would probably also comprise writing about teaching.[27]

Some service is inherently incorporated into Boyer's categories. Indeed, making visible certain kinds of intellectual service that do not fit a traditional understanding of scholarship was a major motivation for Boyer's recommendations. But not all of the service we perform will result in a product that can be evaluated even in Boyer's useful paradigm. If we were to adopt a similar model for service, then it would also need to go beyond, or perhaps add more nuance to, the categories "Intellectual Work" and "Academic and Professional Citizenship" suggested by the MLA Commission on Professional Service. As a starting point, I might suggest the following:

- service of teaching, which would include advising and many other forms of student interaction outside the classroom, such as workshops or talks to student groups;

- service of mentorship and support, which would include professional or personal mentoring of both colleagues and students, as well as professional outreach to K–12 schools;

- intellectual service, which would refer to service that calls on a faculty member's distinct disciplinary expertise and would include program administration, journal editing, manuscript review, and the like; and

- service of integration, service that melds disciplines, brings our expertise or energies to bear on large professional or public issues and could be either external or internal to our institutions.

The advantage of such descriptors could be that something often viewed as monolithically as "committee service" would be able to be parsed and appropriately valued, for certainly not all committees' charges, workload, or impact are the same. Faculty at schools that are more teaching- and service-focused have probably been the most eager to adopt Boyer's refined scholarship categories, as they have sought to highlight the many forms their scholarship take beyond traditional disciplinary confines. Conversely, the impact of more sophisticated categories for defining service might be greatest at research-focused institutions, whose faculty may not have a means of accentuating the important realities of the service they perform. Simply listing "undergraduate advisor," "program head," or "committee chair" on one's CV, for example, certainly does not tell the whole story of the commitment required, a story that deserves to be told on its own merits, and urgently so when it is eclipsed by what is *not* listed in the "publications" section of the CV. Service of any kind produces real benefits—to faculty, students, and institution—but it also requires real hours of real days that cannot also be devoted to the more visible production of traditional scholarship. This is part of the real economy of our workplaces, and institutions ignore it to their detriment.

Elsewhere in this volume Andrea Adolph argues powerfully for an understanding of service as scholarship when the service in question requires deep intellectual engagement within one's field and has impact beyond the institution. From this perspective, one might be able to eliminate the category "Intellectual Service" altogether and instead include these items in the scholarship section of our CV and discuss them with similarly changed emphases in our conversations with colleagues, especially on rank and tenure committees.

Shifting the perspective to increase the visibility and appreciation of service will require time and energy, but the successful impact of Boyer's work offers reason to believe that such a shift is possible. It offers hope that we can move service from the "unwieldy, confused category" that is usually "perceived as sheer labor, at worst despised as thankless scut work"[28] to a part of our work that is not only infused with value but that might even be fertile enough ground for a blossoming of the "golden seed" of desire that many of us probably thought we had lost forever.[29]

Notes

1. Excerpt from my e-mail to an online writing group, October 12, 2007.

2. Nona Fienberg, " 'The Most of It': Hiring at a Nonelite College," *Profession* (1996): 77.

3. David R. Evans, "Small Departments and Professional Desires," *Profession* (1999): 208.

4. John Guillory, "Pre-Professionalism: What Graduate Students Want," *Profession* (1996): 98.

5. Paul Handstedt, "Service and the Life of the Small-School Academic," *Profession* (2003): 81. Handstedt powerfully articulates the sometimes robotic, even smothering, nature of service at small schools, which fosters faculty who "blindly heed the call to service, all the while organizing and chairing . . . [their] way into academic oblivion" or "view[ing] service as a burden." "Service and the Life of the Small-School Academic," *Profession* (2003): 81.

6. Some sectors of the business world may have a better grasp on the benefits of such symbiosis than academe, understanding that employee satisfaction is key for effective functioning. See, as just one of many examples, Geoffrey Lloyd, "Suggestive Behavior," *Accountancy* 124/1272 (August 1, 1999): 60.

7. MLA Commission on Professional Service, "Making Faculty Work Visible: Reinterpreting Professional Service, Teaching and Research in the Fields of Language and Literature," *Profession* (1996): 161.

8. Ibid., 162.

9. Ibid., 174.

10. John Lemuel, "Death by Committee," *Chronicle of Higher Education*, January 9, 2007, Careers section, http://www.chronicle.com/jobs/news/2007/02/2007010901c/careers.html.

11. Stephen Porter, "A Closer Look at Faculty Service: What Affects Participation on Committees?," Report, University of Iowa, n.d., 9.

12. Jeni Hart, Margaret Grogan, Jackie Litt, and Roger Worthington, "Diversity in Curriculum and Pedagogy: Hidden and Sought," Report to the University of Missouri-Columbia, n.d.

13. Katie Hogan, "Superserviceable Feminism," *the minnesota review* 63/64 (2005), http://www.theminnesotareview.org/journal/ns6364/iae_ns6364_superserviceablefeminism.shtml.

14. Marc Bousquet has written some of the most important work available on the economy of academe. See, for example, "The Rhetoric of 'Job Market' and the Reality of the Academic Labor System," *College English* 66:2 (2003): 207–28, in which he argues that "'market knowledge' is a rhetoric of the labor system and not a description of it" (209). For additional discussion of the impact of market rhetoric on higher education, in particular, how it has eroded the "demand" for new PhDs, see Bousquet's scathing description and analysis of "academic capitalism" in "The Waste Product of Graduate Education: Toward a Dictatorship of the Flexible," *Social Text* 70:1 (2002): 81–104, esp. 84–85, where he discusses the inability of the market analogy to provide for the academic workplace anything other than "imaginary solution[s] . . . to real problem[s]."

15. MLA Commission, 161.

16. Lynne Murphy (pseudonym), "At Your Service," *Chronicle of Higher Education*, February 23, 2007, Careers section, http://www.chronicle.com/jobs/news/2007/02/2007022301c/careers.html.

17. The Commonwealth Partnership. "What You Should Know: An Open Letter to New PhDs." *Profession* (1996): 80.

18. Pamela Johnston, "Confessions of a Former FIG Queen," *The Chronicle of Higher Education*, August 2, 2007, Careers section, http://www.chronicle.com/jobs/news/2007/08/2007080101c/careers.html.

19. Dale Bauer, "Academic Housework: Women's Studies and Second Shifting," in *Women's Studies on Its Own*, ed. Robyn Wiegman, 245–57 (Durham, NC, and London: Duke University Press, 2004).

20. Hogan discusses the irony that women who are granted tenure may not only no longer be protected, as they were pre-tenure, but, may, in fact, "experience an increase in service work that often jeopardizes their candidacy for promotion to full professor."

21. Fienberg, "'The Most of It,'" 77.

22. Evans, "Small Departments . . . ," 206.

23. Hanstedt, "Service and the Life . . . ," 81.

24. Ibid.

25. Besides Marc Bousquet's work described in note 14 see also "The Corporatized Research University and Tenure in Modern Language Departments: Notes from Minnesota," *Profession* (1999): 86–95, for an articulation of some of the destructive effects of corporatization.

26. Ernest L. Boyer, *Scholarship Reconsidered: Priorities of the Professoriate*, Carnegie Foundation for the Advancement of Teaching Special Report (San Francisco, CA: Jossey-Bass, 1990).

27. See Jayne E. Marek's assessment of the impact of Boyer's work in "*Scholarship Reconsidered* Ten Years After and the Small College," *Profession* (2003): 44–54.

28. MLA Commission, 170.

29. Jane Smiley, *Moo* (New York: Knopf, 1995), 117. In her novel *Moo*, Smiley's protagonist Cecilia Sanchez grapples mightily with the loss of her desire (in her case for her research).

8

Outreach

Considering Community Service and the Role of Women of Color Faculty in Diversifying University Membership

Myriam J. A. Chancy

Santa Barbara, California, December 2006

It is early December, and I have been asked to give a presentation for a community outreach program run by the Center for Black Studies out of the University of California, Santa Barbara. I am to represent an "accomplished" member of the community. There will be two other presenters—one a resource person in the community, and the other one of the children or youth in the program. The outreach program assists school-age children of color, particularly of African American, Latino, and Native American descent, to improve their grades, as well as their self-confidence, through tutoring, mentoring, and family and academic support, with the aim of tracking the children into appropriate colleges and universities. So far, the program, small in scale, is successful. Mentors are matched by race and gender, however, my first mentee and I have not been able to connect much, so I welcome the opportunity to speak to the children and their parents about some aspect of my work, to be of assistance in some way.

Rather than present on my literature, as is expected, I decide to present a selection of photographs, some published, some not, taken in Haiti, Cuba, California, and Italy. They tell a story about my travels, my hopes, about my well of creativity. I even take my SLR camera to show its inner workings; in this digital age, it is a rare sight. As I had expected, the photographs create an immediate connection; some of the parents find themselves in the photos, remembering cultural details about their own homelands left behind. One

139

mother points to a photograph taken in the Venice canals of laundry sticks and smiles, *lavandería*. A father nods with his son over a photograph of a group of boys playing marbles in an open street in Havana, Cuba. I connect the photographs to my written work, explaining which journey opened up an imaginative window or contributed to finessing a scholarly piece of work, but at the center of it all are the images connecting disparate groups of people through the simple fact of their coexisting humanity.

A Chumash/Latino family presents that same night, their presentation rich with cultural knowledge. They tell us about the uses of fauna in our immediate region, of rites of passage for young Chumash teenagers, of journeys through rapids in traditional canoes. The teenage son reads a poem in Chumash; his father translates. Their presentation is beautiful and inspiring, and it is clear to me that the term *accomplishment* might be otherwise defined, not as professional or worldly success (however we might define the latter as well) but as the ability to succeed in holding on to our integral cultural selves, to be cherished within community, even when such community is fleeting or temporary. After the presentations, as we mingle, both parents tell me, respectively, that they appreciated my presentation, that they hope that it will inspire their son to pursue a doctorate, to travel the world. The thought stays with me, and in a few weeks I suggest that the program allow me to mentor this young man, despite our differences of gender and race.

For a few months, I will be privileged to mentor the young poet who, after our first meeting, sends me a note to tell me that he thinks our encounter will be meaningful, a portal opening for his creative self. Some months after our exchanges, when I will have left Santa Barbara for my own next port of call, I will find out that my mentee has gone on to skip two grades in high school English and has been allowed to do his schoolwork from home. He adores Stephen King and fantasy novels, and now he has all the time in the world to create his own universe.

I saw myself in this young man, despite our differences in age, race, class, and gender, and it had seemed to me then, as it always does in my classrooms, that such differences meant very little in the face of what could be exchanged. I learned as much from this youth and his dedicated family than I had to offer. I was inspired by my mentee's passion for the written word and his depth of readership, which, at age fourteen, was much farther along than most college undergraduates. I was inspired as well by his family, who, despite limitations owing to class, saw to it that their son, one of three, had his artistic inclinations and inspirations nurtured rather than squelched. That form of support is the bridge that made our exchange possible, that will ultimately make possible his entry into the college of his choice.

Some ten years prior, I had quite a different experience with teenage girls in Phoenix, Arizona, with no such bridge to support their efforts. In the fall of 1998, I had been working for two years with an independent organization called Free Arts for Abused Children. The first year, I had co-designed an art course for a girls' shelter with a colleague and fellow writer. The first time we met with the girls, they were well behaved and attentive; everything was in order in their small classroom, and we were full of zeal. I left the first session excited, happy with the choice I had made to extend my teaching beyond the university walls. When my co-teacher and I arrive for the second, planned lesson, the girls are not quite as attentive, nor quite as orderly. It is as if everyone, including the management of the home, has forgotten that we were coming. One of the girls looks up from her desk as we enter the classroom. "I remember you," she says, "weren't you here last week?" We nod. "You're back," another girl says, "we didn't think you'd come back."

Free Arts for Abused Children brings art to homeless, neglected, and abused children, mostly in shelters, most wards of the state. These are the kids that are generically categorized as "at risk." It might surprise you to learn that in Phoenix, this means poor and white. It may surprise you to learn that most of the kids in poverty in the United States are, indeed, white. In these shelters, race has an altogether different potency than in academe or perhaps elsewhere. History is not lost or forgotten but shared. These girls share the same pain of being forgotten, by their mothers, their fathers, their families, and their communities. They do not believe that anyone is coming back for them.

We teach them writing exercises between and with art projects. In one project we decide to have them draw mandalas, symbols of peace and contemplation in various strains of Buddhism and some indigenous spiritual practices; after each girl has created her mandala, we pin or tape it to her back and have the other girls write a word or phrase of positive affirmation on each of the other girls' work, whether or not they consider the others friends or foes. We teach them what they have taught us: that from their losses can be derived strength, that what others consider their brokenness is their worldliness. For now, they are trapped in the group home, made to ingest state-prescribed drugs to keep them calm or to wean them off of illegal intoxicants. They will tell you what works and what doesn't work; they will tell you what they wish they had and what they've lost. Even trapped as they are in the shelter, they are more cosmopolitan than the world traveler. They will tell you how much they love their mothers, even the ones who have beat them or sold their jewelry or stolen their babysitting money for something they were promised that never materialized. And when they look at us, one white, one racially mixed, they don't ask to see our pedigrees. Yes, they test us, but only to see whether we'll truly come back, to test whether or not we truly care.

At the end of it all, one of them asks whether I think she might be able to go to college, and I say yes and explain how this might come about. There is hope in her eyes.

It surprises me, the exchanges I have with these young women. The ones who trust me most, who ask me the questions most important to their developing minds, are not of my age, race, or class, and yet they trust me. I represent something of who they might become. We do share uncertain child-hoods; they pick up on the scent immediately; it's the first clue that they can trust me, but once they realize this, the rest is incidental. These experiences with disadvantaged youth are eerily similar to my experiences in university classrooms wherein the students who most take to my lessons are young males, mature women of all races, white, working-class women, and LGBT students. Affinity is derived from our humanity rather than our sameness.

These experiences working in the community make me wonder about the assumptions that are made in academia about which class of professionals should perform service work on a regular basis (women, people of color, the untenured). On the one hand, we might well ask, who will do this work if we do not, if we care about change, about progress? And yet, my community service also has me think about other assumptions that are made about the forms of service each class can or should perform: Who can mentor, and who can benefit from it? Which forms of diversity do we value? Can we, in this time, in 2008, recognize that diversity is not necessarily shared, but that different points of commonality can enrich our exchanges?

The Engaged Campus and Community Service

According to Campus Compact, a national nonprofit coalition of over 1,100 college and university presidents, whose intent is to promote community ser-vice, civic engagement, and service learning in higher education, an engaged campus can be defined as "one that is consciously committed to reinvigorating the democratic spirit and community engagement in all aspects of its campus life."[1] The co-directors of the University of Maryland Civic Engagement Project further define civic engagement as "active participation (interaction, involvement) in making a difference in the civic life of our communities," adding that "[c]ivic engagement allows us to take what we learn about our world and seek to initiate understanding, change, and growth."[2] Researchers posting the results of a study on the effectiveness of engagement theory and practices at the national level on a University of Michigan Web site report the following:

> An engaged campus has not only lowered the boundaries between
> the institution and its communities, it has established long-term
> partnerships that create both communal and associative relationships.
> Ideally, spending on public service activity is not simply a high

proportion of an institutional budget, but it reflects institutional priorities for civic engagement and is associated with policies and structures in place that guide and direct activities for students, faculty, and staff. In this regard, core leadership support is important in creating a vision of establishing an institutional identity that is engaged in furthering the civic mission of higher education.[3]

The concept of the "engaged campus" thus entails more than simple community outreach or what can often lead to misuse of the community for the advancement of student learning in service-learning opportunities that often turn out to take more from the community than such programs leave behind. What the prevailing circulating ideas on the "engaged campus" suggest is that institutions of higher learning have been failing in their civic duty to encourage the circulation of knowledge for the benefit and use of communities beyond the university walls. Seeking to redress the divide between town and gown, the engaged campus thus takes up its civic duty to export the knowledge and resources of the university to outlying communities. What is not addressed, however, in cursory discussions of the function of engaged communities is the degree to which communities may have knowledge of their own to impart to the university. The model of the engaged campus, as I understand it, suggests a unidirectional conduit of information. The community may serve as a resource, as an object of study, but following in colonial models of valor, it tends to be seen not as an actor but as a subject without agency. This is not to say that all service-learning models for engaged campus are doomed to fail, or that they do fail; it is to suggest that depending on how institutional administrators define their civic mission, that is, whether they understand the civic responsibilities of the university as *missionary* or as necessary to desolving the elitism that has been built into academic endeavors and our reproduction of knowledge largely based (at least in the humanities) on outdated concepts of hegemony, national, gendered, racial, and otherwise, the engagement of any campus will be mitigated by the underlying ideology behind the institution's efforts. By and large, what the available data on engaged campuses suggest is that the increased bureaucracy and business modeling of the institution interfere with the notion of a democratic engagement of campus with surrounding communities. Indeed, institutions of higher learning are, constitutionally, anti-democratic.

On the other hand, current models of community service ask those who serve to offer to community members what they need, to answer to questions rather than only to ask them, to provide assistance rather than to impose it. Without reciprocity, the assistance offered has no purpose; it cannot be taken in but only refused. This reminds me of Paulo Freire's (2000) ideas on the role of love in exchanges between the privileged and the dispossessed, as discussed in his *Pedagogy of the Oppressed*. Without true love for the other, Freire would conjecture, there can be no real teaching, no real exchange. Yet in the context of *university* service, such work, such bridging, has no currency: it is ignored even as it serves to benefit the university (generically).[4] One inspires youth in the community to think about pursuing a college education while also representing the university as an avenue of hope to them, since, after all, as many a postcolonial theorist has argued, knowledge is power. But where is the university in the community? And can the university, with all of its trappings of elitism, effectively become communal, a community *participant* rather than a removed player interacting with the community as its other?

Service and the Tenure Track

In most departments of English and literature in institutions of higher learning, service has become an indispensable portion of a trinity of expectations by which faculty are advanced to or held back from the upper echelons of the tenure-track and tenured hierarchy. Though service is, as Michelle A. Massé and Katie J. Hogan have described in their introduction to this book, a crucial aspect of our work as professionals in this arena, it is also a means by which—especially for those of us dedicated to feminist perspectives—dreams of equality and equal access for those traditionally or economically disadvantaged are realized rather than only theorized. It has also been true that women tend to bear the brunt of such work and, as Hogan, points out, that women of color at all ranks tend to be relegated to more of this kind of work at the expense of their ability to publish and at times to teach at their own or the institution's standards. Both Massé and Hogan also point out that women of all backgrounds at the associate rank, freed from the weight of gaining tenure, can also be overburdened. One can only imagine, then, what this might mean for women who occupy overlapping minority spaces, whether these are women of color, women who have risen from the working classes, or women who are lesbian, and so on, representing other minority groups and looked to for guidance both by students and colleagues. The issue seems to me to be one of competing definitions of "service."

Indeed, in thinking through my ruminative reflections for this modest contribution to this volume,[5] I could not resist the sophomoric urge to seek out dictionary definitions of the term. According to the *Merriam-Webster Dictionary*, "service" has several definitions, some of which are complimentary while others might be thought of as competing. The most pertinent definitions of service are as follows: "1. the occupation of being a servant; 2. help, benefit; 3. a meeting for worship . . . ; 4. the act, fact, or means, of serving;

5. performance of official or professional duties; 6. serve." When performing service for our institutions are we simply performing official duties in order to assist in the smooth running of a workplace, or are we serving our departments and institutions to benefit our students and the wider purpose of disseminating knowledge and skills to our students? Are there instances when, for women and women of color specifically, institutional service becomes servitude? Is there such a thing as "communion," in the sense of worship, in a spiritual sense, attendant to service work? Certainly critiques of women's service, as discussed briefly earlier, suggest that women are forced into an administrative underclass by which they are expected to do the "dirty work" for their institutions so that their roles in the workplace appear to mimic that of the old private versus public spheres of the Victorian age. Service, under this guise, cannot but lose any sense of spiritual "right work" (to invoke a Buddhist conceit), or, in a more plebian sense, to altruistically benefit others. Male colleagues are freed of day-to-day service work in order to publish, attend conferences, and participate in more high-profile service work directly linked to decision making (linked to grants, hires, heading committees or departments). At the other extreme are women of color, said to be a scarce commodity, who not only lack institutional representation at the higher ranks but also, as a consequence, lack the networks and support systems of their male cohorts as well as their white, female cohorts on an ongoing basis; we may, at times, be *included* in the networks of others, but the issues of women of color do not occupy center stage.

For women of color, the strategies for contributing to the health of their institutions while also ensuring their survival within them are fraught. Putting aside for now Kelly Ward's (2003) notion of the "joys" of service,[6] the reality remains that for women of color in academe, opportunities for success are few and far between. And what of service to the larger community or profession? Can "service" beyond the university walls serve as a contribution to the university? In my personal experiences, I have come to believe that community service is essential to the future of universities, especially in terms of increasing the diversity of both student and faculty bodies. Ironically, in terms of my own professional growth, I have little considered the role of my community volunteerism as "service" to the institution. And, as a woman of color occupying the senior ranks very early in my career, I have also not fallen prey to the exploitation faced by most of my colleagues of color whose "service" tasks have often made them servants to their institutions rather than leaders in their fields at the cost of their tenurability and contributions to their disciplines in the form of publications and speaking engagements. For me, throughout the years, the service I hold most dear is that which I have performed *in the community, in addition to,* not in spite of, my work as a scholar, an author, a teacher, and a colleague.

Saying No to Service Work: Women of Color
Surviving in Academe

Over the years, I have performed the requisite service work of a publishing senior faculty member, serving on graduate and graduate admissions committees, dissertation and masters committees, and departmental committees of various stripes, as well as serving on the national level as a reader for various journals and university presses, as a book reviewer and an editor, as a reviewer for tenure candidates at other institutions, and as an NEH expert panelist for grants in the humanities. Unlike the ongoing trend by which faculty of color are exploited in service work, I can report that my experience in the field has been atypical. What accounts for this exception (if it is one)? Are all faculty of color exploited? Are all women of color summarily exploited, or is it that institutions expect to be able to exploit faculty of color? It seems to me that the token representation of people of color on the faculty of most institutions exacerbates expectations based on stereotypes of people of color, which places them in positions of servitude even as they have demonstrated their right to be perceived and treated as equals along with their cohorts in all professorial ranks.

My own atypical experience in academe stems from two interweaving positions, the first being the mentoring I received in Canadian institutions wherein my presence was not perceived as anomalous—or, if it was, it was perceived as a positive one, and the second having to do with the fact that as I obtained tenure at age twenty-seven at Arizona State University, I came under the chairship of a Mexican American department head. That chair sought to recruit and retain me at the institution by strategically assigning service work that freed me to continue the publishing record that had brought me to the department's attention in the first place and that freed me to actively work with graduate students in my field who had long awaited mentoring. As an associate professor, therefore, I was being groomed for a long-term career as a senior professor, and the sensitivity and sensibility of another minority faculty member paved the way for such professional freedom. Such freedom was paired with my own personal understanding of the need to stake my ground, to understand that service to the institution had to be held in balance with teaching and publishing excellence, an understanding I learned as I was mentored by various professors as an undergraduate and as a beginning graduate student in a Canadian context.

I was also privileged to be mentored by a number of senior scholars at the undergraduate level, the most compelling of whom was Evelyn Hinz, editor of the respected journal of multicultural literature, *Mosaic*, and official biographer of Anaïs Nin. While still an undergraduate, Professor Hinz worked with me on my scholarship for over a year while she was on leave from the university and assisted me in understanding how to present my work to editors. Professor Hinz, like many others, taught me the skills that my cohorts were taught by virtue of being "insiders" both culturally and professionally. Being an "insider" meant acknowledging what one did and did not know, acquiring the knowledge one did not have, and valorizing the insights and skills one already owned. Such valorization meant acquiring the ability to defend one's ground; defending one's ground includes the ability to say no to demands on one's time that upset the balance of one's professional work and the triad of publishing/teaching/service. The time that Professor Hinz spent with me during a sabbatical year as she approached retirement age (while I myself was only seventeen years old) demonstrated another aspect of service—that of supporting the intellectual arc of a young, scholar-to-be. This is the kind of service that I'm sure would not have found its way onto Professor Hinz's CV; it was, however, a service that "returned" to the university in multiple ways as I followed in Professor Hinz's footsteps as a teacher/scholar/editor/writer, anchoring as I did, some twenty years later, an international publication sponsored by the Ford Foundation, which focused on transnational women of color. Indeed, my most prized service work is that which I have conducted in the communities in which I found myself, work I did not consider necessary to have counted by my institution. If such work appeared on my CV, then it appeared in a small area near the last pages of that document under a rubric entitled "Community Work" or "Volunteer Work."

In thinking about the issues that Massé and Hogan have raised, I have looked back on such work and realized that it has always centered on assisting younger individuals—as Hinz did me—in disfavored communities (primarily white) to access their creativity and potential as thinkers. Was I disfavored as a youth? Not exactly. I came from a middle-class, educated Haitian household. I was, however, a visible minority and a woman; perhaps mentors such as Professor Hinz already understood the barriers that I would face as I advanced in an academic world that recreates classes of "privileged" and "disprivileged" not solely on the basis of access but on the basis of visible difference. Operating transparently, institutions of higher learning replicate rather than deconstruct raced and sexed hierarchies, often displacing class as a category of disenfranchisement, particularly in the case of women and racial minorities whose difference is taken as their class. To be a woman or a racial minority in academia is automatically to assume a lower class status, thus the institution is able to disempower women faculty and faculty of color of their hard-won gains once admitted within the ivory tower. Ironically, then, I—as someone who might professionally be categorized a "visible minority"—am, in all community work that I perform, operating as one of the privileged, while in the university I circulated as a subaltern. Yet it is my success as a minority—where none is expected—that provides the avenue for assisting community members to *become* successful where otherwise they would be expected to fail. Being both a minority and privileged, professionally credentialed yet also a community worker, I occupy an anomalous position that provides the conduit for transformation. My volunteerism enables a bridging of disparate categories, revealing that whom we serve and why is more fluid than we might imagine.

In the experiences to which I alluded to in the first section of this essay, I came to see that my presence in the community set an important example for possibility. In the U.S. context in which excellence in youth of color is not expected, my minority status becomes a useful tool for change; still, this is a difficult road, for despite my own background and successes, the U.S. climate is such that faculty of color, tenured or untenured, are always faced with doubt regarding their credentials and intellectual contributions. One can only, then, imagine what it must be like to grow up disadvantaged, whether by race, class, or gender in such a society. I came to the United States at age twenty, so I cannot share any anecdotes of my own youth here. The youth with whom I have worked in the last decades have served as unlikely mirrors. In me, such youth were presented with a tangible example of their own possible futures, even if my external appearance belied a different life experience; my interaction with their own lives formed the bridge to those futures that in almost all cases included the vision of attending university at some point or furthering their educations. In some cases, youth thought about becoming professors in a way that had never seemed possible to them prior to such interaction. Being young, gifted, female, and of color, as well as accomplished in my field, and having "returned" in an uncertain sense to communities at risk (being neither American nor from an underclass), provided these youth with a tangible representation of what they might become.

Conclusion: What Can Be Done?

I can only conclude by stating that a return to community, then, through such work, indirectly benefited the universities where I worked at the time I undertook such service, since I was a visible member of the community and such work reflected well upon these institutions; at the same time, the youth with whom I worked began to think of sites of higher education not as hostile (as they usually imagined them to be) but as potential places for their own growth. Why such community work is not counted as service work needs to be examined more thoughtfully (in addition to thinking through why academe is viewed as hostile rather than generative). My guess is that since the results of such work are, in the short term, intangible, little thought has been given (from the institutional point of view) to the gains to be made by the institution from such work. It may also be that not much thought has been given to the competing notions of visibility with which institutions operate, often preferring that minority faculty be visible within its walls and less so beyond them. In my own life experience, I know that such work has been some of the most satisfying I have done in what might be considered "outreach," beyond the classroom. Conversely, given institutions' lack of true progress on breaking down the walls between town and gown, I am unsure of wanting this work to "count"; indeed, I often think of it as subverting the unstated aims of the institution in its cloaked elitism and paternalistic attitude toward the disfavored. Would I want the unenlightened university system of today to monitor and assign value to my community activism? Likely not.

Admittedly, the valorization of my publishing record has accounted for my ability to serve the various institutions where I have been employed without falling into servitude, but such valorization also served to efface my community contributions. In a strange twist of irony, I have benefited from being treated as an "equal" in terms of my publishing record . . . an equal to what, one might ask? The answer is, an equal to white males. White male professionals are not expected to perform service work, especially when they are publishing seriously; professionally, due to my publishing record, rightly or wrongly, I have been held to the same standard, or could invoke it, for similar results. This, however, does not mean that I performed less service, only that I was spared being exploited in "diversity" work on behalf of the university at the expense of my scholarship/writing. Neither did it mean that I was spared the institutional racism endemic to higher education, a reality that takes great pains and energy to counter, live with, and survive. Indeed, the racism that faculty of color must inhabit through most of their professional careers in academia provides an *invisible* form of service: at its worst, it allows the university to fulfill its diversity program through "tokenism"; at its best, if colleagues and administrators are willing to face the critiques provided by such faculty, it allows valuable tools for diminishing racism on our campuses and the force of institutionalized forms of racism in our various disciplines. But for most such service is performed unwittingly, without choice, as a residual effect of unexamined, latent racist and other prejudicial practices that, given the low numbers of faculty of color on most college campuses, often continue to proliferate unchecked or with a very slow process of change. What this "privilege" has also meant is that I have been able to use my relative "freedom" from institutional service work to do the work I do in the community. It is thus unfettered and still remains useful.

It is my contention that even though minority women may need to serve on committees, for example, seeking to address issues of diversity and affirmative action, it actually underserves the university to place them in such positions, as if their only contributions are to be made at this level of racial consciousness-raising. In fact, already highly skilled, such women would better serve and bring a diverse viewpoint to committees addressing structural and curriculum change. More thought, I believe, needs to be given to the ways in which women in general and women of color are "mis-utilized" in service work. The fact that I was spared certain kinds of service work by virtue of my publishing record as untenured faculty meant that I quickly became a senior faculty member. In my case, such a shift in position early in my career (three years out of graduate school) afforded me more weight in faculty discussions. I have, however, observed that, by and large, junior colleagues of color are by and far disadvantaged by a notion in our field that suggests that service to the institution will win one special graces, when it often results in women finding themselves underpublishing and untenured at the end of their tenure-track years and frustrated by the lack of progress with institutional change after their many years of service on committees meant to address such change. The current model of service work, at least for women of color and untenured women, contributes to stasis rather than resulting in growth both for these women individually and for the universities they serve. What is interesting, however, is that research findings show that historically black colleges and universities (HBCUs) disproportionately "spend more on public service than other institutions."[7] This suggests that from a cultural standpoint, faculty of color, and especially women of color, most likely spend more time doing community work. If institutions were to include community service in their indices of "service to the institution" or "service to the profession," then this would undoubtedly result in equalizing the rewards given to women of color and would lessen the pressure on untenured women of color faculty to serve on all assigned committees. They would be more likely to report their community service work in the knowledge that it would count toward their service work and relieve them from being overexpended within the institution. It would also force administrators to put the onus on non-faculty of color and male faculty to bear more responsibility in redressing racial and gender inequity. Unfortunately, such lack of valorization leads faculty of color to operate within their own definition of service. For many of us, "service" often means serving the community and not necessarily servicing the university, though such community work indirectly benefits the university; indeed, such community work necessarily encourages redefining the university as a space of inclusion when, often, such institutions are ill prepared to accommodate new constituents, even as they espouse a desire for inclusion and diversity.

Interesting to me are the ways in which community work might be, and should be, recognized by departments as doing the work of the institution, opening it up to new generations of future students whom the university may not have previously considered serious, future members of its community. Service, then, might be thought of as a means by which not only to get the work of the university fulfilled (in a corporate model that sees universities competing for students, grants, ranking) but as a means by which a utilitarian bridge between the university and the communities that it *should* service is created and kept in good working order. If institutions were made to be accountable to communities (rather than private funding agents, including the parents of undergraduates) through measures that could be measured civically and that would have legal and financial repercussions for those institutions that would reveal themselves to systemically fall short of their *philosophical* civic responsibilities, then and only then might professed engaged campuses fulfill their mandates and overturn their tradition of securing the mantel of the ivory tower. It would allow the institution to be transformed rather than be transformative in its exportation of knowledge. Not only would various forms of service stand to be valorized but so would the communities themselves, communities still yearning to be participants in higher learning rather than summarily tolerated on the outskirts of the institutional vestments of privilege.

Notes

1. Campus Compact, http://www.compact.org/advancedtoolkit/defining.html.

2. See Hickey et al. 2009.

3. N.a., http://www.umich.edu/~divdemo/Final_Engaged_Paper_kinkos.pdf.

4. I speak generically here in that the Center for Black Studies is exemplary in its connecting of the community to the University of California, Santa Barbara; my observations here bespeak the more general apathy of most universities in counting community service performed independently of the institution or on one's own time (i.e., not in service learning contexts) as "service" for faculty; indeed, universities are more likely than not to distance themselves from community volunteerism that does not directly promote a particular institution or its agendas; they do so at the loss of securing a relationship with communities in which they find themselves, which would generate the diversity that many institutions purport to seek with great difficulty. Of the several institutions in which I have taught, all struggles with what some called the "town and gown" syndrome exist at the behest of disenfranchised communities and institutions within their midst. For example, Vanderbilt University exists in a city largely populated by African Americans, as does Louisiana State University; in both cases, historically black universities (Fisk and Southern, respectively) struggle to stay afloat, and integration has all but failed when one considers the low enrollment of African Americans in both institutions. Similarly, Arizona State University is adjacent to the largest Native reservation, the Navajo Nation, and yet Native undergraduates

account for fewer than 2 percent of the student body. The rationale that students from these marginalized communities do not want to go to college simply does not account for the failings of history and the lack of mentoring and bridges provided to these communities to make the university associated with the dominant classes appealing and a natural choice for the college bound.

5. Speculative because this is an experiential rather than a research position, and because I am not a specialist in issues of service to the profession or on community service.

6. In addition to her own work on the subject in *Faculty Service Roles and the Scholarship of Engagement*, in which Ward extols the virtues of service, her comments on others' work in the field suggest a rose-colored view of the strains of service for women and women of color. For instance, in her review of J. E. Cooper's and D. D. Stevens's edited volume *Tenure in the Sacred Grove*, she laments: "Missing are accounts of the joys of teaching, the exhilaration of research, and the gratification of working with students" (Ward 2003, 147–48). What Ward seems to miss is the fact that we all know the joy, exhilaration, and gratification embedded in our work; the issue is that for some, especially women of color, the structures of the institution prevent us from fulfilling the positive rewards of our chosen professions.

7. N.a., http://www.umich.edu/~divdemo/Final_Engaged_Paper_kinkos.pdf.

Works Cited

"Defining the Engaged Campus." 2009. University of Michigan. http://www.umich.edu/~divdemo/Final_Engaged_Paper_kinkos.pdf (accessed January 28, 2009).

Freire, Paulo. 2000. *Pedagogy of the Oppressed*. London: Continuum Press.

Hickey, Georgina, et al. 2009. "Step Up: Initiative Action Leadership Growth, The Civic Engagement Newsletter." University of Maryland Civic Engagement Project, volume 1, issue 1 (January–February). http://www.umd.umich.edu/fileadmin/civicengagement/files/newsletters/civic_engagement_newsletter_jan_feb.pdf (accessed January 28, 2009).

Hollander, Elizabeth, Cathy Burack, and Barbara Holland. 2009. (Compiled material). "Defining the Engaged Campus." Campus Compact. http://www.compact.org/advancedtoolkit/defining.html (accessed January 28, 2009).

Ward, Kelly. 2003. Review of *Tenure in the Sacred Grove*. Ed. J. E. Cooper and D. D. Stevens. *JGE* 52:2: 147–48.

9

To Serve or Not to Serve

Nobler Question

Shirley Geok-lin Lim

Ironically, I am writing this essay about university service while I am at the Institute of Southeast Asian Studies in Singapore on a one-month professorial fellowship. That is, I am as far away from service as a scholar dare dream of and succeed. Even as many other desires have bleached out, reverted to whispers and rumors, or turned mute, the longing for time to read and write drives me, a senior professor, as urgently as it did when I was a young graduate student, and this passion for quiet time and empty space explains why so many academics blithely—if not without internal and familial conflict—abandon their middle-class homes, book-lined studies, high-tech access, and familiar routines for cramped visiting quarters and alien environs. Another, perhaps less acceptable, reason may be the unspoken desire to flee that stepmother-monster of service.

However, when I first left graduate school at Brandeis, I believed myself immensely lucky to have landed a tenure-track position at a community college in the South Bronx. Oh, to be able to count on a regular paycheck when trying to survive in New York, to be paid to read and write at a time when PhDs were driving cabs, to teach literature to undergraduates when my childhood classmates were teaching English grammar to primary school-children—bliss was it even there in the South Bronx to be alive, and to be young was heaven! And, as anyone who has taught in a community college knows, service, whether understood as teaching or continuous committee work, is the essence of the community college profession. A fresh immigrant to the United States, a Malaysian in a giant metropolis where hardly anyone had met a Malaysian, and one of a mere handful (perhaps the only one?) of "Asian Americans" in 1973 to graduate with a PhD in English and American literature, I felt a profound sense of isolation that made me hungry and grateful for any opportunity for community bonding. Service, not research, is where and how daily, ordinary community is to be formed, and so I began my professional life *wanting* to be of service. The Grimms Brothers' folktale of the girl whose stepmother pushes her down a well only to find herself in a world where apple trees beg to be picked and ovens plead for someone to take the loaves of bread out of the oven racks echoed in my imagination: I thought of myself as that little girl, the newly arrived immigrant, eager to work, believing that, as the reward for community service, pearls would then fall from my lips whenever I spoke. At Hostos Community College I began a writing center where Puerto Rican and black students received individual tutorials together with pages and pages of drills and work sheets. I attended rounds of committee meetings in the college and in colleagues' messy living rooms, co-writing grant proposals and churning out reports and memos that no one would ever read a second time. Nights and weekends were spent red-ink-marking students' writing, struggling to comment memorably and usefully on grammar, organization, and ideas. Three years passed by in this hyper-service society, at the end of which, looking at a budget shortfall for the City University of New York, I applied for a position at a State University of New York (SUNY) community college. My department chair wrote in her reference letter that I was "a gem," indefatigable and committed to service and teaching, and thus also with this second position, for the next fourteen years I smiled as I was praised for "working in the salt mines."

A few years later, when I received a SUNY medallion for teaching excellence, I understood that teaching was not separate from service but that the two went hand in hand as conjoined twins, with one heart and one pair of lungs, although with two pairs of hands and legs and two heads. The same motivation, for teaching and service, powered the engine that chuffed "I can, I can, I can, I can," and the ceaseless runs up and down hill drained the same reserves of energy. After a near lifetime of service, I now recognize this baggy monster, service, as uniform and the same everywhere, whether in community college or top research university, whether in New York, Hong Kong, or California. It eats up time like a chocoholic sitting with a box of See's mixed-center chocolates. It spits out co-authored, or at least co-signed, documents like a choleric baby burping up sour milk. From my early instinct for service, intuited as an integral dynamic for community bonding, I have gradually moved to distrust it, seeing how "service" has been institutionalized to serve established power, how its noble identity—as I defined its meaning, "labor, other than research and teaching, dedicated to the operations and advancement of departmental and institutional matters"—has been corrupted to contain and delimit the subject, particularly the minority subject, and how adroitly ambivalent administrators stand in relation to service as a category for reward. As Katie J. Hogan says of her own struggle with what she calls "superserviceable feminism":

> While most human beings, myself included, would not want to "escape" the opportunity to serve others—after all, human connection usually deepens intellectual, creative, political, and emotional development—in the academic world, an insidious and invisible economy of service has for years exhausted the energies of women, with women of color being particularly pressed into service roles. In some instances, this silent economy has cost women their health, jobs, and professional advancement, and it has tragically prevented many from expressing their creative, intellectual, and leadership abilities.[1]

Hogan's complaint underscores that I am not the only academic to have grown disillusioned with the ideal of service that drew us in part to education. Chaucer's clerk, that paragon for the university man or woman in my student days—"gladly wolde he lerne and gladly teach"—as a unit to be measured and evaluated in the contemporary academic labor marketplace—has not a snowball's chance in hell in advancing to tenure in a research university. Andrew Furman urges us "to take a hard look at our ludicrous overvaluation of academic research at the expense of service," but we also know that Furman's suggestion holds no water.[2] At the same time, however, there is sufficient pressure to take up his position that "service" is piously if not seriously expected of faculty members; thus, as in the classic scene in *When Harry Met Sally*, the assistant professor in the face of tenure assessment must make all of the correct glad noises on service while at the same time grinding her teeth and rewriting her tenure book.

My overheated discourse on the role of service in the life of one university woman perhaps marks the bitterness of a seduction gone bad, because for the longest time I believed, as a woman, an ethic minority, and an immigrant outsider, that in service lay true empowerment. Department chairs make decisions, deans rule over faculty, and provosts and vice chancellors, robed in masculine garb, those who individually address faculty as a collective, hold us in their decisive grip. The old boys' network, I was told repeatedly, controlled the levers of university power, and we women subalterns needed to challenge these men to become in our turn administrators, senate chairs, department chairs, and assorted committee chairs. So, yes, today women are to be found as presidents at Princeton, the University of Pennsylvania, and even Harvard University. Yet oddly women are also saying no to offers to serve as administrators and chairs of senates and departments. At least I have said no, and I know of others similarly disinclined.

The situation has parallels with the recent social phenomenon of a growing number of professional women disengaging from the workforce to stay at home to raise their 1.5 children. In the case of these stay-at-home mothers, the pressures and pleasures of child care, together with the economic ability to leave the workplace, explain what must appear as a counterintuitive life decision. But what explains my increasing distaste for service, which, even in my most curmudgeonly moments, I still recognize as both urgently important and potentially self-empowering?

Part of the answer must lie in my experience as chair of a women's studies program and later as head of English and chair professor at the University of Hong Kong. Both administrative appointments brought me tremendous opportunities to make a difference and quite a lot of pleasure in being able to influence the recruitment of young PhDs whose scholarship, teaching, and publications over the years have confirmed my original impression of their promise. Administrative service at its best holds the key for an individual to intervene in the structure of a department, a discipline, or even an entire university; it validates the core commitments that signify her identity, values, and participation in something larger than herself, which is finally what she understands as the meaning of her life. This dynamic of service to the cause of university goals can be as total and absorbing as missionary service: we speak, after all, of the mission of the department, the teaching mission, and so on.

For a number of years, I enjoyed the full conviction that my days were mission-driven. I wrote lists of long-term goals, weekly and daily chores. I had vivid dreams of speeding down lecture aisles, my feet slightly levitated so that the friction of motion was minimized, jetting from place to place, and in my waking hours I hurried, even jogged down corridors and between buildings, racing from one meeting to another, carrying files of paper on which I scribbled all kinds of information and commentary intended to help committees arrive at sound decisions and forward-looking policies. Committees to review faculty and program performance, award grants and fellowships, revise curricula and institutional structure, recruit junior and senior administrators, approve new interdisciplinary centers, decide on the next academic year's courses and teachers, change requirements, consider problems related to minority representation, women's roles, and so on; gatherings to congratulate students, launch books, welcome visitors, meet parents, interface with staff; and so on. And all of this service as an ordinary faculty member, before taking on the duties of a department chair!

Once an administrator with departmental responsibility, I worked in my office more often than not seven days a week, usually from early morning, before 8 a.m., to late in the evening, not including the work in my home study at night. Not all of the hours were in the service of service; after all,

I continued to teach, research, and write. But the heavy lifting was clearly spent on service. Chairing a department, I declared to all who would listen, and these grew smaller and smaller in number as I repeated myself obsessively, was like being the chief servant to all. My job as a department chair was to keep the mission running smoothly (scheduling, recruiting, evaluating, staffing, paying attention to office efficiency, maintaining quality, ensuring competitiveness for resources with other departments and for reputation with other universities, taking care of faculty rewards and promotions, student satisfaction, future growth, disciplinary excellence, and so on) *and* to keep everyone happy, from the top administrators to the lowliest undergraduates. I felt I was both micro-managing (the only way to get an incompetent office manager out was to come in early and to log her hours actually working in the office all day) yet unable to influence the real big picture—as in competing for resources against engineers, bioscientists and the medical school, or even for support from a dean whose administrative philosophy was to let large, strong departments sink or swim on their own in order to throw money at small, weak programs staffed with faculty who never published and that attracted few majors. It was like starving a strong child in order to feed a terminally ill infant, I fumed: it may look like compassion, but it was, in effect, the surest way to destroy excellence and to ensure inferior status for the institution. Yet as an administrator I could never openly engage in such fundamental disagreements. These kinds of frustrations in small and major situations turned me away from the path of administration.

Similarly with committee service: the search committee process seldom ensures that your preferred candidate rises to the top, or even when he does that he will perform in the future as you had argued he would; award, admissions, and grant committees all appear to favor the most voluble or passionate advocate, or, if not, pale consensus hardly presents a better alternative. "The worst are full of passionate intensity/And the best lack all conviction," I found myself muttering at the end of one long stressful committee meeting, knowing even then that quoting Yeats's lines, albeit to myself, was only a cheap shot with no valid relevance to the situation. I acknowledged in moments such as these that I may be approaching that dreaded stage of burnout, when easy cynicism speaks instead of hopeful resolution, when service work leaves me feeling ill used rather than empowered, and when a committee meeting leads to estrangement rather than institutional bonding.

Burnout. For decades I had been skeptical of the very idea of burnout. I scoffed at it as an excuse mouthed by unmotivated, unproductive individuals grasping at a fig leaf to cover up failure. I believed that the internal combustion engine of ambition and social idealism, if it were in any way good, would drive one from mission to mission dutifully and reliably. But now I must confess to some edginess in my acquiescence to requests to serve, an occasional impatience consciously controlled, even if there may be also moments of excitement at the possibility of making a difference, of anticipation at meeting new colleagues, and of reward in learning new information and arriving at satisfying decisions. Service has become a mixed bag for me, an awkward category of work, as clumsy as the mixed metaphors I have been deploying. And yet studying this uncomfortable near-burnout zone critically, I find myself forgiving myself, for what can be more logical than that after over thirty years in the profession, one's priorities change, or that one grows weary of ceaseless calls on one's altruism? Yet I have not grown weary of teaching, and I am today as keen on research and writing as I ever was. What is it about service that has made it so wearisome?

The answer may lie in something as material and practical as the university's reward system, together with the intensifying pace of demand and declining supply of faculty members. Minority women faculty in particular are in short supply in the American research university, but the demand for their service is ever-increasing: their presence on committees safeguards the university against charges of nonrepresentation, besides often ensuring genuinely significant diverse positions to be heard; graduate students of all ethnicities and genders value the standpoint scholarship that minority women bring to their seminars, the different professional networks they can access, the special empathies they display in mentoring; undergraduates flock to courses that fulfill requirements for coverage on ethnicity, or where the instructors offer novel research, are viewed as role models, and otherwise break the mold of uniform homogeneity in the knowledge-learning domain. All of the rationalizations that push service farther and farther into the daily occupations for women of color hold many of us captive on campus. If our very presence—our participation in meetings, forums, readings, office conferences, lectures, talks, studies, evaluations, receptions, and so on—is held as influential, it follows then that our lives are given over to these duties. Yet should we servitors grow disillusioned with the prospect of "influence," then the entire weight of that life of service is cast into doubt. Furman muses, "It is odd that most departments pay so little attention to service, given the crucial role it plays in our efforts to build more coherent, dynamic, and innovative academic programs. . . . We must reward our service heroes with course releases, merit-pay increases, and promotions."[3] In fact, almost all departments do reward certain kinds of services; department chairs, program directors, and chairs of large and important committees often receive release time, and their service work is given partial consideration during merit and promotion exercises. It is therefore not the lack of material reward that turns some of us away from such service; for example, I have enjoyed the prestige and respect carried in the titles of certain service functions, and I have received additional summer salary, research support, and other forms of recognition in my years of administrative service.

So what is it that ails minority women like me, "alone and palely loitering"? It may be in the final analysis the awful isolation and loneliness at the heart of service, particularly for an Asian American scholar whose research and creative writing interests are not shared with a larger department community and whose value judgments concerning excellence and merit are too often subtly and not so subtly viewed negatively as affirmative-action oriented. Instead of community, when the day is done, the university workhorse of a different color finds herself walking alone through the near-empty, dark parking lot. She may dine with a job candidate, but that social experience is hardly ever repeated, even if the candidate becomes a colleague. Long hours and days are spent writing letters of references, but it is rare that anything other than a card of thanks, if that much, follows on those hours and days. Graduate students appreciate the evident time dedicated to their welfare, but they move on to fresh pastures enmeshed in their cohorts. The sad news is that service does not lead to real community, only to busyness, which, in fact, stands in the way to deeper community formation. As an administrator I had repeated with everyone else that inane saying, "For a successful committee, just find the busiest people," but, alas, the busiest people must ultimately lack the time to work on their relationships with their children and spouses. It is one thing to sacrifice an article or even a book for useful service to a university, but when the child is grown and out of the house, the cost of those hours of committee meetings, of reading stacks of reports, of drafting memos and references, and so on begins to show as deep regret. The balance between family and work, already so disproportionate between family and writing, family and teaching, is simply whacked, wrecked, when service comes into the equation.

In writing this essay I had thought I would find equilibrium between idealism and fatigue, between desire and disillusionment, understanding that my age may explain the acedia that eats through my resolve. Instead I find this less-than-comfortable conclusion: it matters who the administrator is for whom you are answering the call to service. Intelligent, straightforward, straight-talking, visionary department chairs, deans, or chancellors are crucial to the outcome of the hours you dedicate, outside of research and teaching, to the mission of the university. Anything less than administrative integrity poisons the well of idealism that is the only sure source for incentive to faculty to give even more of themselves to the institution than they already do. I suspect the chief reason I still remain engaged in committee service instead of being swayed by the cynicism that has accrued over so many occasions of disillusionment is the presence of such administrators at the

University of California, Santa Barbara. The irony, of course, is that these administrators are exemplars of service-centered professionals. Their integrity and commitment appear to me unshakeable, deeply held, and authentic. Their work daily manifests perhaps the clearest model of authority in the university, and so my crossness over the pressures I've suffered from the demands for service in contrast to their model of steady leadership may be read as petty, ill natured, and whiny.

To reframe my major points thus, I must add another relevant countervailing argument in favor of service. Although I have observed that university service does not lead naturally to community formation and may instead result in an attenuation of bonds rising from insufficient attention because of time pressures, nonetheless, serving on committees composed of faculty, staff, and administrators across the entire institution encourages as remarkable a breadth and diversity of social acquaintance as to be found in any profession. The more senior I grow in my university, the more I appreciate the micro-climate, moderated by collegiality, common intellectual interests, and mutual values, which a shared history of service has helped establish. In these institutional spaces, incidental relationships forged over numerous committees, where debate and resolution illuminate character and intelligence, emerge, precariously yet substantively constructed across the potential chasms of gender, class, ethnicity, and discipline.

And a final gloss on the subject of service, having just returned from the Modern Language Association Convention, held yet again in frozen Chicago and between the family holidays of Christmas/Hanukkah/Kwanza and New Year's Day, with a new insight. As much as the MLA Convention is frequently criticized as a market where anxious new PhDs are vetted thoroughly for diminishing tenure-track positions, it also offers an annual occasion that, rather like Thanksgiving for the immediate family, acts as a celebratory gathering of friends and ex-students—catching up and eating and drinking with, thanking, colleagues who'd once or more than once extended their time to oblige our request for letters of references, who'd read our drafts of manuscripts or written evaluations for us; meeting up with once-graduate students, now suited and published; watching fresh graduate students glowing after successful interviews—the convention packs in the rewards of a world in which we have sacrificed, we've thought, invisibly for service, but we now bask in the affect of community created by such sacrifice. There are moments of thanksgiving for service in academia, and as with family, these must suffice. In an increasingly speeded-up, interconnected, fragmented globe, if service can do only so much for our sense of humanity, then it may still be viewed, all things considered, as a noble endeavor.

Notes

1. See Hogan 2005.
2. See Furman 2004, B20.
3. Ibid.

Works Cited

Furman, Andrew. 2004. "Measure Professors' Real Service, Not Lip Service." *Chronicle of Higher Education* 51:1, 5 (November), B20.

Hogan, Katie. 2005. "Superserviceable Feminism." *the minnesota review* 63–64 (Winter). http://www.theminnesotareview.org/journal/ns6364/iae_ns6364_ superservice-ablefeminism.shtml (accessed January 12, 2008).

Martin, Randy, ed. 1998. *Chalk Lines: The Politics of Work in the Managed University.* Durham, NC: Duke University Press.

10

Not in Service

Paula M. Krebs

Women who choose to do academic service have a couple of options that are not usually presented as such: local service, which is usually committee work or administration on one's own campus (and that is what your institution means by "service"), or the one they never tell you about on your own campus—regional or national service, which takes you off campus. Each model is legitimate, and I have done my share of both. But I am going to concentrate in this essay on the latter model, because I think it's a model that's more difficult for women to pursue, for reasons that may be related to the ways traditionally feminine values play out in academic professional life.

Other essays in this volume, as well as Katie J. Hogan's article "Superserviceable Feminism" and Michelle A. Massé's 2004 MLA presentation (which Hogan describes in her article), the works that inspired this book, discuss the various assumptions behind women's inordinate service burden at colleges and universities. And much of that campus service is work we do to keep our institutions running—the housework, if you will. There's nothing wrong with doing housework, as long as everybody in the house is doing it. But too often women faculty members do most of the housework. Such service work has to be done, of course, but women need to be especially wary of local service that does not make change at an institution but instead simply keeps it running smoothly. Local service can be a place to make real political change at an institution, but only when we are willing to throw a bit of grit into the cogs rather than simply greasing them. A progressive model of service is one in which we are willing to force change, even incremental change—to disrupt without destroying. This kind of service is not in service to the institution but in service to the constituencies with whom one's loyalties lie, whether it be women faculty, untenured faculty, or any particular group, configuration, or cause.

Having served my time in service positions at my own institution, I have now moved into service roles that are more national. Perhaps I am reluctant to overindulge in service work on a local level because it feels to me a bit too much like being "in service" in the Victorian sense—being a servant. It also smacks a bit of being "in the service"—like one's whole life is tied up with the institution, à la the military. Another option is to see it as "community service," but that, too, is double-edged—it makes me think of the guys in orange suits picking up litter by the side of the highway. Community service in its more positive sense, however, also feels wrong to me: noblesse oblige does not come naturally to a child of the working classes, and I have never gone in for philanthropy.

That's not to say that I don't do volunteer work. But it's not of the soup kitchen kind; it's more of the phone-bank, picket-line kind. That's the kind of academic service I like to do too—service that feels like politics. Such service can happen at the local level, of course, in collective bargaining, or through various advocacy initiatives. Our institutions push us into a sense that service is what faculty members do for the campus community—the housekeeping work that keeps things running smoothly. Faculty advocacy groups such as AAUP chapters, women's and untenured faculty organizations, and ad hoc groups on campus and off encourage, instead, a sense that faculty members are obliged to make things work better rather than more smoothly. As a child of a union family, I have always identified with the latter sense of service: workers should organize to make things better for workers rather than more smooth for employers, and leaders arise from the ranks of the workers to represent their interests.

Service at the institutional level can be done in ways that maintain the status quo or in ways that make for change. I learned that on the first standing committee to which I was elected at my own institution, the laughably named Committee on Committees. We were the committee that made up the ballots for the other standing committees, and doing such work could be either routine—getting the names of the usual suspects and running them against each other, or it could push the envelope a bit—making certain that untenured faculty members ran against each other for certain committees or that men ran against each other (women would almost always beat men in elections on my campus) so as to be sure the service load (and, in the case of untenured faculty, the power) was spread around. When the ballots began to get noticed and to prompt complaints, we knew we were both good committee members and good change agents.

The impulse to throw grit into the works can lead one into service at a national level. Seeing institutional change result from a resistant model of service emboldens one to push for change via service in bigger venues. Two avenues into regional or national service for women are pedagogy—pursuing teaching-related concerns beyond our own classrooms and institutions, and being pushed—usually by women we see as role models. Through illustrations from my own service history, I'll try to explain both roads and, I hope, encourage some women to see national service as both good for the profession and good for the career.

When I was in graduate school at Indiana University (IU), I avoided student loans by working at the local newspaper, first as a sportswriter, then as an editor. This work came naturally to me, as I had put myself through college as a sportswriter. In fact, I had only landed in graduate school at all because I had seen an ad for an editorial assistantship in the back of the journal *Victorian Studies*. What a great idea, I thought. I could keep going to school and keep writing and editing. I didn't get the job, but I did end up enrolling at IU, and by my second year, I was working at the local newspaper to supplement my teaching assistantship.

I didn't understand this newspaper work to be at all strange until I mentioned it at a faculty-student cocktail party one night. The surprise and admiration from the faculty members I told revealed just how different the world of academics was from the world in which I had grown up. The idea that I could do a different professional job—that I could get paid for writing and editorial work—seemed to startle these faculty members, one of whom actually said that he knew he would be incapable of earning a living at anything other than college teaching.

When I left graduate school for three years after I finished my course work, I worked in Washington, D.C., on a magazine at an education association. The editorial training I got there complemented my newspaper experiences, and upon my return to Indiana, I was able to turn that faculty "I-can't-do-anything-but-write-and-teach" attitude, with its odd kind of professional-class privilege, to my own advantage: I started putting out the word that I would proofread or copyedit manuscripts on a per-hour basis, and I never wanted for work.

That freelance work led me to a kind of service that was as much a surprise to the faculty members in my department as my sportswriting. My grad-school friends and I, seeing a gap in early-eighties feminist scholarship where pedagogy should have been, decided to start a publication to address that need. My journalism experience and the fact that I and another of the founding editors worked at the local newspaper and so had access to typesetting equipment (it was that long ago) meant that we could take almost the entire production process into our own hands. Mary Burgan, chair of the English Department when we started the magazine, arranged for funding to help support one of us to work on the publication. A publication aimed at serving the profession as a whole—and we aimed *Feminist Teacher* at teachers from preschool through graduate school—surely counts as service. But it was not the kind of service to make things run more smoothly—it was service aimed, rather, to disrupt. Our fund-raising coffee mugs boldly proclaimed "Politics and teaching *do* mix."

The magazine grew out of our commitment to pedagogy, so we founding editors didn't see our project as bold or arrogant. It wasn't like we started a journal of literary criticism or cultural theory. We as women graduate teaching assistants were confident in our teaching abilities and commitment, so we never worried about taking the bold step of starting a national publication that had to do with teaching. The unexpected bonus of the project was that it proved to be an incredible opportunity for professional advancement. Every member of the publication's editorial collective, all of us grad students at Indiana, got a tenure-track job in what was then, in the late 1980s and early 1990s, a very tight job market.

This very long story aims to make a very particular point about the origins of my own service work in academe—it arose from more than the desire to "do good" that motivates all service work. I think it arose from a sense of self strongly conditioned by (1) a sense of confidence in myself as a teacher—an area in which I felt I had cultural permission as a woman to excel, and (2) a working-class identification that produces an alienation that is a genuine gift to the working-class academic. Feeling like an outsider means that you can do all kinds of things you don't know better than to do, from starting an academic journal with strips of typeset copy and a waxer to applying to a major foundation for a grant to start a national program (on which more later). It's about wanting to make things better, like most service work, but it's also about knowing that, hey, you're in foreign waters anyway, and you could always make a living doing something else, so what do you have to lose?

Of course, after you get tenure, the sense that you might ever make a living doing something else tends to diminish. At my college, after you get tenure you serve your time as department chair, and when I started my term, I attended a summer seminar for chairs sponsored by the Association of Departments of English. I found the group to be exciting and fun. Here were academics who were interested in sharing—not their research but their advice and experiences with managing people, budgets, and administrators. And they talked about policy issues—about how English departments compared across types of institutions, about standardized tests and English teacher education, about what the English major looks like nationwide, and about the national overdependence on contingent labor. That organization of English department chairs seemed to be able to make a difference in a lot of areas.

Never one to sit quietly in class, I spoke up quite a bit at the seminar and asked a lot of questions. I loved the coffee breaks and nightcaps, at which I could meet other chairs and find out how they handled the same issues I was facing. I was learning to be a good chair, but I was also meeting some great chairs from all over the country and seeing my own institution in comparison and relation to lots of others.

I was thrilled when a year later I was elected to the ADE's Executive Committee, and I enjoyed every meeting, even the work between meetings. This was exciting stuff—seeing humanities education from a national perspective and feeling as though you could make some impact, through setting priorities for your national organization, gathering data about issues that hadn't had enough national attention, and reaching out to department chairs all over the country to affect curriculum and hiring.

During my chairing and consequent involvement with the ADE, I returned, in a peripheral way, to the career I had forsaken for academics—journalism and publishing. As I started gaining a broader perspective on higher education issues, I started writing occasional pieces for *The Chronicle of Higher Education* and *InsideHigherEd*. When my college started a minority hiring initiative, I started reading and writing about issues of race in higher education, and I was thrilled to be appointed to the ADE Ad Hoc Committee on the Status of African American Faculty Members in English. The work of that committee led us to the conclusion that to increase the proportion of faculty of color in English departments, we needed to find a way to increase the numbers of students of color going to graduate school in English. Our research showed that summer institutes for students had great success rates in lots of different contexts, so we decided that what the profession needed was such an institute. I was no longer chairing my department by this time, and such a project sounded like a politically useful way to do some service work, so I offered to write the grant proposal, which was, fortunately, funded.

It's important to point out that what enabled me to become active in the ADE, to work on the ad hoc committee, and to feel that I could apply for a national grant was other women, mentors, and role models and colleagues. My first experience of speaking up at the ADE seminar was in a meeting of women chairs, where I felt taken seriously by every person in the room, despite my newness on the job. The women who served as ADE presidents in my last two years on the Executive Committee saw me as a valuable colleague, sought me out, encouraged me, and befriended me. I look to them and other women chairs and former chairs I have met through the ADE as a new national mentor/friendship network, a way to keep my vision extended beyond my own campus.

The advice and feedback I get from these great women colleagues is supplemented by a couple of women role models. One teacher of mine from graduate school went on to head up a national organization—her activism reminds me that you can move from academics into national advocacy and live to tell the tale. I've stayed close with another former teacher of mine, this one from my undergraduate institution. Watching her career from faculty member at an undergraduate teaching institution to vice president of an important national higher education association, I could see a potential career path for myself. And when I had a chance finally to chat with her about the grant I had secured to start the summer institute, she didn't seem a bit surprised. Instead, she immediately started talking about what my next grant would be.

But it has not only been academics who have mentored me as I have gone into national service work. Our building secretary at Wheaton, Marilyn Todesco, advocated for staff interests at the college and pushed me to put my money where my mouth was in terms of solidarity in the workplace. When I found myself on a joint faculty-staff committee on benefits, Marilyn reminded me of how privileged the faculty were in relation to the staff and how we needed to use our power to advocate for interests beyond our own. She encouraged me to write for *The Chronicle* about faculty-staff relations, and when I took over the editorship of *Academe*, she gave me lots of advice and feedback on articles I was commissioning and editing that dealt with staff issues.

Marilyn gave me perspective on my role as a faculty member that has helped me see faculty as coworkers with staff, has helped me take a closer look at the structures of power at my own institution and then in higher education more generally. Still another perspective came from my sisters, who work at a branch campus of Rutgers, near where we grew up in New Jersey. One sister is in charge of campus parking and supplies the family with endless stories of faculty arrogance and cluelessness that keep me humble. The other sister is taking graduate classes on the campus where she works in the facilities office and also teaching part time at a nearby urban community college. When she and I wrote a series for *InsideHigherEd* about the differences between teaching at a selective liberal arts college and teaching at a two-year college in a city that's been named the nation's most dangerous, we both learned a lot about how social class informs educational contexts and issues.

The traditional way to move beyond one's own campus is through research and publishing, through which we connect to a larger network of scholars in our field. But, as Hogan points out, it is still the case that a very low proportion of women scholars makes it to the level of national visibility. Alternately, and increasingly, women can move into administration on campus and then into larger circles of deans and provosts. That is a particular version of women's service that I leave to others in this volume to explore. Either research or administration can open up professional opportunities that could move a faculty member to another institution. But that's not the kind of off-campus I mean. What's happened to me through service work is that I've moved my center of gravity off campus without changing jobs. Getting involved in national educational initiatives has given me a new perspective on my own institution as well as on higher education in general.

Of course, national organizations need housekeepers too, and a quick glance at the 2008 membership of MLA committees that are all work and no glamour makes the gender politics clear: for example, the Delegate Assembly Organizing Committee and the Elections Committee have eighteen members between them, two of whom are men. All national service is not world-changing. But, as with local service, you can always throw a bit of grit into the wheels of an organization whose smooth running benefits only certain constituencies. It is important not to be seduced by being drafted for national service. After the initial thrill of being noticed and being part of an important national or international cause (the analogy to military service is a bit creepy) comes the realization that maybe you aren't so special after all. Maybe you're just the smart (or mouthy) kid in the class who got chosen to be the class monitor to make sure everybody did their busywork. The committees that you serve on in your professional associations predate your membership and will go on long after you. The trick is to make something lasting out of your work on them: to be slightly annoying, to make the bureaucracy consider another way of doing something, to form a subcommittee, a study group, or an ad hoc committee, and then to develop an action plan. Robyn Warhol-Down, whose work in English and in women's studies always pushes boundaries, did just that with her ADE Ad Hoc Committee on the Status of African American Faculty Members in English. Instead of writing a report that summarized our reading and our work on the committee, Robyn pushed us to develop a real plan, a bullet-pointed series of recommendations for English department chairs, the adoption of only one or two of which by most chairs could really change the profession over a few years. "Affirmative activism," she calls it. I call it grit in the wheels.

One final point about moving into a national arena with one's service: don't expect the folks on your own campus to like it. Additional barriers that women must overcome in higher education can sometimes include their own friends and colleagues. When you move into national arenas in academe, you can make people in your home arena uncomfortable. After all, service you do nationally comes directly out of the time you might have spent doing service locally. And if women are the ones doing the lion's share of the service, then the service you don't do at your own institution is service that will be done by your female colleagues. In addition, you can't underestimate the "too big for her britches" factor. "Who does she think she is, running off and doing consulting (or missing class to attend off-campus meetings, or applying for national grants, etc.)?" Pay careful attention to the balance in your professional obligations, especially if your national service is all volunteer (as most is). It won't do to give up all service obligations at the institution that signs your paycheck. But there's nothing wrong with being forthright with your dean and your colleagues about the advantages to your home institution of the work you do elsewhere.

It can be difficult for women faculty members to make the leap into national service, to trust that they have something to offer a larger professional context. National service for me has been an extension of my pedagogy as well as my politics. I wouldn't have imagined a few years ago that I would be doing what I'm doing now, but it all came quite naturally from work I was already doing and women with whom I was doing that work. National service work may not be every woman's service of choice, but it is a kind of service that can be good for your career—and it can do a lot more than housekeeping. Instead of being in service like a Victorian parlor maid, you can be in the public service like a senator, responsible to the constituencies from which you come and working to make real change, on a large scale.

Works Cited

Hogan, Katie. 2005. "Superserviceable Feminism." *the minnesota review* 63–64:95–112.

Hubbard, Dolan, Paula Krebs, Valerie Lee, Doug Steward, and Robyn Warhol. 2007. "Affirmative Activism: Report of the ADE Ad Hoc Committee on the Status of African American Faculty Members in English." *ADE Bulletin* 141–142 (Winter–Spring):70–74.

11

Experience Required

Service, Relevance, and the Scholarship of Application

Andrea Adolph

Most faculty members who are (over)committed to professional service can attest to the various passions and ethical issues that drive their endeavors, but there is real need for an overhaul when it comes to acknowledging and rewarding professional service, regardless of the altruisms that often lie at the hearts of our hard work and that are often used to insinuate that those good works should be their own rewards. Personal commitments—to social justice, to identity groups, to solving public problems—do not necessarily negate the need for professional acknowledgment, particularly when those commitments enable and overlap with other, more traditional professional activities. Links between certain forms of professional service and activities that are traditionally rewarded do exist, but embracing a defined model for assessing these efforts is imperative if the full range of academic work is ever going to be acknowledged and rewarded.

In his attempt to blow open the uneven tripartite against which most academics are evaluated, Ernest Boyer (1990), in *Scholarship Reconsidered*, created a new model for understanding academic labor that outlines four components of scholarly activity in addition to the kind of professional service that he calls "university citizenship."[1] "There is growing evidence," he then wrote, "that professors want, and need, better ways for the full range of their aspirations and commitments to be acknowledged."[2] His model attempts to acknowledge a multiplicity of scholarly endeavors as it complicates the long-standing emphasis on the products of academic labor rather than on its processes or, importantly, on forms of work such as service that are invisible, because the product often *is* the process, because the end result is rarely tangible and quantifiable in direct proportion to the efforts expended along the way. Service is performative, and in many cases, the act itself is its own dissemination. Capturing its importance can be a transitory act that needs to be clarified in order for this work to gain value in faculty review processes.

Many have addressed the issues related to the time that service activities can take away from rewarded work such as research and publication, but that conversation only reifies the old paradigm. The time taken to perform these other functions should be viewed as part of the composite of one's scholarly profile. If service is to be valued as a contributory aspect of a scholar's professional activity, then the terms of service, so to speak, must be clarified, and its assessment must be guaranteed. Those traditional final products, such as publication, should still be valued highly as a chief method of communicating scholarly discovery and new ideas; however, the intellectual and discipline-related activities that infuse *all* of Boyer's quadrants should be explored as faculty are assessed and rewarded for their achievements. Accepting a new model for faculty assessment will allow the emergence of a more nuanced, accurate portrait of academic labor.

While all forms of service should be valued as a part of faculty profiles—in fact, institutions need the services of academics in order to function, making such services inherently valuable—certain forms of academic "service" are actually tightly integrated with the field-specific, intellectual labor that has traditionally formed the bulk of what has been considered "scholarly," and thus of what faculty are already rewarded for. These kinds of service endeavors, then, at least parallel the kinds of scholarship that have defined faculty roles-and-rewards systems in the U.S. academy. Following Boyer, I propose that not all service is created equal, and in this essay I will outline how certain kinds of service—service that requires field-specific knowledge and that impacts a world beyond a department or an institution—are in actuality a form of scholarship akin to what Boyer calls the "scholarship of application." In his work, Boyer makes clear the difference between activities that are themselves scholarship and the kind of functional service that Kelly Ward (2003) calls "internal service": that which "supports the internal functioning of the academic profession and higher education as a whole and is tied to the premise of shared governance."[3] According to Boyer, service that is scholarly and linked to the goals of discipline-specific study creates a site where "theory and practice vitally interact, and one renews the other."[4] "To be considered *scholarship*, service activities must be tied directly to one's special field of knowledge and relate to, and flow directly out of, this professional activity. Such service," he continues, "is serious, demanding work, requiring the rigor—and the accountability—traditionally associated with research activities."[5] While most forms of faculty service can be assessed and rewarded, forms of scholarly service are already a part of this ongoing conversation about how we evaluate faculty labor.

Scholarship Reconsidered and its companion volume, *Scholarship Assessed*, make clear the importance of distinguishing between citizenship (traditional service) and the scholarship of application, which is meant to define scholarly activity that directly impacts external communities.[6] What I will call in this essay "applied service" (to riff on Boyer's "scholarship of application"), if conceived of as a form of scholarly activity, is already imbued with qualities—disciplinary knowledge, impact on a specified audience or organization, rigorous and documentable methods—that allow for such work to be evaluated alongside traditionally disseminated scholarship such as journal articles and academic monographs. A result of the call to accountability that American academic institutions faced during the late twentieth century (and that they continue to face), Boyer's model can be productively malleable for those academics who are heavily engaged in "service" that differs from the day-to-day mechanics of departmental and institutional functioning. While many, including some who advocate for Boyer's legacy in and through engagement-related initiatives, will continue to prioritize the peer-reviewed article or scholarly monograph as the *sine qua non* of academic life, there are additional facets and outcomes of faculty work that are scholarly and that can be assessed as such.

This essay, in part, draws upon my experiences with developing and coordinating a service-learning initiative on my campus, which is a regional campus of a larger research university. My work, too, extends beyond my own campus and into our larger, eight-campus system as we attempt to institutionalize forms of learning through public service vis-à-vis our accreditation process. My large-scale responsibilities have moved from faculty development to constructing university policy, too, since I refused to develop more faculty as practitioners without working simultaneously to create a structure through which they can be recognized. The nomenclature here—the use of the term *service* in relation to work with external constituencies—should not, however, confuse the details of my discussion of academic service or limit this discussion to issues of service-learning or of a more lateral community outreach, because my work parallels other forms of academic labor in ways that I will discuss throughout this essay. The separate definitions of service-learning, a pedagogical approach through which *students* serve the community as a way of addressing course goals, and what I will call "applied" as a domain of faculty labor, too, are critical to this essay. While I speak from the standpoint of someone engaged in service-learning practice and oversight, I seek here to discuss broadly how certain forms of academic work that might historically have been construed as "service" are actually connected to our academic training and can be conceived of as scholarly, assessable forms of labor. The conversation that has been ongoing in service-learning circles and central to defining issues related to outreach and engagement activities holds many models of possibility for others whose professional service is truly "applied service" and whose activities remain invisible because they are not embraced as scholarly.

I became involved in applied service early in my pre-tenure career, but actually this work stems from pedagogical training that I undertook while a graduate student. The use of service-learning in the classroom, especially in the composition classroom, became so central to my philosophy of teaching that when I took my first full-time academic position and was unable to use service-learning as a teaching method, I was more than a bit adrift. Without knowledge of the area, it took me several months to assess community needs and to become acquainted with people with whom my students and I could partner. Once I learned more about my new community and was able to connect with our largest, relatively (for small-town Ohio) urban school district, I was able to create my own partnerships with local underserved schools, where my first- and second-year writing students tutor and mentor youth, most of whom are considered "at risk."

Greater than the challenge of beginning again as a service-learning practitioner, however, was the lack of programmatic efforts within the university system that would have provided me with a context for my teaching methods and for my interest in service-learning assessment and theory, which has crept its way into my research agenda. This also meant that my colleagues lacked a rhetorical framework for understanding my work. At institutions where programs exist that match our interests, scholars have access to vocabularies that most colleagues will at least recognize as validated within the institutional framework, even if those colleagues do not quite agree with the goals of the work itself. For instance, if an institution houses a women's studies program, then faculty who are engaged in teaching and research about sex and gender can point to particular curricula and institutional goals as they speak to and report on their own work; even if anti-feminist colleagues don't agree with the content of such scholarship, they know where it fits within the design of their institution. But lacking that structural validation, I feared (knew) that my work would be invisible, noncountable in annual reviews and at the all-important career juncture of tenure and promotion review. I had enjoyed too much pedagogical success as a practitioner of service-learning to abandon it, but I had to educate those around me whose review of my work depends on their ability to grasp what it is that I do. (Within the Kent State system, this process includes annual reappointment balloting by colleagues and one-year pre-tenure employment contracts, which made it immediately necessary for me to create my own context.) It was important for me to create a paradigm that my colleagues could use to understand my work, and as my efforts led (quickly) to invitations to become more engaged in campus and university leadership, it became important to me to ensure that my efforts would not be ignored simply because they do not fit the typical list of efforts for which faculty are rewarded.

Benjamin Baez discusses how service has been codified as pretty much anything that cannot be fit into the structures that govern teaching and research,[7] and this murky definitional attitude has created much of the difficulty that is faced by active scholars whose work it is to serve professionally. Because I wanted my work in this area to "count" when I would stand for tenure, and because "service" rarely counts for much in that process, I attempted to ensure that this work could stand separately from my other, more typical service on faculty committees. My efforts as a service-learning coordinator (and in faculty development), while they "serve" both the university community and the communities that surround campuses in seven counties, are also part of my paid workload. I not only wanted my work to be understood, but I held out and lobbied hard to receive reallocated workload (from my 4/4 teaching contract) for the efforts, something that does not happen too readily on my campus, and likely not in many academic settings. The fact that I am paid to do work that can doubly be construed as "service" begins to point to some of the problematics of the ways in which academic institutions have lumped so many disparate activities into the catchall service container. In the best possible world, when one is paid to do "service," it can then be conceived of as actual work that is assessed and rewarded. Payment for labor means that the label of "service" cannot stick as easily as it can when the work is performed gratis, and even if this argument does not fully extend all paid labor of this sort into the arena of "applied service," it certainly illuminates the fact that there is no name for much of this kind of work, and without a name, the work remains easy to ignore.

Service in all forms, save the martial—whether in volunteerism, the helping professions, or academic housekeeping—is typically feminized and thus low in the hierarchy, and as a pre-tenure, female faculty member, I fit the profile of the faculty member who typically becomes involved in these kinds of activities. According to Antonio, Astin, and Cress:

> Women faculty are five times more likely than men to teach courses with a community service requirement . . . lower-rank-ing faculty members generally demonstrate the highest levels of community service activities . . . [and faculty] at the lowest ranks indicate support for a community service requirement at nearly twice the rate of full professors.[8]

But what are those of us to do who wish to become involved in new or innovative initiatives? Wait for tenured, white, male, middle-class, heterosexual

colleagues to take the reins and *then* join in? For anyone who has formed
the cutting edge of any movement within academe, this has hardly been
the appropriate modus operandi. Because it is easier for many to dismiss
work that is not endorsed by those with institutional power, however, it
is important to find ways to engage in a constructive dialectic with the
power structure, even as one circumvents or attempts to alter that structure.
Although my choice of service-learning as a pedagogical approach does stem
from a sense of altruism and a desire to interact as a true member of my
community, as well as from a desire to offer my students a route toward
high-quality learning, my extended work in what I identify as the scholarship
of application stems from something far more entrepreneurial. I knew that
if my work were ever going to be granted the visibility locally that it could
have in a national field of scholars and practitioners also engaging in such
activities, then I would have to help make that happen. There was a need
for some infrastructure that would allow for an assessment of my work at
critical professional moments such as tenure time.

   What has resulted from my work far surpasses any benefits that I can
reap from it, and I am more than pleased with what these efforts have meant
for the university, as well as for the community organizations that have partnered with the many faculty whom I have helped with course development.
My own service-learning practice is fairly static, although I have created great
community partnerships from which my students also benefit as they learn
more about issues related to educational and socioeconomic access than I
could ever hope to teach them through assigned readings alone. The work
of my colleagues, though—work that they have undertaken to some degree
because we now have a paradigm and a vocabulary upon which to base such
work—has collectively had a far-reaching impact: funds into the thousands
of dollars have been raised for a local food pantry by business classes, and
an annual Hunger Awareness Week was created and is implemented now by
marketing students each year; deliverable writing projects such as a newsletter
and pamphlets have been created for a peer-support group that assists families
and individuals who are affected by mental illness (this organization is so
small that it lacks even a physical office location); communications students
conducted focus groups with parents of some of my community's poorest
students to uncover what they need to receive from our public school district.
The impact of these and other service-learning projects extends far beyond
the fifteen weeks of a single semester. I am proud of this work, as well as
of the many other projects that I have helped facilitate, but I cannot deny
the fact that I was motivated to create such a paradigm so that I myself can
utilize it as I make my way through the academic ranks.

   As a quasi-administrator, I am responsible for day-to-day tasks that
ensure the running of a small, unincorporated program—data gathering,

paperwork, the scheduling of meetings—and that actually are "internal" service functions that on their own would not necessarily comprise scholarly activity. Beyond the mechanics of daily programmatic functioning, though, this work is also tied to a dynamic field of scholarly inquiry,[9] and in order to perform my duties with validity, I must keep abreast of the ongoing research in a field unrelated to my own traditional field of twentieth-century British literary studies. How can I adequately perform community-needs assessments, direct student reflection, or help faculty design courses if I do not keep abreast of trends in this field? The necessity for a scholarly foundation from which to perform the work posits this kind of non-teaching- and non-research-related activity as related to Boyer's scholarship of application and illustrates, in Boyer's terms, how such work surpasses the functions of "university citizenship." Like many others whose duties include applied service that necessitates faculty multilingualism with respect to scholarly fields of study, I must be active in more than one field in order to perform my job well and with integrity, since this knowledge is critical if I am to be aware of best practices in the field. As a pre-tenure faculty member, it is important that all of my areas of expertise be valued as relevant components of my scholarly profile, especially since any publications that might follow will likely, in my case, be based in issues of institutionalization or program assessment, concerns that cannot easily correlate with the literary scholarship that I will continue to pursue.

Many literature faculty already know the derision with which pedagogical scholarship is often met; I cannot imagine many of my disciplinary colleagues embracing research that lies even farther afield from text-based theory and criticism. And yet this kind of activity sometimes challenges me more readily than does my own discipline, since few who publish in engagement-related fields are humanists; much of the research in service-learning comes from scholars of education, sociology, and psychology. Research methods are often quantitative, totally foreign to someone formerly most comfortable with a Virginia Woolf novel in one hand and a hovering pencil in the other; I have had to learn to understand the basics of a chi-square test. A distinct effect of my immersion in service-learning, both as a practitioner and as someone committed to this multidisciplinary field, is my increased awareness of other disciplines and of research methods other than my own, something often lacking within academe. I am poised now more than ever to collaborate and to work collegially with others from across the institution, from faculty to professional staff to administrators, and I have gleaned a level of institutional knowledge that usually comes much later in one's academic career.

Because language- and literature-related disciplines generally have not (with some exceptions, such as linguistics and education-related curricula) had to consider ways to include applied scholarship in personnel evaluations, these types of departments are perhaps more in need of a model for evaluating nontraditional scholarship than are those departments that have more experience with evaluating similar activities. Unlike departments that house English and foreign languages, disciplines more rooted in application or in working with external audiences "share the common characteristic of simultaneously having to combine practical and academic goals."[10] It's not that the goals of language and literature study are opposed to meeting community needs, or even to research that is multidisciplinary or interdisciplinary in design. On the contrary, English and language departments are increasingly sites of all of these things, and they increasingly value the cultural production of multiple communities. This reason alone is cause to view an evaluative model based on Boyer's outline as useful beyond the sphere of engagement-related practices.

Many forms of academic service that now infuse our departments are founded upon similar goals. Academics who are involved in "applied service" that attracts us politically and personally are often connected and responsible to external audiences, even if serving those audiences is only a tertiary goal. Likewise, many of our most passionate acts of professional service are founded upon affinities for constituencies beyond our institutions, and because of this, models such as those proposed by Boyer and perpetuated by those working specifically in engagement/outreach are also applicable to areas of faculty work that, while perhaps not particularly community based, is definitely community influenced. Those engaged in writing-center administration or in heavy student advising often have links to local public schools or have an investment in the recruitment and retention of students who are not traditionally college bound. By their very natures, these kinds of efforts implicate issues of socioeconomics and social/educational access, social justice issues that are tied to Boyer's notion of the scholarship of application. Many colleagues engaged in this kind of work belong to related professional organizations, participate in professional meetings, and publish in the publications germane to these fields, and thus they are active scholars in the traditional sense, but there are also countless gestures and daily practices through which scholarly activity is performed regularly. At my institution, our contractual obligation to use Boyer's categories for our scholarly activities allowed our very active writing-center director, whose primary field of inquiry is literary, to address as the scholarship of application his other activities and publications in writing-center theories; a coordinator of women's studies on our campus made use of this scholarly category to document her activities too.

Those who run academic programs or who generate curricula devoted to studies in race, ethnicity, or sex/gender almost always have direct contact with and at least indirect accountability to communities beyond the campus, and perhaps a model for assessed service is most critical for these faculty. As with practitioners of service-learning and their heavy concentrations within the less powerful strata of the academy, nontraditional faculty—women, nonwhite faculty, working-class colleagues—are notably more likely to perform service tasks and to be called upon to serve as representatives of their sex/gender/race/class groups. Ward borrows A. M. Padilla's term *cultural taxation* to discuss this issue,[11] and additional studies have shown that this service-based inequity exists.[12] One way to counter that lack of parity is to allow faculty to define some of those activities as scholarly when the activities do in fact overlap with a field of scholarly inquiry. Baez states that "service is important and valuable when it furthers social justice,"[13] and in his discussion of nonwhite faculty and their service issues, he links the idea of social justice with an increased need for new ways to reward faculty for their community-based activities. His language provides a route for connecting applied service performed in the name of personal affiliation with the work done by scholars who advocate for Boyer's overarching approach to a "scholarship of engagement" that would be "particularly relevant to the nation's most pressing civic, social, economic, and moral problems."[14] Baez continues, " 'social justice' service, for lack of a better term, arguably considered 'the downfall of faculty of color,' might resist institutional structures, and in resisting these structures presents the possibility of redefining them."[15] At the heart of both conversations lie the same important issues: How can faculty, as representatives of the academy, use their cultural capital for the public good without harming themselves in the process? These are not mutually exclusive impulses. If the work of women, nonwhite faculty, and others who have been traditionally underrepresented within the academy is ever going to be addressed in all of its manifestations, then a broader context for such evaluation is warranted.

In order to move toward such a model, though, applied service must be defined such that its dissemination can be documented and evaluated. Ward points out that Boyer's work, though, falls short, in that he "never actually defines the essential elements that constitute scholarship" but simply provides a new structure for expansion of scholarship. "Scholarship," she clarifies through a restatement of the Portland State University definition, "is considered to be creative intellectual work that is validated by peers and communicated."[16] The importance of dissemination here is underscored, as is peer review, but a truly reformed model for assessment can focus on the essentials of scholarly activity—inquiry, action, reflection—rather than only on prescribed artifacts of scholarly activity. There is no shirking from rigor here, and in some cases rigor is actually increased when scholars (as with service-learners in the classroom) are accountable to others in the "real world" with regard to the quality of their scholarship, and Boyer suggests, that in "documenting *applied* work . . . faculty should include . . . the evaluations of those who received the service."[17] The review of peers should not be trumped by community review, but there are multiple ways to disseminate and assess one's work, and some of that dissemination occurs as communication through practice. Just as the scholarship of teaching surpasses pedagogical publication and is in part enacted in a scholarly classroom that "both educates and entices future scholars,"[18] the scholarship of application is partly defined by the act of doing. Because of this, documentation can be a challenge, since there is not often a deliverable product at the end, and since there are not always means to quantify the outcomes of such applied service. But valuing multiple means of dissemination is key in order to move on toward assessment and, ultimately, faculty rewards.

From among a chorus of voices asking what the humanities in particular can do to fight the shrinking market for publication and thus the tightening field of traditional reward, the MLA Ad Hoc Committee on the Future of Scholarly Publishing reports that electronic publication may be a route to reinvigorating the field, but even that digression from traditional ways of meeting scholarly criteria, they find, "will likely be viewed with suspicion unless a widely accepted system of quality control is in place."[19] Even this mild deviation from the norms of faculty review will be hard won. There is much resistance to change within academe, and it is hard to imagine that without some serious efforts on many parts and some significant acquiescence to new ways of identifying scholarly work, labor such as applied service will not go very far within faculty reward systems. Regardless of the additional issues addressed earlier—inequities across ranks and faculty groups, the need for addressing public problems—there is in our fields of study an ongoing "crisis" in publication opportunities that affects the traditional routes to faculty reward structures such as tenure, promotion, and merit-based raises. John Guillory points out that publication "claims to *be* scholarship, and not just a means to make scholarly work public."[20] He goes on to address the "misrecognition of publication as the only evidence of accomplishment"[21] and heads straight into the center of a debate that is necessary, but that is going to be difficult for our profession to conclude until the definition of scholarship is not merely expanded to include new-media venues for old-school dissemination but to truly allow for the exhibition of all forms of faculty endeavor that are tied directly to faculty knowledge and study. For Baez, "Race-related (or social justice) service . . . might provide the context for the kind of agency that subverts institutional structures,"[22] and this shift in emphasis might indeed be one way to divert the monumental difficulty faced by those intent on maintaining (or even ratcheting up via increased demand for publication) the status quo in faculty review and reward structures. Baez acknowledges that the applied service of nonwhite faculty might not always effectively resist the cultural expectations of academe but, he suggests, in trying to "they make *possible* the subversion and redefinition of these structures,"[23] and I concur that this possibility lies within all forms of this kind of work, regardless of its moniker: scholarship of application, scholarship of engagement, social justice service, applied service, or just plain service.

Assessment of this work will be critical if any of it is ever going to "count" toward achievement within traditional faculty rewards structures, and *Scholarship Assessed* provides a significant outline that can allow for this model to maintain the rigorous expectations of tradition but that departs from it in spirit. These guidelines emphasize that the same evaluative goals should be worked toward regardless of whether the scholarly output is a traditional journal article or an applied act of scholarly service. Six standards for evaluation are outlined in this volume—clear goals, adequate preparation, appropriate methods, significant results, effective presentation, and reflective critique—that can encompass all forms of scholarly activity. These standards are already in use—at least in theory—at numerous universities and in many discreet academic units nationally; my own institutional system, Kent State University, adopted this model over a decade ago, and other institutions such as Portland State have also broadened their definitions of scholarly activity. As the standards move beyond rhetorical gestures and begin to formulate an actual reward system, they will allow for standards to be adhered to as changes are made to what is measured and assessed within the academy. Some organizations do exist that will provide peer review of nontraditional scholarly activity—especially useful during tenure and promotion review—since not all institutions may have enough people working in certain fields to provide adequate assessment. In the areas of service-learning and outreach, the Scholarship of Engagement Review Board was established to provide exactly this kind of assistance for those whose scholarship does not fit neatly into the traditional three categories; however, the mission of this board is still focused upon traditional scholarly outcomes, primarily publication.[24] Venues for the assessment of a multiplicity of scholarships should be established, and this will at the very least encourage dialogue about what constitutes scholarship and how we can acknowledge the efforts of colleagues if those efforts are not so easily identified as the fruits of intellectual labor. We must "focus on how faculty members repeat institutional structures that constrain the choices of other faculty"[25] so that maybe, once exposed, these constraining practices will be abandoned and replaced instead by constructive evaluations of scholarly work that will resonate far beyond our usual audience.

Notes

1. See Boyer 1990, 22.
2. Ibid., 75.

3. See Ward 2003, iv. Ward argues that both internal and external service can be tied to scholarship (113), but for the sake of the present argument, I choose to focus on the ways in which these projects differ. I do not mean to argue that internal service cannot be scholarly, nor that it should not be recognized and rewarded, but that there are subtle differences that, using Boyer as a guide, allow me to present a model for evaluating service that reaches beyond the immediate university community.

4. See Boyer 1990, 23.

5. Ibid., 22.

6. See Boyer 1990, 22–23; Glassick, Huber, and Maeroff 1997, 12. There is much discussion and confusion as to Boyer's use in 1990 of the term *scholarship of application* and his later term, coined in 1996, *scholarship of engagement*. Although scholars who work in related fields will differ, the majority of influential thinkers in service-learning research agree that Boyer's term *engagement* was not meant to be an additional category only related to serving the public good, but that it is a quality meant to infuse all four of Boyer's earlier categories: discovery, integration, application, and teaching. In "The Scholarship of Engagement," completed by Boyer before his death but published posthumously, he extends his work for the Carnegie Foundation by reemphasizing the very public nature of academic labor on the whole. He suggests in that essay that "the scholarship of engagement . . . means creating a special climate in which the academic and civic cultures communicate more continuously and more creatively with each other" (20), and in this way, he redefines (again) the academy as an institution meant to further the public good and to solve public problems.

7. See Baez 2000, 364.

8. See Antonio, Astin, and Cress 2000, 380, 382.

9. In addition to published monographs and articles in the field, during the period 2004–2006 alone, 131 doctoral dissertations were completed in the multidisciplinary field of service-learning research; see Smith and Martin 2007.

10. See Ward 2003, 94.

11. Ibid., 66–67.

12. Antonio, Astin, and Cress (2000) discuss this phenomenon in both institutional and community-based contexts; Baez (2000) focuses on nonwhite faculty in his article.

13. See Baez 2000, 364.

14. See Boyer 1996, 14.

15. See Baez 2000, 385.

16. See Ward 2003, 108.

17. See Boyer 1990, 37.

18. Ibid., 23.

19. MLA Ad Hoc Committee 2002, 181.

20. See Guillory 2005, 32, emphasis added.

21. Ibid., 33.

22. See Baez 2000, 386.

23. Ibid., 387.

24. Information on the board can be found at http://www.scholarshipofengagement.org.

25. See Baez 2000, 388.

Works Cited

Antonio, Anthony Lising, Helen S. Astin, and Christine M. Cress. 2000. "Community Service in Higher Education: A Look at the Nation's Faculty." *The Review of Higher Education* 23:4 373–98.

Baez, Benjamin. 2000. "Race-Related Service and Faculty of Color: Conceptualizing Critical Agency in Academe." *Higher Education* 39: 363–91.

Boyer, Ernest J. 1990. *Scholarship Reconsidered: Priorities of the Professoriate*. New York: Carnegie Foundation for the Advancement of Teaching.

Boyer, Ernest. 1996. "The Scholarship of Engagement." *Journal of Public Outreach* 1:1: 11–20.

Glassick, Charles E., Mary Taylor Huber, and Gene L. Maeroff. 1997. *Scholarship Assessed: Evaluation of the Professoriate*. San Francisco, CA: Jossey-Bass.

Guillory, John. 2005. "Valuing the Humanities, Evaluating Scholarship." *Profession 2005*. New York: MLA, 28–38.

MLA Ad Hoc Committee on the Future of Scholarly Publishing. 2002. "The Future of Scholarly Publishing." *Profession 2002*. New York: MLA, 172–86.

Smith, Liberty, and Heather J. Martin, eds. 2007. *Recent Dissertations on Service and Service-Learning Topics: Volume IV, 2004–2006*. Washington, DC: Learn and Serve, America's National Service-Learning Clearinghouse. Online. http://www.servicelearning.org/filemanager/downloads/Dissertations_VolumeIV_v2_web.pdf.

Ward, Kelly. 2003. *Faculty Service Roles and the Scholarship of Engagement*. ASHE-ERIC Higher Education Report. San Francisco, CA: Jossey-Bass.

12

Humble Service

Margaret Kent Bass

The Call to Service

The language of service and the imperative to actively serve others have been as essential to my growth and development from childhood to adulthood as food. My first stories were collections of "Bible Stories" in which Jesus, the Good Shepherd and Suffering Servant, was the model for living a good life.

My father Daniel, a minister in the Christian (formerly Colored) Methodist Episcopal (CME) church, and my mother Maggie, daughter of a CME bishop and academically trained theologian, provided a devoutly Christian upbringing for my brother Danny and me. We prayed before every meal and recited one of the many Bible verses that we'd memorized after the "blessing." We learned to pray as toddlers, on our knees, hands folded, parent kneeling with us: *"Now I lay me down to sleep. I pray the Lord my soul to keep. If I should die before I wake. I pray the Lord my soul to take . . ."* followed by a long list of "God bless" my relatives and friends, known and unknown. One sign of growth and maturity was our transition from this early childhood prayer to "The Lord's Prayer." I knew "The Lord's Prayer" before I knew how to read, and I learned to read long before I entered first grade.

For the first thirty-five years of my life, I prayed before every meal—three times a day, at home or school, at relatives' and friends' houses. Praying was like going to the bathroom. It was a necessity; something I didn't have to think much about. I just did it because it was one of those things essential to life.

Jesus was the central figure around whom my early sensibilities and notions about service to others and the commitment to self-sacrifice, particularly in the face of abject poverty, oppression, and injustice, developed. In

Sexuality and the Black Church, Kelly Brown Douglas notes that Jesus' "ministry was characterized by giving himself to others so that they might experience justice, healing, belonging, self-worth, life and/or empowerment."[1]

My instruction to love those who hate me, turn the other cheek, and do unto others came not only from what Jesus said but also from the examples of his own life and death. My life, all human behavior, had as its model the "perfect" life of Jesus and, to a lesser extent, my father.

Although I stopped praying when I entered the academy, this is the tradition from which I've come. My jobs in academe have, more often than not, physically removed me from the black church and black communities, and my own intellectual and theological maturation (some would call it *whitening*) has moved me far, far away from that early Christian training.

I can live with this, but I've not been able to move away from the life of Jesus as a model for my own life. There are many other historical figures, good men and women, whom I choose to emulate. Perhaps Jesus ranks high among them because he's all I have left from the church and the tradition I love. I've known Jesus for as long as I've known myself, and I'm inspired not only by his life but also by his words.

It is this early Christian call to service that not only led me to this work that is teaching, service, and self-sacrifice for the good of others but also keeps me in it. Even though the service may appear to be institutional service, it is human service, service to my people, and service to the cause of social justice locally, nationally, and internationally.

There is a precedent among black women scholars and intellectuals to respond to the call to service. Serving others and serving black people is deeply embedded and historically traditional among middle-class black women scholar-activists.

Stephanie Y. Evans (2007), in *Black Women in the Ivory Tower, 1850–1954*, notes that service has always been a priority for black women intellectuals and scholars. In her chapter on "Service," Evans examines the lives and words of Anna Julia Cooper, Mary Church Terrell, and Mary McLeod Bethune. Of Cooper, Evans says: "Earning an education was a form of service, and those who had formal training owed their gains to the community. . . . Her [Cooper] idea of service was far more profound than current definitions of campus-based committee work. She insisted that educators engaged in community service for the purpose of social justice.[2]

Mary McLeod Bethune was another of my childhood heroes. I spent five years as a child in Jacksonville, Florida, living under "Jim Crow." Bethune was an exemplar for us. She was not only an educated woman, but she founded Bethune-Cookman College to educate her people. Evans tells us that Bethune "affirmed that community service and social responsibility were core tenets of higher education."[3]

Although these early black women felt the tugs of race and gender, and the blows of racism and sexism, they fought tirelessly against all oppression and injustice. Of particular concern, however, were black people and the notion of racial uplift. Like it or not, we are often perceived to be "representatives of our race," and under that circumstance, Cooper and other black women of her time "thought her role as a black woman required her to be above reproach in order to be a moral compass for all black people."[4] Education not only offers access to a world that we would otherwise not be able to inhabit, but its premier function is that it allows us to teach and to lead by example. We become "a credit to our race."

These commitments to racial uplift, giving back to my people, and social justice for all people are commitments that facilitated my escape from "Jim Crow" untarnished. There was work for me to do in the world, and I couldn't do the work with credibility unless I had an education. My education was for my family, my people, and me. This reality was demonstrated time and time again as long as I was in the South. In Baton Rouge and Nashville, older black women would often stop me: "Chile, I heard you is a teacher here." "Yes, ma'am, I am." "Praise God! I'm so proud of you!" The women and I would embrace, as though we were borne from one body. I felt as deeply connected to those women as I did to anyone in my biological family, and I enjoyed tremendous satisfaction in what I represented to them. The inescapable fact was and is that I owe an inestimable debt of gratitude to the ancestors for making it possible for me to attend Louisiana State University (LSU) and to teach at the institutions with which I've been affiliated. I'm standing on their backs, and I've got to stand tall.

These sensibilities and commitments to social justice, strengthened by my study of African cultures and my travels, confirmed my deep connections to others in the African diaspora.

My father taught us to speak out in the face of injustice. We never feared "Jim Crow" or white people. My brother and I never felt inferior to anyone. The system was flawed. We were to speak when we witnessed injustice, even if it meant that we had to suffer the consequences. We were not to be silent.

This outspokenness was further encouraged during the late sixties and seventies. The shouts of "Black Power" and "Power to the People," and the fists raised in solidarity told us that justice and all of the privileges of citizenship were on the horizon. I've never recovered from the shock and deep disappointment of realizing that my climb up the ladder of success and my attainment of a place in the ivory tower were big steps back in time. I and others like me are among the first critical mass of black women to integrate white academe, and the sentiments against our arrival are as strong as those our foremothers encountered in Birmingham, Selma, or Boston. When white administrators sought "diversity," they had no idea for what they were asking; in turn, we had little idea as to what was in store for us.

New Job, New Life, New Understandings:
An Introductory Note on Diversity

Diversity is not a word I or anyone I knew used consistently before my entry into the academy. I knew the word, but I neither used it in the way I do now nor ever imagined it would come to mean *me*. In the "academy," which is always white, I *am* diversity, and I mean exactly that. I do not, in the minds of most of my colleagues, merely *represent* diversity. I *am* it. The "I" to which I refer in this essay is that collective "I" common to African American and other "ethnic" autobiographies; it means we, in this case, "faculty of color." Not all of us, mind you, but enough of us to matter. Diversity is code for several words that we do not use comfortably in the academy. Diversity is a word for race, but more than that, diversity is a word for anyone who is not white—or *non*white, as white colleagues often say. White is always the norm. If one is not white, then one is something else: "diverse, ethnic, of color."

I grew up thinking that diverse meant many variations of the same or similar things. When my family went to the zoo, we saw a diverse group of animals. They looked different, had different eating habits and sleeping patterns, and were born and bred in various parts of the world, but all were animals—not good or bad animals (of course, some were more ferocious than others), but animals. Although we knew the lion was the "king of beasts," I don't think we took that hierarchical term seriously. The lion was just another big guy in the animal kingdom. When my family went to the aquarium, we saw a diverse group of fish—all swimming, all fish doing fish things. The flowers in our yard were diverse: roses, pansies, daisies, gladioli, all beautiful with sweet smells, and all flowers. The point is that I never, ever heard the word "diversity" used to define people until I entered the white academy. That is when I first learned I am diverse, but the term had taken on another meaning. I am diverse because I am "different." I am not white, but what follows is not the suggestion that, despite external differences, we are all the same. In addition to being not white, the word diversity has taken on meanings that suggest inferiority, incompetence, and inadequacy. I am diverse because I am not white. I am diverse because I am black. I am diverse because some believe they were forced to bring me here, while others simply felt morally obligated: "It was the right thing to do." Many believe I do not belong.

I am diverse because I am an "affirmative action" hire. I was recruited, and sometimes white colleagues must figure out complex ways to retain me. Sometimes I think diversity, recruitment, retention, minority, and nonwhite are synonyms.

The problem with this new meaning of diversity—this academic meaning of diversity—is that it is both pejorative and essentialist. It means "let us figure out how to bring these people into our midst and keep them here," and the problem with this is the pronouns: us, them, our. These pronouns set up a dichotomy that continues to exist once the "diverse" people are in their white academic midst. I, diverse person, am *invited* into white academe: "We invite this one into our house because she, unlike all the other blacks, is exceptional. She is almost like us. What is important is the fact that she looks different. She is clearly not us, but she is enough like us to *pretend* to be like us while she is with us. We will have this stranger in our midst. She uses our language, but there are certain conversations we cannot have with her; certain words we cannot say to her, and although she is not quite ready to be here, with our care and concern, guidance and mentoring, she will be all right. Aren't we lucky to have found such a prize?" And so I arrive, and the continuing problem of diversity in the white academy is solved for the moment. I am not fooled. I have heard the pronouns, and I know this ain't nothing like my trip to the aquarium. Ain't nobody looking at me and thinking "Well, we're all human" 'cause I wear the sign of diversity on my face. I become not just a faculty member but a *minority* faculty member, a *faculty member of color*, and that, my friends, just ain't the same as a *regular* faculty member.

Diversity comes in handy in the classroom as well. Many of my students have never exchanged a word with an African American until they speak to me. I get to assure them that they can talk about race in my presence. I get to listen to them use "they" and "them" when they talk about black people in exactly the same way that I now use those pronouns to refer to my white colleagues and students. Perhaps, as my friend Peter suggests, the we/they dilemma is one of the inescapable ironies of American race relations, but the power of my pronouns is limited. My use of these pronouns in the community in which I live and work is meaningless and without the force of majority power. I believe, however, that the pronouns just might have some power on the page, and that is why I write. I am not unlike my forebears in that way.

To continue: I get to assure students they have no reason to be afraid of me. I am not as "intimidating" as I look or sound. I have to listen to stories about racist parents and families. I get to offer absolution for past racial sins and injustices, and I have to assure them that I do not hate them;

I will grade them fairly; I am not easily offended. Finally, I have to endure the racist remarks of the most conservative ones and defend myself against the occasional student who clearly feels superior to me and believes I do not know much. I get to remind them, as I did one student in my class, not to deal with my blackness by making me invisible.

Sometimes my diversity leads to compliments. The most consistent compliment I receive is about my ability to speak—to express myself orally, but using " 'good English' don't make me smart or nothing." I have *presence* rather than intellect. I have the power "of a preacher" instead of the power of a scholar. I can "speak white," and it doesn't get any better than that for them. They all tell me I speak so well, and it seems odd that they make a point of this, since I have a degree in English. I actually have two degrees in English—a BA and a PhD. If the BA did not convince them, then the PhD should have, but I guess their folks tell them the same thing my folks tell me: "Chile, there is a plenty fools out there with all them degrees. Ain't no fool like an educated fool."

I never hear them telling each other *they* speak so well. Speaking well comes naturally to white folks. They leave the womb speaking well, I guess. When they tell me I speak so well, it means I speak like they do. It means I use the English language "properly." I know that verbs and subjects must agree. I have a fairly decent vocabulary. I speak in complete sentences, and my syntax is usually good too. My voice is strong and forthright. I do not slur my words in a Steppin' Fetchit kind of way, and this is particularly amazing to them because they know I am a Southerner; that I spent a good part of my early education in all-black schools in the South.

The best thing about me is that I do not use "Black English." This is the best possible attribute a black faculty member can have. Diversity doesn't include diverse ways of speaking English. Many of my colleagues have absolutely no evidence that I can speak "Black English" with great fluency. Most of them do not know that I love that language they believe to be substandard and inferior, incorrect and improper, just plain bad. They do not know how that language allows me to express my deepest feelings and emotions in a way the language we speak together, American *Standard* English, could never do. They do not know that if I do not ever speak that lovely nonstandard language with them, then they will never, ever be my friends. But that ain't the point of diversity, now is it?

I digress; the subject of this essay is service, and this badge of diversity comes with certain privileges that mostly have to do with service. I get to serve as the representative diverse person on more committees than I care to name. When I taught at research universities, I got to serve on the thesis committee of every student in any discipline who studied "diverse issues." I get to serve as mentor for African American students from every academic discipline. I get to introduce nearly any African American speaker who comes to campus. I am invited to all of the minority student functions and events. I am invited to speak to numerous student and community groups. I get to listen to their racist remarks. I get to endure their inability to figure out "how to talk to me." I get to "help" them understand things about race. I get to do so little research and writing that my colleagues "worry" about my progress toward promotion to full professor, and I get to continually reassure them that I am "happy," because if I am not, they will worry about losing their "diversity." I get to talk to them about black literatures because they do not know anything about what I do. I get to prove, however, that I am competent in their specialty areas. Imagine an Americanist who doesn't know anything about Hemingway or Faulkner, Shakespeare, Milton or Chaucer? Imagine that! I get to undergo certain kinds of competency testing: *"Happy to meet you, Margaret—to have you as a colleague. I'm told you specialize in autobiography studies. Ummm, let's see. Can you name the historical figure that is considered the first autobiographer? Take a moment to think about it. I'm sure you'll figure it out."*

Charmaine C. Williams (2001) applies W. J. Wilson's interpretation of the racial dynamics in the plantation and the later industrialized economy to understand the place of people of color in academia. In the close quarters of academic departments, those in power can develop intimate symbiotic relationships with beginning scholars that take on a paternalistic quality through the tradition of supervision and mentoring. Emerging scholars of color are disadvantaged in challenging the authority of those in power because the power differential is so broad. Women scholars of color, working as others, do within interlocking discourses of oppression, face significant challenges in attempting social change within the institution or in using (borrowing?) institutional privilege to effect social change beyond the institution.[5]

Williams knows of what she speaks. I refer to the administration building of my university as the "Big House." The institution itself is "the plantation." I am the jovial, nurturing "mammy" or the intimidating, boorish "Sapphire." They dislike my "rhetorical style." I'm what Southerners would call an "uppity nigger." I've had to recall all my resources and resolve from the days of dealing with "Jim Crow," but this alienation, this marginalization, sexism, and racism, is covert. One can easily tell you that you've made an error; that you haven't really experienced racism. You're "defensive, hostile, overly sensitive." You suffer blow after blow alone, misunderstood until your dismissal from the ranks, the shunning and the silencing.

I didn't get a PhD to do "institutional housekeeping."[6] That labor that is "much like the unpaid, domestic housekeeping performed by women in family units [or house slaves], institutional housekeeping is usually performed without resources and recognition." My service, as I suggested early on, serves the people, the race, and those who suffer from oppression, discrimination, and injustice.

St. Lawrence University is a small, private liberal arts college in upstate New York. Most New Yorkers can't locate Canton, New York. Canton is about twenty-five miles from the Canadian border. It is closer to Ottawa, Ontario, than it is to any city in the United States. One's only direct access to Canton is by bus or car. Even Amtrak is 130 miles downstate in Syracuse. There are few people of color at St. Lawrence among faculty, staff, and students and even fewer in Canton. The area is very rural and very white. Our student body is overwhelmingly white as well, and for many of the students from Maine and Vermont, our own "north country," I am the first black teacher they've ever had. My service and my duty to them is to make black people real, human, loving, intelligent individuals; to share my knowledge and experiences with them; to help them understand why race and gender matter in a world that increasingly suggests they don't.

For students of color, I do all of this and more. When they ask me why I stay, I tell them I stay for them. Much as I resist the role of "nurturer" and "mother figure," it is both cultural and inevitable that many students of color see me as protector, as guardian of their interests, and as "one who understands and cares." I identify with their loneliness; I know their stories of racism in the classroom are true. I listen. I tell them to "hold on."

Most students of color come from urban areas, and the cultural shock and subsequent disorientation lead to all kinds of problems. The overt and covert racism is wounding, and many experience it here for the very first time. They, too, have often lived such sheltered and insular lives that they live under the illusion that racism was "a long time ago."

Only a small portion of my service is for the good of the institution itself. The institution doesn't need me beyond my ability to "represent diversity." Even good liberals don't want to engage or entertain my perceptions of events or situations, my anger or my constant vigilance with regard to racism, sexism, and homophobia. I define my service, and I ain't cleaning no institutional houses.

My experience over the past eighteen years reveals that the "honeymoon" period between "angry" black women and white institutions lasts about five years. My first academic appointment was in 1990. I was, according to the local newspaper, the first African American hired in the English Department at Vanderbilt University in Nashville, Tennessee. My time at Vanderbilt was the most pleasant of the three academic appointments I have held, and I am convinced that my three-year stay is the sole reason for the success of the experience.

My honeymoon with the University of Iowa ended after five years, and I fell from grace here at St. Lawrence just about five years after my return in 2000. At both institutions I lost status, stature, "friends," and respect because some colleagues and I did not come to consensus on the process and method by which we further "diversified" the faculty. I saw up close and personal the racism and presumption that allowed white colleagues to tell me how to effectively recruit and retain faculty and staff of color. I balked at the manipulations of affirmative action language and laws, and most important, I vociferously and publicly disagreed with their practices with regard to "minority" hiring. In short, I became an "angry" black woman, "hostile and mean," an "ungrateful Negro," to use the dated term. After all, I'd been given the privilege of serving the academy in a meaningfully diverse way. I mistakenly assumed membership in a club in which I ultimately learned that I really didn't belong.

The retaliation in the white academy is the most effective method of alienating and silencing that I have ever experienced, and the most painful. It literally puts one in her place by a collective white wall of sanction and shame. I have grieved my human losses and wondered why I continue to trust and continue to care.

The integration of white academe replicates the movement of glaciers, and I need all of the resolve and determination that I learned from my father more than fifty years ago. Sometimes I want to give up; other times I begin to wonder if I'm really the person they say I am. On occasion, I question my sanity, but then I recall the lives of Anna Cooper, Mary Bethune, Sojourner Truth, and all of the women before me who have been subjected to similar kinds of disregard, disrespect, and misunderstanding. I continue to heed the call to service in the ways that I've learned from them. Evans says of Mary Bethune, "While she was aware of her marginalized position as a black woman in America, she saw service as a duty and struggle as an honor."[7] Thank you, Mrs. Bethune, so do I.

Notes

1. See Douglas 1999, 115.
2. See Evans 2007, 180.
3. Ibid., 184.
4. Ibid., 182.
5. See Williams 2001, 89.

6. See Bird, Litt, and Wang 2004, 196.
7. See Evans 2007, 185.

Works Cited

Bird, Sharon, Jacquelyn Litt, and Yong Wang. 2004. "Creating Status of Women Reports: Institutional Housekeeping as 'Women's Work.'" *NSWA Journal* 16:1: 196.

Douglas, Kelly Brown. 1999. *Sexuality and the Black Church: A Womanist Perspective.* New York: Orbis.

Evans, Stephanie Y. 2007. *Black Women in the Ivory Tower, 1850–1954: An Intellectual History.* Gainesville: University Press of Florida.

Williams, Charmaine C. 2001. "The Angry Black Woman Scholar." *NWSA Journal* 13:2: 89.

13

Welcome to the Land of
Super-Service

A Survivor's Guide ... and Some Questions

Phyllis van Slyck

First, a Little History

It is a truth (almost) universally acknowledged that if you want to have an academic career devoted to teaching and service, you should apply for a job at a public community college. Here are a few more generally acknowledged truths about community colleges in the United States. From the 1960s through the 1990s these institutions have traditionally attracted and retained women faculty, though, consistently, they have been paid less than their male colleagues.[1] Community college faculty have accepted, and continue to accept, high service demands as necessary for tenure and promotion. The kinds of service undertaken include departmental administration, writing program coordination, college-wide professional development leadership, coordination of women's centers, direction of Phi Theta Kappa programs, development/ coordination of special academic programs such as learning communities, and advisement of students and mentoring of new faculty. Except for administrative work such as that of department chair or writing program director, much of this service is considered part of the job and is, therefore, uncompensated—or very modestly compensated. From the 1960s to the present, women faculty at community colleges have helped define and deepen this extraordinary and, in many ways, valuable emphasis on service. Yet they have accepted service on the job in the same way they have long accepted it in the home—without much struggle for recognition of their work.

Because, for many years, community colleges hired faculty who had master's degrees rather than PhDs, service was implicitly, and often explicitly, understood as a substitute for scholarship. However, since faculty at community colleges have also consistently been required to. teach more courses than faculty at four-year institutions, it is clear that service has never been considered as arduous or time consuming as scholarship. And even though community college faculty have contributed substantially in the last two decades to traditional scholarship, to the field of composition and rhetoric, and to the scholarship of teaching, as Ernst Boyer has noted, the latter, especially, is regarded as second tier to traditional scholarship in literature, for example—a kind of distinction that perpetuates the second-class status of many community college faculty.[2]

As community colleges have expanded and diversified their mission, and as students, increasingly, have come to these colleges with the intent of transferring to four-year schools, there has been a parallel (and an appropriate) increase in the kinds of scholarly demands placed on faculty, and many new faculty are being hired with PhDs in hand. While expecting faculty to be active scholars in their fields is a good thing, the problem confronting growing numbers of community college faculty is that the demand for service has also increased. Add to this the fact that community colleges are the last place where there is genuine open admission for students, and that class sizes are often larger than at four-year institutions, and we have an almost perfect recipe for faculty stress and burnout—especially in departments such as English, where faculty teach four to five courses each semester and are required to give as many as eight essays per semester in writing courses.[3]

I teach at Fiorello H. LaGuardia Community College of the City University of New York (CUNY), where these realities are evident. Women faculty and administrators have consistently played a major role in defining the quality of teaching and service at our institution: women outnumber men, both in my department and in the college; a majority of current department chairs are women, and the highest-ranking administrator, the president, is a woman.[4] And while the student population (64% female; 36% male) may not seem *directly* related to the service issue it is important, because faculty, women faculty in particular, are modeling for women students what it means to be an academic. At LaGuardia, excellent teaching is the faculty's primary responsibility, but substantial service to the institution has always been an explicit part of our contract.[5] When LaGuardia first opened its doors in the 1970s, professional scholarship was not particularly encouraged, as it was believed it would interfere with our primary responsibilities of teaching and service; however, in the last five to seven years, professional scholarship has been deemed essential for tenure and promotion, and we have hired faculty in English, in the social sciences and in the humanities who have a strong commitment to publishing in their professional fields.[6]

Despite this new emphasis on scholarship and despite significant changes in student goals (80% of students entering LaGuardia plan to acquire higher degrees than the AA) and in faculty credentials (50% of current LaGuardia faculty have PhDs),[7] service expectations for new faculty have become even greater than they were in the 1970s and 1980s. Our English Department rarely considers a candidate who does not have the PhD in hand, or nearly in hand, because the combined teaching and service demands are so great that most would not be able to complete their degrees before a tenure decision is made, and we would be condemning them to failure.[8]

As LaGuardia faculty are mentored in the march toward tenure, they are expected not only to excel in the classroom and to contribute substantial service to their departments but also to find a particular "niche" or significant project that will define their contribution to the larger college community. But a new emphasis on scholarship has been added to this already substantial set of service demands. Recently a faculty member who had an excellent teaching record and who had performed superior departmental and college-wide service over more than a decade was denied a promotion because she had failed to publish adequately. Conversely, a junior faculty member whose scholarship was more than adequate but who took a year's leave because of the demands of child care (breaking her march toward tenure) was discouraged from returning on the grounds that her service to the college had not been significant.

The message to faculty at institutions like mine is that they had better do all three things well—teaching, scholarship, and service—and not complain if they hope to earn tenure and promotion. However, the culture of our college community offers little room for an open discussion of service issues and concerns: untenured faculty and even tenured junior faculty do not feel comfortable indicating to their chairs or to tenured colleagues that they are overwhelmed by the teaching load, by service, or that they are anxious about finding time to pursue their scholarship—but the stress level is palpable.

This profile of faculty expectations at LaGuardia may differ from national norms, but I would like to suggest that it represents the direction community colleges are headed; as such, our situation raises a number of important and difficult questions. How can new and junior faculty begin to address the competing demands and the fundamental inequities of their situation—specifically, that they are asked to perform service and publish while teaching two to four more courses, annually, than their colleagues at four-year institutions? How will the generation of women currently being hired at community colleges address issues of child care at institutions that, despite extraordinary professional service demands, have not acknowledged (or only minimally acknowledged) personal service demands?[9] What steps can new faculty take to challenge the status quo without risk to their positions? And how can leadership at community colleges today become more responsive to the multiple demands being placed on faculty? How might senior faculty, department chairs, and even college-wide administrators be encouraged to support this generation and to understand the pressures they are facing?

Equally important, how can junior faculty themselves begin to take greater ownership of the priorities and vision of public community colleges? Women faculty at community colleges have traditionally taken a leadership role in defining—often redefining—approaches to pedagogy. Student-centered learning, deeply connected to feminist scholarship and revitalized and re-envisioned since Dewey, in large measure by the women's movement, has changed the way faculty at community colleges think about teaching and the way they mentor new colleagues. Collaborative pedagogy and attention to the social and cognitive aspects of learning have been embraced by those of us who teach first-generation college students (the vast majority at community colleges) and by scholars advocating attention to diverse students' learning styles; yet this pedagogy's association with feminist privileging of "community" over "competition" has associated with it "soft" scholarship with second-tier institutions and with community colleges. How can faculty at community colleges begin to challenge these perceptions? And might taking on this challenge become an instance of meaningful service? In other words, what kinds of service, especially for women in the profession, would decenter assumptions about community colleges and help promote a deeper understanding of the significant role these colleges play in educating students for transfer to four-year institutions?

My Story

Hired in the early nineties at LaGuardia, I did all the things required of me as a faculty member and more; I did them, for many years, as a single parent without questioning or challenging any of the priorities being set for me. Despite a heavy teaching load, I found service both inspiring and career defining precisely because that service was directly related to the kind of teaching I was learning to value. I became involved, initially without really knowing its roots, in a deeply feminist attention to student learning. In faculty professional development seminars we read and discussed constructivist learning theory from Dewey to Kolb; Schoen's work on reflective practice; Belenky's ideas on women's ways of knowing and Shaughnessey's critique of errors and expectations for basic writers; MacIntosh's reflections on white privilege, Palmer's "inner landscape" of the teacher's life; and hooks's ideas about teaching in community. We immersed ourselves in these inquiries because we hungered for conversations about teaching: we were engaging with students for whom college was an entirely new, or entirely different, kind of territory from their past educational experience, and we needed to find the best strategies to reach them.

My colleagues and I were, and are, aware that there is widespread suspicion, at least at the senior college level, about the value of scholarship devoted to student-centered learning, that some of our four-year colleagues feel it would be better simply to fail students who have difficulties learning in a traditional classroom. But active learning approaches helped us improve the engagement and retention of first-generation students, and, contrary to assumptions that there is a tremendous *difference* between community college and public four-year college students, the community college population today constitutes 49 percent of the total U.S. college population; increasingly, these *are* the students who are entering the four-year college classroom at both public and private institutions.

Attention to teaching methodology is a political, gendered, equity issue for all of us, most of all for our students. Emily Lardner, co-director of the Washington Center for Improving the Quality of Undergraduate Education, recently summarized the inequities for economically disadvantaged and minority students who arrive at senior colleges: "At four-year colleges 26 percent of freshman drop out before their sophomore year; only 7 percent of young people from the lowest-income families earn four-year degrees by age twenty-six; 59 percent of white students earn a bachelor's degree within six years of entering college versus 39 percent of African Americans and 37 percent of Latino students" (12).[10] We would all be well advised to reflect on our positions as educators in the face of these statistics—and to consider the wisdom about student success that has developed—through attention to pedagogy and professional development related service—at two-year institutions. Community colleges are especially aware of student equity issues precisely because the gendered model of service that they have defined and promoted focuses attention on alternative curricular structures and fosters valuable dialogue about teaching and learning.

My interest in pedagogy led me to learning communities, a curricular and pedagogical initiative guided and refined by women in the profession from the seventies through the nineties.[11] Teaching in learning communities led to service work: for almost two decades I have coordinated, expanded, and assessed learning communities on our campus. Learning community leadership not only gave me opportunities for personal and intellectual growth, it connected me with a community of like-minded individuals within the college and university, people who were deeply committed to service. The importance of these relationships is rarely discussed, yet it is something we should support more purposefully in our profession. I developed connections with faculty and administrators from other disciplines and colleges across the country, individuals I probably would not have otherwise known, and some of these connections developed into ongoing professional and personal relationships. Such connections were initiated and sustained by women leaders in the field of learning communities, in particular, by institutions such as the

Washington Center for Improving the Quality of Undergraduate Education at Evergreen State College, for example.

Because much of my service helped me deepen my understanding of pedagogy and provided me with valuable opportunities for dialogue with colleagues on my campus and nationally, it contributed substantially to my own professional advancement—a significant benefit I did not anticipate when I began this work. The kinds of service I became involved in at LaGuardia led to national presentations, first at conferences and later in venues we created for ourselves in both regional and national networks. These networks, combined with LaGuardia's long-standing reputation in the learning communities field, led to invitations to give workshops on campuses across the country and to a variety of pedagogical publications in monographs and refereed journals. I now regularly encourage new faculty to find the kind of service that will do "double duty," that is, contribute broadly and deeply to their professional growth—and to their resumes.

At different stages in my career I received a modest amount of released time for the coordination of learning communities, for professional development seminars, and for co-coordinating a writing program, but a good part of my service, both to my department and the college was, and continues to be, voluntary. So was it possible to perform service, to teach effectively, and to pursue my scholarship? Yes, but it was not always easy: I produced articles in both my "scholarly" field (Henry James studies) and in pedagogy (composition studies and learning community design and assessment). But to publish at all, I had to learn how to set limits on service demands, to say no to meetings held on days I wasn't on campus, for example. I also worked to create a teaching schedule that gave me a block of time several days a week for writing; and I learned not to answer any kind of communication until I had put in the requisite three to four hours of writing four to five days a week. However, I could only afford to do these things after I was tenured, and I earned tenure primarily on the basis of my service, something that would not be possible now. Today many of our new hires have arrived with a number of articles already published and book contracts within their first two years, but their commitment to scholarship is seriously challenged once they begin teaching and service at LaGuardia. Junior faculty tell me that they get up at 4 a.m. to complete writing projects and then put in a full day of teaching and service at the college; even with a three-day teaching schedule, most put in four-day weeks because of service commitments. We need to come up with better solutions.

Challenges Today for Junior Faculty at Community Colleges

Let me return to my initial questions about service at the community college. If I have made my peace with the balance between service, teaching, and scholarship, as I mentor new faculty, then I wonder how they are going to balance and fulfill demands that are much greater than those I faced. I wonder how young women, particularly, are going to confront increasing demands for meaningful service, demands for visible scholarship, a heavy course load and large class sizes, and a continued lack of real support for family concerns. In my department, three junior women faculty currently coordinate our very large writing program (and one of them has not finished her doctorate). Another half dozen have taken on substantial committee work that involve such things as the development of an English major articulated with a four-year sister college, the development of a series of literary lectures for our English major, the coordination of a common reading program for all entering students (this includes the development of a Web site, teaching materials, and faculty seminars), and the facilitation of year-long faculty development seminars on a variety of pedagogical topics. Junior faculty at LaGuardia today are less likely to be given course release for the service or professional development that I received (the money is simply not available), and although they may receive a stipend, there is no getting around the fact that such service only increases the workload.

I am concerned about the pressures we place on new faculty, that we will lose them to institutions where the demand for service is lower and where they will be better able to pursue their scholarly interests. New faculty at my college are afraid to speak about "service overload," or what some have come to call "shadow workload." How do you say no to service without putting yourself at risk, they ask. Will department chairs listen, or will they insist that new faculty simply learn to do more? (Faculty at our four-year sister colleges who are publishing scholars receive released time from teaching for their professional work, something community college faculty have never been granted.)

New faculty at LaGuardia have told me, in confidence, that their first and second years feel like a kind of "hazing" process, an experience designed to test their stamina and commitment: they move from graduate school with its intermittent stress to continuous high stress and a work environment that seems to have hidden rules: they learn quickly that there is a difference between the letter of the law and the actual way things work. If you follow the letter of the law in our writing program, for example, teaching four composition courses a semester and requiring eight essays plus revisions in each course (with a class size of twenty-eight to thirty), then you would be grading between five and ten hours a day: it simply can't be done. Yet faculty recognize that they are being taught not to question the cultural norms of the institution: the message they are getting from faculty one step ahead of them is, "I went through it, so you can too!" Service pressures are so great that competition is subtly replacing a spirit of collaboration. The need for junior faculty to be visible and self-promoting also creates what is perhaps an unfair resentment of "superstars" who "set the bar too high"; this, too, fosters a competitive spirit that clashes with the kind of genuine collegiality and support we espouse in our work. Faculty who perform extraordinary service without complaint, and who are playing into the corporate agenda, are often rewarded, ironically, by being given more administrative projects. Junior faculty need to examine the political implications (not to mention the professional consequences, i.e., less time for scholarship) of playing by these new rules.

Equally problematic is the fact that there is no real internship period: you are hired, you sign the papers; everyone is welcoming; then, suddenly, you must hit the ground running. Yes, you receive mentoring in some departments, and you are welcome to visit your colleagues' classes, but the emphasis on performance, both in the classroom and college-wide, tends to promote a sense of inadequacy. Recently a junior faculty member commented that a new faculty member's recently announced service project made her feel somewhat anxious: "I didn't do anything like that in my first year; should I have?" The hiring of large numbers of new faculty at LaGuardia in the last seven years has also created complex and subtle tensions as new faculty confront old traditions in the culture of the college in general. Some of this is inevitable, and we know that it is a nationwide issue, as 30 percent of the senior faculty at both two- and four-year institutions will retire over the next decade.[12] The tensions that arise in an institution with large numbers of new faculty will affect service and collegiality in numerous ways, yet so far this remains a privately discussed, but publicly unacknowledged, issue.

In a well-meant effort, LaGuardia's administration initiated a new kind of unnamed service a few years ago, a required year-long professional development seminar for faculty in their first year at the college, designed to acculturate them to teaching in our community. While the seminar offers beneficial discussions of pedagogy and helps create a community and network for new faculty, it is time consuming (Fall, Winter, and Spring institutes, in addition to bi-monthly meetings), and some faculty complain, privately, that they have too much work to do to make this additional commitment, that they would become acculturated more effectively if they could devote themselves more thoroughly to teaching in their first year.

What Conversations Do We Need to Have, and Who Should Initiate Them?

Having examined what I see as some major problems related to service at my institution, I want to state that if faculty were to cease their involvement in service, then a very important part of the culture of the community college would be lost. Service provides vision, new directions, and it grows the leadership of the institution; it helps faculty think together about what is most pressing, about changes in our student population, about the kinds of pedagogical initiatives that will best address student needs. Most important, service also offers the necessary space for deep community to develop; ideally, it creates faculty-centered leadership both within departments and college-wide.

Today, perhaps as never before (although this is always a naïve assumption), the radical changes in information technology, to give just one example, are having a profound impact on teaching methodologies as well as scholarship itself: from blackboard to blogs to second life.com, faculty are having to catch up with a techno-savvy generation.[13] This is not to say that we should in any way be abandoning our commitment to traditional forms of scholarship but, rather, that we need to meet students where they are—to have a deeper understanding of their language—if we hope to inspire them. The profound shift in the *means* of communication that is taking place will need to be incorporated into the academic community. Who will help faculty understand this shift, these tools, and how to use them if not the newest generation entering our departments? This *could* be an extremely valuable kind of service.

Junior and senior faculty need to work together to take on the challenge of communicating the need for various kinds of support, from intellectual validation to released time. LaGuardia's English Department recently created a "State of the Department Committee" so that faculty would be able to talk about these kinds of issues. We invited faculty to respond—anonymously—to a questionnaire in which they described their best experiences in the department (and at the college) and what they were most concerned about; we also solicited suggestions for change. In what might be a good model for other community colleges, the CUNY Union, the Professional Staff Congress, achieved an important victory in its most recent contract: all new faculty receive twenty-four hours (the equivalent of six to seven courses) of released time to pursue scholarship; this is spread over a five-year period and may not be taken in a large block, but it is a beginning. However, in this same contract, the union leadership conceded a move in the tenure clock from five to seven years—a change that will inevitably increase the service demand for new faculty. A group of mostly, but not exclusively, junior faculty is also fighting for a better family leave policy from the university, in coordination with the union. Perhaps the most difficult problem for community college faculty at CUNY is the continued inequity in the teaching load between junior and senior colleges—an issue that remains unaddressed.

Finally, there is a fundamental disconnect between the requirements being placed on faculty and the messages faculty are receiving about how best to achieve them. Part of this disconnect is based on a widely discussed shift to a corporate management model at both public and private institutions of higher education.[14] Recently our college president notified one of our union representatives that she could no longer use college e-mail to send out notices of union meetings, because "union business is not part of the performance of an employee's duties and responsibilities." This ban is currently being challenged in court by our union. Why is it threatening for faculty to seek better conditions, conditions that will enhance their ability to teach, to perform service, to do their scholarship—precisely those things that are being demanded of them? An increasing tension is emerging at LaGuardia and elsewhere between an original faculty-centered culture and an administratively driven set of strategic goals demanding measurable results (such as high pass rates in basic skills courses within a semester—regardless of the level of proficiency with which students enter a given course). From the administration's point of view, only such measurable results translate into "productivity."[15] But faculty know that this kind of pressure to provide successful "data" interferes with good teaching practice.

A related problem at two-year colleges is a new emphasis on service-related scholarship—as being more "relevant" than other kinds of scholarship. Senior administrators (including, in some cases, department chairs) who have long since ceased to be publishing scholars tend to privilege service research over scholarly research. Sabbatical proposals that promise research into new pedagogies that will be piloted on campus, for example, are more easily approved than scholarly projects whose direct application to teaching at a two-year college is less obvious. While my colleagues and I have completed many pedagogy-based research projects, we know that our scholarly projects are equally valuable and worthy of support. Students at community colleges need and deserve the same exposure to current intellectual currents and methodologies, and their histories, as their peers at four-year institutions. For administrators to argue that such scholarship is not relevant to community college curriculum is simply a belated form of colonialism: it patronizes and diminishes our students.

Despite these problems, new directions in national leadership are already visible. I was heartened to note that the December 2007 MLA Convention offered a panel discussion on released time, teaching, and publication at community colleges, and that a national organization of community college faculty is also forming through the MLA. I was also pleased to see that the MLA is considering revising the format of the annual convention. Proposals for this new format suggest a heightened attention to service (and its implications) in the college and university, including "workshops focused on the vast range of professional interests, responsibilities, and proficiencies—pedagogical issues, institutional facilitation (preparing dossiers for tenure cases, mentoring graduate students and junior faculty members), disciplinary and administrative issues (academic freedom, gender and diversity, departmental governance), and so forth."[16]

The assumption on the part of our four-year colleagues and our college administrators, that community college faculty do not need time to pursue scholarly interests, may well be tied to the long-standing bias that this group of faculty, especially its majority of women faculty, is primarily committed to service. So we need to move beyond discussion and consider actions we can take to support junior faculty on our campuses. An important local step would be for us to begin to document—and then to challenge—the multiple demands being placed on us. But if we want to change the culture at the community college, then we are going to have to mobilize and win the hearts and minds of new colleagues who, for the most part, have evinced little interest in union activities. (When asked about this, the standard response is, "I can't get involved in political action until I am tenured.") We all want, and our students deserve, college faculty who are not only current in their scholarly fields but also conversant in the best pedagogical practices for a changing student population; we also want college administrators who are supportive of their faculty—in relation to teaching, to scholarship, *and* to service. Most important, we want college communities in which everyone has a voice; communities that are committed to open and thoughtful dialogue about the major changes in leadership and vision that are already taking place in our institutions. This anthology of writings offers the beginning of a broader, deeper conversation about service for women faculty, for all faculty, at both two-year and four-year institutions.

Notes

1. "Gender differentials in salary remain a problem: Male professors at community colleges average $66,030, compared to $62,357 for female professors" ("American Association of Community Colleges, 2005," in *National Profile of Community Colleges: Trends and Statistics*, ed. Kent A. Phillipe and Leila Gonzalez Sullivan, 98 (Washington, DC: Community College Press, **2005**).

2. See Boyer's *Scholarship Reconsidered: Priorities of the Professoriate* (Baltimore, MD: Carnegie Foundation, 1997). At my institution, the scholarship of teaching has been explicitly encouraged as "preferable" to traditional scholarship, because it is considered more "relevant" to the kind of teaching we do, although this assumption is being challenged.

3. The class size for basic or pre-college level writing at LaGuardia is twenty-eight, almost twice that recommended by the National Council of Teachers of English. One third of entering students need ESL courses, and more than half need pre-college writing and math courses. (Students at LaGuardia come from 150 countries and speak 115 languages.)

4. "Women Now Constitute Nearly 27% of Public and Private Community College Presidents, Up from 11% in 1991" (*National Profile*, 2005, 97).

5. Article 15b of the Collective Bargaining Agreement between the Professional Staff Congress and the City University of New York (2002–2007) reads, in part, "Employees on the teaching staff of the City University of New York shall not be required to teach an excessive number of contact hours, assume an excessive student load . . . it being recognized by the parties that the teaching staff has the obligation, among others, to be available to students, *to assume normal committee assignments, and engage in research and community service*" (26–27, emphasis added).

6. Currently, department chairs at LaGuardia, and the president of the college, explicitly demand that new faculty publish in order to earn tenure; outstanding teaching and service are also essential. This message is reinforced at college-wide tenure and promotion information meetings for new faculty. In contrast, a former chair of my department in the 1970s and 1980s told me of this illuminating exchange with the then dean of the faculty. "How much does publication count in promotion decisions?" Long, long pause. Then the irony-free answer, "Well, it won't really hurt them." The chair also explained that giving talks at conferences was accepted as the equivalent of publication.

7. *2007 Institutional Profile*, Office of Institutional Research, Division of Information Technology, LaGuardia Community College, the City University of New York (ix).

8. Our president, like other presidents at CUNY, has indicated to department chairs that she will no longer reappoint instructors who have reached the tenure decision year without completing the PhD. Previous presidents often appointed these faculty as lecturers with a tenure equivalent, the Certificate of Continuing Education, allowed under the Collective Bargaining Agreement between our Union, the Professional Staff Congress, and CUNY.

9. In the most recent contract, the Professional Staff Congress of CUNY awarded its members eight weeks of paid maternity leave and then up to three months of paid use of sick days.

10. See "The Heart of Education: Translating Diversity into Equity," in *Diversity, Educational Equity, and Learning Communities: The Washington Center for Improving the Quality of Undergraduate Education*, ed. Emily Lardner, 1–35 (Olympia, WA: The Evergreen State College, Summer 2005).

11. Learning communities are courses clustered around a common theme and taught to the same cohort of students within a given semester; they encourage a high degree of integrated, and interdisciplinary, learning. The founder of the learning community movement in the United States was Alexander Meiklejohn, who established the Experimental College, a school within a school, at the University of Wisconsin in 1927. But the faculty who advanced and disseminated the pedagogy we associate with learning communities from the seventies through the nineties were (and continue to be) predominantly women. See, for example, Barbara Leigh Smith et al., *Learning Communities: Reforming Undergraduate Education* (San Francisco, CA: Jossey-Bass, 2004).

12. "Full-Time Faculty's Years to Retirement by College Type 1999–2000" (*National Profile*, 117).

13. In this context, see, for example, Michael Berube, Sven Birkets, and blogs such as bitchphd.com.

14. See, for example, Cary Nelson and Stephen Watt, "The Corporate University," in *Academic Keywords: A Devil's Dictionary for Higher Education*, 84–98 (London and New York: Routledge, 1999). More recently, see Marc Bousquet, *How the University Works* (New York: New York University Press, 2008).

15. A recent English Department faculty meeting was devoted, almost entirely, to the question of how to improve the pass rate in our Basic Writing courses. Some of our newer colleagues expressed dismay at the illogic of this administratively driven goal, especially when told that smaller class sizes were not an option that would be considered.

16. See interim reports submitted to the MLA Executive Council and Delegate Assembly on Proposed Changes in the Convention Structure at http://www.mla.org.

Part 3

Service Changes

14

Service and Empowerment

Patricia Meyer Spacks

Received wisdom has it that the ambitious young academic should try to avoid entanglement in committee assignments and administrative tasks, distractions from and obstacles to the research and writing that can further a career. My experience tells me something more complicated, about the advantages as well as disadvantages of academic service. Sometimes, at least, service too may further a career.

First, my experience. Then, more about what it tells me.

When I began my postdoctoral teaching career, at Indiana University, I thought I knew quite a bit about eighteenth-century poetry, but knew that I didn't know much about anything else. In particular, I knew almost nothing about how universities work. I had won my instructorship (in those days one started as an instructor, PhD or not) under peculiar circumstances. The department chair from Indiana came out to Berkeley to interview graduate students, and certain students were assigned, regardless of their wishes, to meet with him. I began my interview by announcing, "I should tell you at the outset that I have no interest in teaching at Indiana." "That's fine," the chair said, "because we have no interest in hiring women." I didn't know enough to be offended. We had a pleasant conversation, and then he offered me a too-good-to-refuse job, and there I was in Bloomington.

As I remember, the large department contained two other women, one of them, like me, a newly hired instructor. I can't speak for the other women, but during my two years at Indiana I was not asked to serve on any university committee, and I can't recall any departmental assignments either. Perhaps the powers that be—whoever those powers were, I didn't know—wished to protect me from distraction. Perhaps they doubted whether a young woman could contribute to committee deliberations. Or maybe they just hadn't noticed that I was there. When I left Indiana, after two years, I think I could at least recognize everyone in the English Department, but I had never met anyone from elsewhere in the university.

My career restarted at Wellesley, where the faculty of the college—a women's college, of course—and of the English Department were divided roughly fifty-fifty between men and women. Among the faculty, deliberations were as nearly gender-blind as any I've encountered. I remember a Jewish male colleague observing that he never noticed how many men and how many women were in a room, he only noticed how many Jews. It was not hard to understand how that might happen—not because Jews were discriminated against, but because they, unlike women, constituted a minority.

I served on many committees at Wellesley, college committees and departmental ones. Some seemed tedious and meaningless, and many specialized in unnecessarily long meetings which often struck me as being inefficient. Still, they performed much of the real work of the institution. Men and women served equally on them. The committees established curriculum, made appointments, adjudicated disputes, ordered books for the library, and arranged public lectures. They pondered policy issues and possible new directions for the institution. They figured out who should be the next department chair. Although, like my colleagues, I complained about endless meetings and about being overworked, I found many of the committee deliberations rewarding. For one thing, they enabled me to grasp how the college functioned, to understand the lines of power and how to get things done. For another, they introduced me to people throughout the community whom I probably wouldn't have met under purely social circumstances. The committee work made me believe that I had a stake in the institution's procedures. I felt deeply connected to the college—and not only because it was much smaller than the university where I started.

Was I institutionally rewarded? I don't know. In due time, I received tenure, perhaps partly because of those committees. In subsequent deliberations on personnel matters that I participated in, we talked seriously about service, but no one was ever promoted or given a raise for service alone. Like every other academic institution I know of, Wellesley claimed the tripartite requirements of scholarship, teaching, and service. During my untenured years, one of my colleagues failed to win reappointment on the alleged grounds that he focused too much on his scholarship, at the expense of teaching and service, but no one that I know of was fired only because of failure to "serve"—although people *were* fired for failing to teach well.

The notion of "service" struck me (and strikes me) as puzzling. Why did it constitute service to devote hours to planning the curriculum, whereas the greater number of hours allotted to grading freshman papers did not count? It was "service" to act as faculty adviser to the campus newspaper but not to hold conferences with 100 students—including conferences involving advice about how to make career choices. Of course I understood that grading papers and holding conferences make up part of the enterprise of teaching, but surely planning the curriculum provides the foundation for that enterprise, and the campus newspaper supplies important educational opportunities. The line between teaching and service seemed hazy. Even the line between teaching and scholarship didn't make much sense, since scholarly enterprises, even in an undergraduate institution, were both fueled and tested in the classroom. In any case, it seemed fair enough that all three categories should count, however blurry their boundaries.

In due time, I became department chair—at Wellesley very much a service position, since the chair bore great responsibility, had little power, and accrued no financial gain. Partly as a result of my holding this post, my concept of service started to enlarge. I began to worry that my perspective on academic questions was becoming too narrow. I didn't know much about what went on at other institutions. Gradually, purposefully, I became active in national organizations. I served on MLA committees; I read countless manuscripts, for book publishers and for journals; I eagerly participated in departmental evaluations, and on occasion I served as a consultant to other departments; I also read fellowship applications.

I learned that terrific people were teaching at non-elite institutions, that many departments shared the same problems, and that some depart-ments were better than others at solving them. I saw that many institutions burdened their faculty far more heavily than Wellesley did, and I admired the good grace and determination with which overworked faculty labored for those institutions. I got ideas for dealing with departmental difficulties at home. I met a lot of people I liked, some of whom became lasting friends. I acquired a vivid sense of what was going on in the publishing world. I found myself increasingly interested not only in the fortunes of my own discipline but in the situation of the humanities at large.

After twenty happy years at Wellesley, I moved to Yale, wanting to teach graduate students and to see if I could fathom the workings of a university better by this time. To figure out Yale wasn't easy, and over a ten-year period I never altogether mastered the institution's ways, but I learned a lot about how to get things done—again, largely by committee work, by serving as director of undergraduate studies soon after I arrived, and by my three years as chair, years occupied with such matters as trying to get the electrical wiring in our building upgraded, as well as with more intellectual pursuits.

Of course the ratio of women to men was less comfortable than at Wellesley. Men greatly outnumbered women, and they were active in what I had learned to think of as "service." They worked productively on committees; they participated consistently and fruitfully in staff meetings for introductory courses; and they willingly served as directors of undergraduate and graduate studies and, of course, as chair, a far more powerful position than it was at Wellesley, in spite of the mundane worries it entailed. Some of my male colleagues gave me valuable tips regarding the appropriate persons to call about problems in the building and how to deal with intractable staff conflicts. I got the impression, though, that most of them thought of service in rather different ways from those I had become accustomed to. To put it in crude terms: they appeared to see most departmental and university responsibilities as avenues to power.

When I moved on to the University of Virginia, I found a comparable situation. Here, too, men outnumbered women, although not so radically as at Yale. And here, too, they vigorously participated in service activities. Because, I think, of the felt need to have women on important committees, I quickly found myself involved in making vital institutional decisions. I served as director of graduate studies the year after I arrived and then became department chair, a position I filled for six years. I also continued and expanded my commitments beyond the university, working with other departments, with publishers, with fellowship-granting organizations, and with groups concerned for the welfare of the humanities—as, indeed, post-retirement, I continue to do.

I tell this story not because I think it exemplary (I don't), and not because I wish to demonstrate that everything is for the best in this best of all possible worlds (it isn't). I'm quite aware that I have taught mainly at privileged institutions and thus avoided various hardships, that others have taught more courses each semester and served on more committees and found their opportunities for intellectual exploration constricted as a result. I'm also aware that I'm negotiating a minefield here: I may appear to be suggesting that the activities labeled "service" are so much worth doing for their own sakes that they don't need to be externally rewarded or to be ignoring the degree to which women new to the profession (as well as men) can be pressured into working for a department or an institution rather than pursuing their own scholarship. Let me postpone these issues, though, in order to specify what morals I draw from my reminiscences.

First, it seems to me important to acknowledge that engaging in service gratifies self-interest, even if self-interest focuses on building an academic career. To begin with perhaps the most trivial benefit—trivial, but not negligible—service activities can provide a useful distraction, a change of pace, ultimately valuable to one's scholarship and teaching. I had a colleague at Wellesley, an unmarried woman much older than I, who told me that when she got really stuck on a problem, she'd scrub her kitchen floor, even if it was the middle of the night. She found herself more lucid afterward, she said.

Discussing the curriculum or who should be invited to lecture can work like scrubbing the floor. Breaking your concentration is not necessarily a bad thing: it allows intellectual problems to drop into the unconscious, after which, retrieved, they may appear more soluble. But the personal benefits of service do not lie only in the change of pace. The opportunities to encounter new persons, forge new communities, engage with fresh ideas—these are enormously valuable, both personally and professionally, and so is the wisdom one gathers about the institution one inhabits and the experience of engaging in common enterprise with one's colleagues. Scholarship is usually a solitary activity, and although our classrooms contain many persons beside ourselves, those others are not fully our peers. To work with your colleagues may be exhilarating, comforting, or irritating, but it will certainly be enlightening. Service endeavors often provide the significant satisfaction of getting things done—within a much more compressed time frame than that in which you see results from teaching and scholarship. Moreover, the multifarious activities lumped together under the category of service draw on and develop different skills from those demanded by the classroom, enlarging both competence and a sense of competence. And simply knowing more people in your home institution constitutes a form of power. My male colleagues at Yale were right: you get power in the institution by doing things for it. That's a matter to which I shall return.

To extend your service outside the home institution extends its personal benefits. It can broaden perspective: the guy from poli-sci who has been driving you crazy by refusing to sign off on your committee report recedes into insignificance. You see more clearly not only the daily workplace but your position in it. Sometimes outside service proves astonishingly useful for solving knotty local problems. It can also facilitate the enterprise of writing, providing a sense of audience both broader and more precise than the one a young writer might develop alone at the computer. Furthermore, to learn about other institutions, to become more fully aware of what is being written, what is being studied, and what is being imagined and done around the country—this kind of knowledge increases your agility and effectiveness, as well as, arguably, the respect of your colleagues. Diminishing myopia, it enlarges possibility and encourages daring. Other people, other institutions, have done things in different ways: Why can't we?

Most important, perhaps, the broader kinds of service help prevent individual participation in institutional parochialism. Working hard within your own college or university, you can come to think of it as the center of the universe: it is, after all, the center of your personal working universe. Still, its ways of doing things are not the only ways, perhaps not even the best ways. A double realization develops from cooperating with inhabitants of other colleges and universities: a new awareness that you are alone neither with your difficulties nor with your aspirations. We readily acknowledge a community of scholars, especially within specialties or subspecialties: Renaissance drama, Romantic lyric. The community of teachers is larger. Throughout the country—doubtless, throughout the world—men and women struggle to persuade students that the principles of good writing remain relevant beyond the freshman English classroom, or that books matter even in an electronic age. To become more fully aware of our common pedagogical and administrative endeavors and common difficulties not only makes you feel better; it provides fresh impetus toward solving problems, as well as a kind of knowledge that increases personal and professional confidence.

I'm not trying to glorify the activities lumped together under the category of "service"—dull meetings and recalcitrant colleagues remain facts of academic life—but, rather, to suggest that they include built-in bonuses. Their rewards, clearly grasped, contribute to a solid academic career, inasmuch as the capability for developing skills and forming alliances translates into forms of competence useful for writing, teaching, and making a name in the profession. The rewards have value, though, only if recognized. If you don't realize that you've acquired new proficiencies, then you're unlikely to use them; if you don't understand that the examples of other institutions may be productive for your own, then they won't be.

I've alluded in passing to power as an issue connected to service, and to the fact that my male colleagues at Yale often appeared to understand service as an inlet to power. Power does not necessarily imply control over others; it may entail simply the ability to do or act effectively. The variety of skills you cultivate in the course of academic service manifestly increases your ability to act effectively. As you acknowledge that fact, your colleagues are likely to do so as well. Your clout increases along with your effectiveness, but the necessary first step, the step those men at Yale understood so well, is to recognize what you're getting from what you're giving. In at least a limited sense, surely we all want power: the power to achieve what we want to achieve. To think of service as a form and source of power, to understand how it enlarges your capacities, makes it possible to use those capacities to advantage. Service, in other words, can empower.

In contrast, if you experience service as pure burden, then it becomes exactly that. Everyone knows that institutions tend to undervalue the faculty's service, but I wonder if in a sense women in particular tend to undervalue it first and to be especially ready to think of it as a burden. Perhaps I speak only for myself in confessing that analogies to housework occur to me all too readily when I think about the actual work that figures as service within a college or university. Tidying up the curriculum, looking for the right department chair, chairing a department myself—these things I associate readily with dusting the furniture, searching for a nanny, and managing a bunch of toddlers, who say no first and don't play well with others. It's not accidental that I thought of my colleague's floor-scrubbing as a metaphor for service. The housework analogy is partly a joke, but it also conveys a real perception.

Not all academic women associate committee work with housework, but it's my impression that many women, thinking of service activities as work that must be done, think also (perhaps with good reason) that the doing wins no respect. By extension, it's easy to believe that such work, conceived as drudgery, hardly merits respect. To believe, however, even to suspect, that our work is mere drudgery quickly disempowers us. Institutional cultures often encourage such disempowerment: institutions, after all, can thrive on their inhabitants' drudgery. Every department in which I've worked has contained at least one man who in effect pronounces himself too good—too rarefied of intellect, too absorbed in his scholarship—to serve on committees. Such men typically support their positions by showing themselves utterly incompetent for committee work, forgetting meetings, showing up late, ostensibly incapable of the requisite degree of organization. They get away with their irresponsibility, and they even appear to accrue a certain degree of prestige as a result. (My experience is limited, but I've never seen a woman behave in this way.) Good departmental citizens suffer in consequence, not only because there's extra work to do, but because they have in effect been labeled lesser beings, not altogether dedicated to the life of scholarship, and they may be tempted to internalize such a label.

Women have no special aptitude for service work. It's equally certain, though, that women are socialized to accept responsibility for the kind of labor that keeps the wheels turning and socialized as well to believe that such labor will win no recognition. Even those who grasp the personal as well as institutional importance of service activities—men and women alike—may talk about them in deprecatory terms. They may suspect themselves of saying yes to too many committees in order to avoid grappling with hard scholarly problems, or they may worry lest their colleagues think them better suited to supportive rather than innovative enterprises. I don't think I've ever heard anyone celebrating the joys of committee work, and "joy" is not a term that readily applies, even if one tries to make the best possible case.

Service may not be immediately joyous, but it can return a lot to its performer, if she is willing and able to take it seriously as a productive and an important use of personal power. In this respect, as in others, service is comparable to scholarship and teaching. All three can and often do amount to strenuous and exhausting endeavors; all three empower those who pursue them wholeheartedly. Intertwined activities help constitute the institution their participants inhabit. In defining these categories as the criteria for individual advancement, the institution acknowledges this fact. Both personal prestige and tangible reward, however, accrue more readily to the charismatic teacher or the productive scholar than to the efficient organizer. It is the nature of much academic service to be largely invisible, and even good academic citizens can find themselves wondering whether it's really worthwhile spending hours in unsung labor.

True, service is sometimes coerced. I have heard troubling accounts of untenured or recently tenured faculty, of both sexes, effectively compelled to spend far too large a proportion of their time in committee or administrative service. The work of the institution demands doing. When long-tenured faculty members refuse to shoulder their share, the most vulnerable get fingered. Departmental administrators, under pressure from higher authorities who may themselves be suffering the constriction of tightening budgets or multiplying programs, find their human resources depleted, and in desperation they apply their own pressure to those with the fewest resources for resisting it. As a result, they distort their younger colleagues' possibilities of accomplishment, a shortsighted and destructive tactic.

Service should not be compelled—and such a self-evident statement should not require making. Service (in conjunction with teaching and scholarship) should be acknowledged and rewarded. *Should*s offered to institutions, however, forceful though they may be, do not necessarily translate into changed procedures. My emphasis throughout these reflections has focused on individuals, and individuals bear their own responsibilities for managing their commitments. The untenured have relatively few options, dependent as they are on the benevolent understanding of department administrators for humane teaching and committee assignments. Once officially secure in the profession, though, we confront enlarged possibilities and greater choices. If we understand scholarship, teaching, and service as roughly comparable significant contributors to our personal professional growth, then we occupy a strong position from which to make choices. Each of the three forms of activity by its nature seems to demand every moment of our time; each can readily occupy whole days and nights. Striking a balance among them requires a capacity to say no as well as yes—and in all probability, whatever we say, we will always feel, and no doubt be, overworked. Ideally, though, we will be able to see the commitments we embrace as forms of replenishment as well as demand, of opportunity as well as necessity, of pleasure as well as obligation.

15

The Hermeneutics of Service

Donald E. Hall

Academic, indeed all, intellectual activity is by its very nature dialogic. In our research we enter conversations within our disciplines and with scholarly predecessors in ways that we overtly signal, or at least tacitly acknowledge, and then attempt to supplement with originality and insight. Our teaching, even if we are tethered to the podium and yellowed lecture notes, is necessarily engaged with voices outside and inside the classroom: those of writers, thinkers, and researchers who cite, and to whom we respond, and those of students with whom we interact and whose questions and thoughts (should) help propel our courses. This dialogism is the phenomenological basis of all intellectual life and, in varying degrees, of human existence itself (according to Husserl and Heidegger), as we navigate through our day by processing data and exchanging information with everyone and everything that surrounds us.

Yet much of our training in the academy and certainly many of our acculturation processes lead to forms of professional behavior and self-conception that are decidedly monologic in nature. Our research, especially among those of us working in the humanities, is most often conducted alone in archives or in solitary reading and then disseminated through writing produced in the quiet of our offices, staring at a computer screen or pad of paper, with no one around to distract or converse with us (there is a certain irony to this, of course, as those most "human" of disciplines are the ones with the least human contact in the research process, while the cold, "hard" sciences are the disciplines with research conventions rooted in collegial behavior and collaboration). Similarly, our teaching, as convivial as it may be in the classroom setting itself, is usually based on hours of preparation and grading done, again, in the silence of our offices and without a word being uttered, beyond perhaps a running commentary in our own heads.

Our careers—from job application to promotion, tenure, merit raises, and accolades—are almost always built on individual achievements. We are trained and professionalized to operate as solitary agents whose primary responsibility is to and for the self; after all, no one is going to do the hard work for us of research and publication, of preparing classes and grading papers, and of applying for grants and sabbaticals. Our evaluation processes are based firmly on the assumption that we are responsible for our own successes and failures, for our choices and priorities. I too have issued pointed reminders of that fact, most explicitly in my 2002 book *The Academic Self: An Owner's Manual*, which urges its readers to "own up to" their responsibilities for choosing wisely in planning and advancing their careers.[1]

Yet at the same time I believe that there is a clear and fundamental disjunction between the demands of our careers as judged for their successes in self-interested and solitary activities and the fundamental, lived reality of our professional lives in necessary dialogue with others. In *The Academic Community: A Manual for Change*, my 2007 sequel to *The Academic Self*, I explore that tension and how best to respond to those multiple demands with collegial awareness and ethical responsibility.[2] Of course, nowhere do I suggest that we should or could simply renounce our solitary professional activities (even minimally collaborative research and occasional team teaching are not for everyone and certainly should never be mandated). However, I do think that our failure to recognize and address that tension between "community" and "self-interest" in our profession contributes to the most egregious instance of misplaced prioritization therein: a devaluation of service, the most overtly dialogic of all of our activities. In re-theorizing academic life as inherently dialogic, we can also rethink the hierarchy of research, teaching, and service to find in service the clearest, most laudable manifestation of the very process that is intellectualism. Service, in theory at least, becomes the sin qua non of an academic life.

My own thoughts on this topic have been generated by and honed through conversations with many peers and diverse predecessors. One of the most compelling voices to which I've attended in my recent work on the profession is that of the late German philosopher Hans-Georg Gadamer, one of the preeminent theorists of conversation as a principle governing intellectual, professional, and ethical social life. In *Truth and Method*, Gadamer's magnum opus from 1960, he offers an anti-methodological "method," one that embraces dialogue among varying perspectives and processes, with each allowing access to a very limited and circumscribed "truth," but in their interplay and fusion they generate a broader, if always still evolving, "truth." Though addressed primarily to other philosophers and classicists, Gadamer's "philosophical hermeneutics" has much to say to us in the humanities and throughout the academy today. What Gadamer asks of us is a revised notion of the academic and intellectual self, in which learning about one's own methodological, presuppositional, and disciplinary limitations, while adding to the knowledge base of others on similar quests, is one's primary task and goal. At once anti-hubristic, anti-solipsistic, and anti-monologic, Gadamer provides a theory base allowing for a reconception of our professional lives as ones in which the degree of one's commitment to and participation in dialogue is the chief indicator of one's "success" as a teacher, researcher, and colleague.

Gadamer's specifically "philosophical" hermeneutics bears some explanation here. Hermeneutics, first theorized in the nineteenth century by Friedrich Schleiermacher and Wilhem Dilthey, focuses intensely on the individual reader's response to print texts as she or he works toward understanding. The hermeneutic circle, as originally conceptualized by Schleiermacher, points to the way in which individuals make sense of texts through anticipations of the meaning of the "whole," which will then allow one to understand provisionally a passage or other subunit as it is encountered. The circle is also fundamental to Gadamer's "philosophical" hermeneutics, in which the dialogic process, as one enacts it within communities of fellow citizens, professionals, and intellectuals, will allow one to revisit the limited perspective that is the "self" and its standpoint epistemology. Gadamer finds in conversation an encounter with an expanded, even if a provisional, "whole" (the multiple perspectives of community), which will allow a return to the self-generated perspective with a new ability to critique and revise it. He reminds us, however, that the "whole" of the communal interplay of perspectives never will allow complete access to "truth" but, rather, that the self and its surrounding other/s shift and (ideally) expand constantly as the broad conversation reflects enhanced individual perspective/s and as individual perspective/s change through new encounters and additions to the conversation. This is what happens ideally in research as I add to the community of scholarly voices in my field by incorporating and responding to the work of others (and as they do the same); it is what happens in teaching as I learn through encounters with my students and hone my teaching skills through exchanges with fellow pedagogues. Finally, and to the point of this essay, it is what happens in service as I come to the departmental, institutional, or professional task or challenge at hand with a desire to interact with my colleagues in ways that are fully invested in the conversational dynamic and in which my voice is only one of many, all with limited perspectives, but each adding productively to an expanding group perspective.

Indeed, before Gadamer was an internationally known philosopher and lecturer, he was first a successful faculty colleague and administrator. *Truth and Method* was published when Gadamer was sixty years old; his preceding three decades in the academy were spent as a modestly well-known writer of essays on classical literature but also as a successful department chair, dean, and university president. Much of this early work is recounted in Gadamer's few autobiographical writings, the most notable of which is *Philosophical Apprenticeships,* published in 1977. In it we find that Gadamer's professional praxis reflected the basic tenets of philosophical hermeneutics but predated by several decades his inauguration of the field in *Truth and Method.*

In detailing dialogue-based processes and practices in his development as a teacher, a scholar, and an administrator, Gadamer demonstrates how his version of the "hermeneutic circle" can work within a university context and in collegial activities. In fact, this figuratively circular process is manifest explicitly as a concrete practice in a venue that Gadamer notes was called a "home circle," in which faculty, when he was studying at the University of Marburg, would invite into their homes on a set evening every week colleagues, students, and visiting scholars to converse on a chosen topic. It was a dialogic mechanism that he later adopted as a professor. In such a conversational circle a form of a hermeneutic circle is enacted, when, as he discusses in *Truth and Method,* the interlocutor puts her or his "prejudices" or presuppositions at risk in seeking out others with whom to share ideas, to test notions of reality, and to come, through an exchange of viewpoints, to some (even if always imperfect) expanded understanding of one's own mistakes and misapprehensions. Risk taking, especially in this way risking one's core beliefs and sense of self-satisfaction, demands a certain conscious, even chosen, privileging of the communal over the solipsistic or self-serving. Thus I suggest in *The Academic Community* that Gadamer's dialogic model presents us with an *ethics* of engagement with colleagues and others. As Jean Grondin, his biographer, notes, "As Gadamer often says . . . 'the soul [of his philosophy] consists in recognizing that perhaps the other is right,' "[3] or, as Gadamer himself states in *Truth and Method,* we must remain "fundamentally open to the possibility that the [other] is better informed than we are."[4] Gadamer's is a conversational practice that explicitly values differences in perspective rather than a communal homogeneity of belief or outlook. His ideal community is one in which we learn constantly through encountering those who disagree with us.

Gadamer relates this dynamic explicitly to the various aspects of our work in the academy and points to clear implications for a classroom practice centered on developing "people's sense of judgment and ability to think for themselves by 'engaging in the primacy of dialogue in the theory and practice of teaching.' "[5] However, these were pedagogical lessons that he learned slowly over time. As a novice teacher in the 1930s, he knew of only one mode of possible interaction with his students—the lecture. He admits: "The beginning of every semester was filled with anxiety: . . . At the podium I was very shy, and I heard later that people occasionally characterized me as . . . 'the one who never looks up.' "[6] But over time he adopts more interactive techniques as he refines his research-directed theories of dialogical interaction and consequentially becomes a very popular instructor and innovative discussion leader. In doing so, he anticipated many of the emphases of recent commentators on a communally invested academic praxis. No one may seem more distant from the dry classicist Gadamer than bell hooks, but in her discussion of the classroom as a venue for risk and transformation, she too reminds us that the "engaged" pedagogical voice "must never be fixed and absolute but always changing, always evolving in dialogue with a world beyond itself."[7] For Gadamer too, that world is expansive as he explores how an enhanced commitment to dialogue can contribute to a process of community building and intellectual productivity well beyond, as well as within, the classroom.

For Gadamer, dialogue should suffuse an academic life. In *Philosophical Apprenticeships*, he explores how he gradually learned to become a colleague in a department by attending to how others conducted themselves in conversational interactions. He devotes chapters to the major philosophers whom he encountered as a student and an academic-in-training, and he pinpoints precisely what they taught him, focusing specifically on their dialogic style. In Hans Lipps, for example, he discovered a "resolute original" who had an "impetuous manner with which he applied himself to his conversation partner: without restraint, without flourish, totally concentrated"; in Max Scheler, he found a passionate intellectual whose "reading so devoured him that whenever he met a colleague he would compel his participation simply by ripping pages out of whatever book he was reading and pressing them into the hands of his astonished companion."[8] Out of these and many other scripts of a teaching and an intellectual life, Gadamer constructed a "life plan," a phrase that is not actually Gadamerian, but one that is used by his friend and fellow hermeneutic theorist Paul Ricoeur in his book *Oneself as Another*.[9] While never objectifying other human beings, Gadamer nevertheless examined them as texts of sorts, as complex conveyers of meaning whom he must interpret and from whom he could learn. This is a putting into lived practice his theory of hermeneutics, which, to my mind, provided a praxis-based coherence and honesty to a successful and multifaceted professional life.

Gadamer as institutional citizen, not as world-famous philosopher, offers us also a text from which we might learn. Unlike Angela Davis, another exemplary academic I discuss in *The Academic Community*, Gadamer was not a revolutionary. However, much like Davis, he did discover that "politics and intellectual life are not two entirely separate modes of existence."[10] During the war, Gadamer taught at the University of Leipzig, where he was under constant threat of imprisonment if he challenged the party more than implicitly in his lectures, which he did subtly but unmistakably. He was denounced by students for encouraging subversion and interrogated by the local SS, though not finally charged with treasonous behavior. After the war, Gadamer, who had served already as a department chair, was singled out by occupying forces as someone particularly untainted by Nazi policies and beliefs. He soon learned, "I would be the rector [president] chosen to reopen the university. I was duly elected and now began the exhausting, interesting, illusion-rich, and disillusioning work of construction—or was it deconstruction?—of Leipzig University."[11] In the middle of an intellectual career of widely recognized, but still largely unrealized, potential (his major works were published decades later), Gadamer, in his mid-forties, chose to devote himself to the mundane and extraordinarily hard work of institutional reform and service. His devotion to his community, at the temporary expense of his own research and writing, may make him a particularly compelling role model for some of us contemplating a department chairship, a university leadership role, or some other time-consuming assignment.

Gadamer's commitment to dialogue and critical agency had immediate payoffs in his work as an administrator and a participant in diverse service responsibilities. In *Philosophical Apprenticeships*, he discusses at length the particular necessity that he perceived as a department chair and dean, of working to create dialogue-based communal interactions across and within academic departments, going on to note, "Today, in the face of the fragmentation of the giant universities, such interdisciplinary efforts have a new [even greater] significance."[12] He writes of his work on the faculty of Marburg in the 1930s in organizing and participating in "one-hour lecture[s] on something of interest from one's own discipline," "for listeners from all faculties."[13] After he left Leipzig, which he found increasingly uncomfortable when it was placed under Russian jurisdiction (and which is why he mockingly referred to his work there as "deconstructive" rather than "constructive"), he took a post as professor and dean at the University of Heidelberg, where he created a "home circle," modeling it on his memories of the productive exchanges among faculty, students, and others that occurred in his own student years, and in which a dozen or so people would gather weekly to discuss texts of common interest. He concludes, "There was no 'teacher' among us; it was always a free exchange, and we all learned a good deal from it."[14] He notes, "Another feature that I introduced into . . . Heidelberg . . . was that of regular guest lecturers . . . because I wanted to give the philosophy students an opportunity to get to know other teachers, and the discussions that followed were good tests for both participants and listeners."[15] While these may seem rather unremarkable administrative moves and forms of service to us today, they were quite revolutionary in Heidelberg during the 1940s and 1950s and developed organically from the theory base underlying his own evolving research. Much as we do today, he performed all of this administrative work and service while also teaching and attempting to pursue research. As

Gadamer says, "This is in any case not easy for an academic teacher, and even in those times it demanded a consistent budgeting of personal time, although the number of students and the whole style of the university were not yet comparable with those of today's mass universities."[16]

Obviously, we today, especially those of us teaching in mass universities, need even more active attention to that process of community building. And that, I would argue, is exactly the promise and project of "service." What Gadamer theorized and lived was a hermeneutics of academic community that manifested itself in micro-level commitment to roundtables, speakers, and other conversation venues, but that I would like to extrapolate from and see as applicable also to the myriad of other service tasks we routinely perform: work on curricular and program committees, work on senates and other governance bodies, service on advisory boards and task forces, and participation in strategic planning, assessment, and program review processes. All of these venues provide opportunities for intellectual engagement and an enhanced understanding of our institutions and our "selves" as they operate within those institutions. All provide forums for a hermeneutic activity that places our circumscribed knowledge in conversation with others who will challenge, change, and augment our perspectives, even as we do the same for them. Through service I can learn about the limitations of my point of view—determined as it is by my personal history, departmental and disciplinary norms, and position in a variety of hierarchies of age, gender, race, and professional standing—and I can add, as well, to the perspectives and limitations that others bring with them.

Service is always potentially a deeply meaningful set of intellectual activities. Our perception of it, however, can be otherwise. Service is often denigrated as "busy work," "a waste of time," or simply tedious. To the extent that it draws us away from that which we too often define narrowly as our "real work"—research or, more rarely, teaching—it is regarded as a necessary evil, but one that should be avoided if possible or performed only in the most perfunctory way. Missing from this undervaluation is the recognition that service always involves the same critical faculties that we draw upon in research (close reading, interpretation, the consideration of preceding arguments, and a careful marshalling of evidence to support our own arguments) and in our teaching (the education of others out of our own knowledge base and skills sets and an attentive listening to others and appreciation of the knowledge that they bring to the task at hand). All service should involve a critical interaction with the texts of our institutions, disciplines, and professional communities, though of course that is not necessarily the case. Just as we can interact with any other text in passive or intellectually disengaged ways (film, television, books, or magazines), so too we can "switch off" our intellectual curiosity and quickness when approaching service. However, I think that we are far better served individually and communally when we switch "on" those intellects.

This is true, I believe, in all of the venues in which we are called upon to render service: in our departments, institutions, communities, and disciplines. Curriculum committees, tenure and promotion committees, strategic planning committees, and even regular department meetings offer the potential for deep intellectual attachment to the "texts" of our professional lives. In negotiating over the design of our majors/minors/graduate programs, in reading critically and judiciously the texts of our colleagues' achievements and activities, in thinking creatively about the future of our departments, and in engaging with each other attentively and reasonably during meetings we contribute to an ongoing process of community building and nurturance that represents the Gadamerian notion of "understanding" as an always unfinished dialogic process. Similarly, in serving on university committees, we can find singular opportunities to learn about the limitations of our own disciplinary epistemologies and presuppositions, while in working with the public or in surrounding communities we have the chance to denaturalize our academic behaviors and participate in a public intellectualism that can be as exciting as that which we perform in our research arenas. Finally, in serving our profession through participation in review bodies, accreditation committees, and disciplinary or cross-disciplinary task forces, we engage in conversations that can alter the future of institutions and entire professional fields. These are stunning opportunities for applied intellectualism if we approach them as such.

Thus hermeneutic theory challenges us to rethink the bases of our academic identity, shifting from an inward-looking, careerist notion of academic selfhood to an energetically outward-looking, community-based notion of academic and intellectual activity. In doing so, we alter the bases of our valuation of all of the component parts of that activity, but we can find in service a set of processes and interactions that represents the best of what we do as engaged intellectuals. This allows us as well to reclaim a significantly redefined notion of "collegiality" as a valued aspect of academic life. Collegiality, in the Gadamerian sense, is not about "fitting in" or demurely following one's senior colleagues directives; it is instead the successful enactment of the conversational commitments and behaviors discussed earlier. Collegiality means a vigorous participation in institutional conversations, ones in which disagreement and interpersonal differences of perspective are highly valued. While collegiality of the most nondialogic sort was an often abused and is now a regularly excoriated category for the evaluation of faculty (used in the past to enforce homogeneity and to deny tenure to individuals who challenged the norms of a department or an institution), dialogic collegiality is a commitment to the interactive processes and projects serving the department, institution, public, and profession. This does not mean that we should reinsert "collegiality" as a fourth category for evaluation; it means recognizing service as a highly valued category that encompasses all of the collegial activities that support the entire structure of our profession and depend always on the dialogic investment of colleagues. Those who refuse to participate in committees, department meetings, senates, and task forces fail to meet their professional obligations and fail as praxis-based intellectuals.

However, it is necessary to address here a likely rejoinder to the aforementioned addition to this volume's conversation on service, namely, that collegiality has been used often in the past as a category to punish women, and that service is deeply imbricated within gender power systems (as women are often called upon to perform extraordinary service because of deeply ingrained, sexist assumptions and social/professional norms). I well recognize that the legacy of gendered expectations regarding service leads to differential demands and assumptions, both in the valuation of service and the career paths of women and men in the academy. However, by reappraising service as central to our academic and intellectual lives, what I hope to do is make it the responsibility of all in the profession, not a few. If service is too often implicitly considered "women's work" and tied to essentialist notions of femininity, then I would suggest that we link it instead to the baseline duties determining the category "academic intellectual." If a commitment to and successful participation in a myriad of service activities are required of all—for tenure, promotion, and pay raises—then I would expect new patterns of service activity to emerge that would be far less dependent on gendered expectations.

Yet this may still beg the question for many of this volume's readers of how compatible hermeneutic theory—and specifically Gadamerian theory—is with identity politics and the academic projects that follow from such politics: feminism, queer theory, race theory, postcolonialism, and so on. It is a fair question, since Gadamer himself did not write about or participate in identity political movements, beyond his support for Jewish colleagues before, during, and after World War II. As Lorraine Code writes in a volume of feminist assessments of Gadamerian theory, "feminists . . . have to work hard to find in Gadamer a social-political ally, or even a silent friend of feminist politics."[17] However, she goes on to suggest that hard work pays off: "Gadamerian hermeneutics . . . has much to offer feminists and other theorists of subjectivity, agency, history, and knowledge."[18] In emphasizing dialogue, an active interrogation of the self and of received wisdom, and a commitment to allowing the other to alter us (as well as be altered by us), Gadamerian theory, she argues, "can initiate changes, however, minuscule, in the social order, with incremental effects that extend beyond the places of their enactment to interrogate the assumptions and prejudices that hold larger, macropolitical institutions and structures in place."[19] It is for that reason too that Mae Gwendolyn Henderson finds in Gadamer's work an emphasis on "mutuality and reciprocity" that is very useful in discussing the successful creation of community among marginalized peoples.[20] I see a discussion of hermeneutics and service working also as a fulcrum that allows for a thorough rethinking of what it is to be and act as an academic and intellectual in the twenty-first century.

This may sound idealistic, but so be it. Gadamer encourages us to commit ourselves to a conversational dynamic and transformative potential that is idealistic but grounded in the real world of human interaction. "Understanding," as he posits it, is never fully achieved, only pursued. Yet the pursuit of understanding as an interactive process (not product) is the basis of all ethically responsible and intellectually engaged activity. Service to the "other" is our attempt to allow the "other" the same potential for growth, change, and increased awareness that she or he always allows us (if we allow ourselves to be challenged and changed). That circle of responsibility is the hermeneutic circle of enhanced understanding through self-displacement and learning. At its best, all academic activity is hermeneutic activity.

Notes

1. Donald E. Hall, *The Academic Self: An Owner's Manual* (Columbus: Ohio State University Press, 2002), see esp. xi–xxiii.

2. Donald E. Hall, *The Academic Community: A Manual for Change* (Columbus: Ohio State University Press, 2007), see esp. 1–16. Some of its discussion points overlap with those here, although the specific purpose of each is quite distinct.

3. Jean Grondin, *The Philosophy of Gadamer*, trans. Kathryn Plant (Montreal: McGill-Queen's University Press, 2003), 100.

4. Hans-Georg Gadamer, *Truth and Method*, 2nd rev. ed., trans. Joel Weinsheimer and Donald G. Marshall (New York: Continuum), 294.

5. Quoted in Susan-Judith Hoffman, "Gadamer's Philosophical Hermeneutics and Feminist Projects," in *Feminist Interpretations of Hans-Georg Gadamer*, ed. Lorraine Code, 103 (University Park: Pennsylvania State University Press, 2003).

6. Hans-Georg Gadamer, *Philosophical Apprenticeships*, trans. Robert R. Sullivan (Cambridge, MA: MIT Press, 1985), 70–71.

7. bell hooks, *Teaching to Transgress: Education as the Practice of Freedom* (New York and London: Routledge, 1994), 11.

8. Gadamer, *Philosophical Apprenticeships*, 89, 33.

9. Paul Ricoeur, *Oneself as Another*, trans. Kathleen Blamey (Chicago, IL: University of Chicago Press, 1992), 157–58.

10. Angela Davis, "Reflections on Race, Class, and Gender in the USA," in *The Angela Y. Davis Reader*, ed. Joy James, 319 (Malden, MA: Blackwell, 1998).

11. Gadamer, *Philosophical Apprenticeships*, 104.

12. Ibid., 122.

13. Ibid.

14. Ibid., 140.

15. Ibid.

16. Ibid., 139.

17. Lorraine Code, "Introduction: Why Feminists Do Not Read Gadamer," in *Feminist Interpretations of Hans-Georg Gadamer*, ed. Lorraine Code, 3 (University Park: Pennsylvania State University Press, 2003).

18. Ibid., 4.

19. Ibid., 34.

20. Mae Gwendolyn Henderson, "Speaking in Tongues: Dialogics, Dialectics, and the Black Woman Writer's Literary Tradition," in *Feminists Theorize the Political*, ed. Judith Butler and Joan W. Scott, 147 (New York and London: Routledge, 1992).

16

Rewarding Work

Integrating Service into an Institutional Framework on Faculty Roles and Rewards

Jeanette Clausen

Preamble

Service has been and still is central to my career. I accepted my first administrative appointment, as coordinator of women's studies, several years before being tenured. From then on, I had an administrative assignment, in addition to many committees and other service responsibilities, every year except for two sabbatical leaves. As I gained experience in academic administration, I began to amuse colleagues with my informal theory of service as women's work. It went like this:

Administrative work is like housework because

- it is never done;

- no one notices it, unless you don't do it; and

- no one thanks you for it.

(How many family members thank you for clean socks and underwear? How many faculty members thank you for writing the department's annual report?)

Service is like mothering because

- it is assumed that no particular expertise is needed to do it;

- people who have never done it don't hesitate to tell you how to do your job; and

- you get little praise for a job well done, for it is assumed you
  have a natural gift or knack for it, but if you do it poorly, you
  are blamed.

My ironic attitude toward the gendered aspects of service and administration
notwithstanding, I continued to accept and even seek such assignments. I
found the work rewarding. It was satisfying to find solutions to problems,
to influence decisions, and, best of all, to create something new—launch a
new program, organize a new event, draft a policy. Success in my service
roles usually led to rewards at merit raise time but not, of course, to refereed
publications in my discipline—the coin of the realm. Not until fifteen years
after my first promotion did I finally have enough publications to apply for
promotion to professor. By then I was an associate vice chancellor in the
Office of Academic Affairs, and I welcomed the opportunity to participate
in the process of integrating service into my university's system of faculty
roles and rewards.

Service in the Context of a Campus Culture

Most colleges and universities have well-articulated criteria for rewarding
faculty achievements in research and, increasingly, for rewarding high-quality teaching as well. A framework for documenting and evaluating service
is usually lacking. Such was the case at Indiana University Purdue University Fort Wayne (IPFW), where I was employed for many years. IPFW
is a regional, public, comprehensive university with about 12,000 students.
Tenured and tenure-track faculty have a 3-3 teaching load, with 25 percent
release time for research/creative endeavor. No portion of faculty time is
specifically allocated for service. Yet at IPFW, as elsewhere, service expectations increased throughout the 1980s and 1990s even as the percentage of
tenured and tenure-track faculty decreased.[1] IPFW governance documents
created in the late 1980s specify "a record of satisfactory teaching, research,
and service" for tenure. Excellence in one of the three areas is required for
promotion: "Favorable action [on a promotion case] shall result when the
individual has demonstrated, in one area of endeavor, a level of excellence
appropriate to the proposed rank" (IPFW 1989). Other sections of the
governance documents also address service as a possible basis for promotion.
The promotion and tenure (P&T) criteria are the basis for faculty annual
evaluations for reappointment and merit raises as well as for tenure and
promotion specifically.

Although the basis for rewarding service was stated in IPFW governance documents, policy did not necessarily translate into practice. Chairs and

deans might recommend a higher salary increment for faculty with excellent service records during any given year, but such decisions were on a case-by-case basis rather than criterion driven. Moreover, no one had ever applied for promotion to associate professor based on excellence in service. One or two faculty members in the professional colleges had achieved promotion to professor on records of service and leadership, but those were isolated cases that had no impact on policy or practice elsewhere on campus.

Creating a Framework for Rewarding Service

The creation of an IPFW-specific framework for defining and valuing service was initiated by Vice Chancellor for Academic Affairs Dr. Susan B. Hannah, who served from 1998 to 2008. The framework for service was part of a more comprehensive project to expand the definition of faculty work and at the same time provide guidance for how the work might be rewarded.[2] The framework is elaborated in an Academic Affairs Memorandum titled "Examples for Documenting and Evaluating Faculty Service," online at http://www.ipfw.edu/vcaa/promotion/default.shtml. The document contains typical examples of service activities and rubrics for distinguishing between satisfactory and excellent performance. It begins as follows:

> The goal of this document is to help faculty, chairs, and other administrators distinguish between satisfactory service that is expected of all faculty and service that represents a contribution of some significance. The rubrics can be used to identify individual service contributions that merit recognition and reward; they can also help faculty who wish to do so build a case for excellence in service over time. Faculty, chairs, and deans/directors are encouraged to discuss the rubrics and modify them as appropriate in order to clarify the standard expected in their units. (Examples for Documenting 2005)

Note that the document is presented first and foremost as a framework for discussion, not as a policy document. Definitions and rubrics could become policy only if they were adapted for or incorporated into departmental or college-level P&T criteria.

"Examples for Documenting" (2005) was written by members of the vice chancellor's staff (of whom I was one) with input from both external and internal sources. Ernest L. Boyer's (1990) categories of scholarship provide a first framework for integrating service into a rewards system. Boyer's expansion of the word "scholarship" to include integration, application, and

teaching as well as research has since been further refined: the search for
new knowledge is now widely referred to as "discovery"; the scholarship of
teaching has become the Scholarship of Teaching and Learning (SoTL); the
scholarship of application—"applied research"—and service on behalf of the
public good are variously defined as "outreach," "engagement," or "outreach
engagement." These categories, together with standards articulated by Glassick
et al. (1997), provide a basis for integrating service work into an institutional rewards system. The Glassick standards include clear goals, adequate
preparation, appropriate methods, significant results, effective presentation,
and reflective critique. Other external sources included the publications and
Web sites of associations such as the (now-defunct) American Association
for Higher Education (AAHE) and the National Review Board for the
Scholarship of Engagement (http://www.scholarshipofengagement.org).

Citing national associations and authorities such as Boyer and Glassick
lent a certain legitimacy to our project, but it was equally important, if not
more so, that the framework for rewarding service be relevant to the campus
mission and consistent with criteria stated in IPFW governance documents.
To these ends, we sought input from many sources on campus, notably the
Senate Faculty Affairs Committee, deans and department chairs, and faculty leaders. In addition to the IPFW Senate documents, cited earlier, we
reviewed P&T criteria from numerous departments. Our document went
through multiple drafts over a period of about a year and a half before being
published as OAA Memorandum 04-2.

The key features of excellent service that we found in IPFW P&T
policies are *faculty expertise* and *a contribution of special value to the constitu-
ency/ies* served (Senate Documents SD 88-25 and SD 94-3). In other words,
value is placed on work that faculty are able to do well because of special
disciplinary or other expertise that they have, and on work that results in
a benefit to the group or organization served. Given that past practice had
often devalued or simply ignored service, it was important to specify levels
of achievement in service comparable to definitions of competence or excellence in research and teaching. OAA 04-2 states the following rationale for
defining service as part of a scholarly agenda:

> When a faculty member's disciplinary expertise is brought to bear
> on initiatives that serve the community, the profession, or the
> university, the work may have a scholarly dimension that is evident
> in the approach to the task, the results of the service (products,
> policies, organizations, etc.), or in work that feeds back into the
> discipline (new areas of research, or new approaches to teaching
> or scholarship, etc.). (Examples for Documenting 2005)

What does the aforementioned mean in real life? One example is the field of women's or gender studies, where activism on behalf of women inside and outside the academy led, over time, to profound changes in teaching and scholarship. The work of infusing new feminist research findings, theories, and practices into curricula and scholarly societies requires knowledge of one's discipline as traditionally understood, in addition to expertise in feminist approaches to the discipline. Examples of a scholarly dimension of service in the foreign languages include developing and implementing standards for teacher preparation and certification, organizing professional development workshops for K–12 foreign language teachers, and serving as university supervisor for student teachers. Such activities provide the opportunity to advocate for changes in curriculum, pedagogy, and scholarship, such as greater attention to gender and diversity issues, student-centered classrooms, and active learning, among others. If the scholarly dimensions of such work can be defined, then a more compelling argument can be made for rewarding the work.

Documenting and Evaluating Service

The authors of OAA 04-2 attempted to identify all the types of service that faculty do and, for each category of service, to distinguish between evidence of contributions, on the one hand, and criteria for valuing them, on the other. This distinction may seem too obvious to warrant attention; however, our review of departmental promotion and tenure policies taught us that activities or products that count as evidence of achievement in teaching, research, and service were usually specified, but criteria for evaluation usually were not. Reasons for such an omission are not far to seek: with research/creative endeavor and the scholarship of teaching and learning, it is understood that scholarly and creative products will be subject to peer review. Most faculty undergo peer review of their scholarship and teaching at regular intervals as part of their progress toward tenure and promotion, thus standards are at least implicit, even if not always entirely transparent. Meaningful peer review of service was almost entirely lacking at IPFW, so the task was to articulate a means of documentation and sample criteria analogous to those used for research and teaching.

A partial model for defining and valuing service had come out of an Indiana University Strategic Directions Initiative.[3] The multiyear project, titled "Defining, Documenting, and Evaluating Professional Service" (1996–99), involved faculty from all the IU campuses in a process of research on, discussion of, and writing about service. Outcomes of the project were a set of recommended quality indicators for evaluating service and a booklet containing self-reports, with analysis and reflection, on exemplary service projects by faculty at several IU campuses. The quality indicators and the booklet were distributed to deans, department chairs, and faculty at the various campuses, including IPFW, and discussed in workshops on tenure and promotion. However, lacking explicit connections to local governance documents, they had little, if any, impact on either policy or practice.

The quality indicators from the aforementioned project, adapted for IPFW and included in the introduction to OAA 04-2, are as follows:

1. The impact or significance of the service, indicated by:
   - an identifiable outcome relevant to the university's mission and goals;
   - a measurable impact upon particular constituencies; and
   - relevance of the service to the faculty member's professional development and/or to the faculty member's teaching and research.

2. The intellectual work required to perform the service, indicated by:
   - the application of relevant knowledge, skills, technological expertise, and so on;
   - contribution(s) to a body of knowledge;
   - imagination, creativity, and innovation; and
   - sensitivity to and application of ethical standards.

3. The importance of the faculty member's role(s), indicated by:
   - creative and responsible leadership that has an identifiable impact on the project;
   - increasing levels of responsibility;
   - consistent and sustained quality of contributions; and
   - taking the initiative to build consensus, solve problems, and so on.

4. Analysis of and reflection on the service, indicated by:
   - responsible representation of work during and after completion;
   - communication with appropriate audiences; and
   - using audience-appropriate modes of communication and dissemination.

Note the similarities to the Glassick et al. (1997) standards: clear goals (#1), significant results (#1, #2), appropriate methods (#2, #4), and effective presentation and reflective critique (#4). The aforementioned quality indicators also mesh well with the IPFW categories of faculty expertise and work that measurably benefits the constituency served (#1). The emphasis on intellectual work and leadership (#2, #3) provides a basis for identifying scholarly dimensions of faculty service. References to sustained effort and increasing levels of responsibility over time (#3) recognize that faculty will be able to document growth resulting from high-quality service, much as faculty are expected to demonstrate continuing growth as scholars and teachers throughout their careers. The emphasis on communication and dissemination of results (#4) recognizes that service may result in knowledge or processes that should be shared with others in the field; in this sense, it is a positive step that looks beyond traditional scholarly publications. On the other hand, it also tends to replicate the traditional bias toward valuing publications more than other activities or products. This is a thorny issue that will not be easy to resolve.

Citizenship, Scholarship, and Leadership

Another quandary that must be addressed when defining service that will be rewarded is how to value the university's "good citizens," those faculty who always step up to the plate and do their share of the work. Driscoll and Lynton (1999), following Boyer (1990), write that some institutions view committee work and faculty governance as lacking "the intellectual content and other attributes to be 'scholarly'; that is, it is good citizenship rather than good scholarship" (1999, 6).[4] The authors of IPFW's framework for valuing service chose to make a somewhat different argument, namely, that good citizenship also requires expertise of various kinds—leadership skills, negotiation, understanding of short- and long-term planning, and so on. Skills such as these may not have been acquired as part of a faculty member's formal training in her or his discipline, but they are valuable—indeed, essential—to initiatives for change in the academy. A leader who is effective in her or his role will produce results that can be evaluated by peers. In this view, leadership is a legitimate basis for excellence in service.

Categories of Faculty Service

As mentioned earlier, the authors of OAA 04-2 attempted to identify all the kinds of service that IPFW faculty do. The familiar categories—service to the university, the community, and the profession—did not seem differentiated enough to encompass all that we wanted to recognize. The finished document has seven partially overlapping categories, as follows:

1. *University service*: serving on committees, participating in faculty governance, contributing to projects that help the university meet strategic goals

2. *Administrative service to the university*: serving as department chair, program director, associate dean, directing a multisection course, and similar roles

3. *Service to students*: counseling and mentoring students, advising student organizations, and other activities that contribute to improving the quality of students' college experience

4. *Significant project development and management*: planning, leading, and implementing projects or initiatives that may require years of work, such as entrepreneurial activities, creation of a freshman-year experience program, collaborative partnerships with K–12 or with local agencies

5. *Community service/outreach engagement*: participation in a town/gown partnership; consulting for businesses, organizations and agencies locally, regionally, and nationally

6. *Professional service*: refereeing of manuscripts, writing reviews, journal editing, organizing conferences, serving as program evaluator for other institutions or for accrediting agencies, and similar activities

7. *Professional leadership*: holding office in professional associations

The categories of service were meant to help faculty make visible the work they were doing as well as its scholarly and disciplinary dimensions.[5] Not only do the aforementioned categories overlap with each other, but categories 3–7 also overlap with teaching and/or research. The intent was to encourage faculty, chairs, and deans to look more closely at work usually defined as service to uncover how it intersects and even merges with teaching and scholarship. For example, is student counseling and mentoring "only" service, or is it another facet of teaching? Depending on how the question is answered, a department might choose to expand the definition of teaching roles to encompass advising, or adapt criteria from the evaluation of teaching to reward advising as service to students. In the category of community service or outreach, one could ask whether entrepreneurial activities do not require, à la Boyer, the application of disciplinary expertise to initiatives that benefit both the university and the community partner. An example of the latter might be the Small Business Development Center, which provides service learning opportunities for students, meets a need in the community, and benefits from the disciplinary expertise of the faculty mentors.

Note further that leadership roles (categories 2, 4, and 6) are separated out, rather than being lumped together with other service roles. Separating administrative service (category 2) from other university service, for example, allowed us to create rubrics for recognizing and rewarding leadership that produces results. This is a qualitative shift from the old-fashioned view of administrators as paper-pushers whose job it is to "keep the train running" and not waste faculty time with committee work.

Rubrics for Evaluating Service

For each of the seven categories, there is a rubric to define what constitutes satisfactory service and what constitutes excellence. Evidence typically consists of self-reports and reflections, evaluations by peers who were in a position to judge the quality of the individual's contributions, and products or changes ("impact") resulting from the service. The rubrics consistently define "competent" as doing one's share of the work and making a contribution, for example, "The candidate participated regularly and contributed to the outcome," or "The candidate performed necessary tasks on behalf of the unit's normal operations." The rubrics for identifying "excellent" consistently make reference to exercising leadership, assuming greater levels of responsibility, negotiating a process, effecting change, and creating new policies, products, or initiatives that can be measured by relevant standards of peer review.

Creating a framework for defining and documenting excellence in service opened the door for faculty to define their service as work that should be rewarded. The definition of satisfactory ("competent") service was groundbreaking as well because, as mentioned earlier, criteria for valuing service had been absent or, at best, less fully articulated than for teaching and scholarship. Spelling out what is meant by satisfactory service that is expected of all faculty in effect raised the bar, for even though OAA 04-2 was not a policy document, it had the effect of saying that some of the emperors wore no clothes. Articulating a basis for competent service challenged chairs and deans to recognize and reward their good citizens. It also sent a message to faculty who pad their annual reports with committees to which they were appointed but did not attend. As already mentioned, the authors of OAA 04-2 encouraged departments and other units to adapt or refine the rubrics as appropriate to the kinds of service done by their faculty.

Responses to OAA 04-2

Because OAA 04-2 had not been formally sanctioned by the Faculty Senate or any other faculty body (though Senate committees and faculty leaders had been consulted often during its development), a mix of responses was to be expected. Not surprisingly, there were negative reactions from some faculty, who argued that defining service as a basis for rewards, including promotion, signified a "watering down" of standards. Those who hold this view do not accept Boyer's (1990) arguments that application and integration are also a form of scholarship. At the other end of the spectrum were the responses of several deans, who saw the criteria and rubrics of OAA 04-2 as potentially raising the bar for excellence in research and teaching as well as in service. The basis for this response is the consistent use of "impact" as a basis for excellence in service, a standard that the deans saw as *higher* than prevailing criteria for evaluating scholarship. Whether the impact of scholarly publications and creative products can be measured in terms comparable to measuring leadership of a process that resulted in observable changes is too large a question to be answered here.

Faculty members who did not express negative reactions to OAA 04-2 seemed to read it in terms of what it could do for them. Those who responded most favorably tended to be female associate professors who had devoted several years and much creativity to service, especially while serving as department chairs or associate deans. One had written a grant to fund an area health education center, a project in collaboration with a local hospital to provide health education and services to underserved populations; she had also done a significant share of the work to staff the center and get it open. Another had led the process of creating a new master's program designed to serve the needs of the region in which IPFW is located, securing approval through all channels, and recruiting students. A third had led the development and implementation of a program assessment process for her college that aligned with the requirements of their national accrediting association. In each of these three cases, both disciplinary expertise and leadership skills were essential. These and other faculty members were able to draw on the language of OAA 04-2 when preparing their promotion dossiers and, to my knowledge, all were successful in their bids for promotion to professor.[6] However, I should add that none based her promotion case *solely* on service but instead chose to make an argument based on excellent service and strength in another area. Time will tell whether faculty in the future will be able to present a successful promotion case based only on documented excellence in service, with competence in teaching and research/creative endeavor.

Valuing Service at Other Universities

Another IU campus that has integrated guidelines for documenting and evaluating service into its reward system is Indiana University Purdue University Indianapolis (IUPUI). Criteria for evaluating teaching, research, and service are published as appendices to the Dean of the Faculties' Guidelines for P&T dossier preparation and review, online at http://www.faa.iupui.edu/common/uploads/library/FAA/APPD735652.doc. The service section of the appendices lists the types of evidence to be provided and where to include it in the candidate's dossier. In contrast to IPFW's seven categories, IUPUI divides service more or less along traditional lines into three types: University Service, Service to the Discipline, and Service to the Community. Criteria that echo the quality indicators from the Strategic Directions project mentioned earlier are specified for four levels of achievement: unsatisfactory, satisfactory, highly satisfactory, and excellent. IUPUI excludes "citizenship" from the category of professional service (cf. endnote 4). Thus IUPUI's guidelines are both less specific in defining the different types of service and more specific in defining additional levels of achievement and excluding citizenship from the category of professional service.

A university that recently adopted Boyer's (1990) model is Western Carolina University (WCU). As reported by *Inside Higher Ed*, integration of the Boyer model into promotion and tenure policy was approved by the WCU Faculty Senate, then endorsed by the campus administration, and finally approved at the University of North Carolina system level in the fall of 2007 (http://www.insidehighered.com/news/2007/10/02/wcu). This is a significant difference from the IUPUI and IPFW models, where approval at the system level is not a factor. When the *Inside Higher Ed* report was published, WCU had not completed what was seen as the next step, namely, the creation of an external review panel to evaluate service. The Boyer categories have been inserted into the promotion and tenure document, but criteria for evaluating contributions in those categories are not specified (http://www.wcu.edu/facsenate).

Blog postings in response to the *Inside Higher Ed* article about WCU represent a familiar range of opinions on the value of Boyer's model. No less than six respondents wrote to say that their institution, or some departments at their institution, had adopted the Boyer model, and that it was working well. One went so far as to say that this approach had improved the quality of the faculty at his institution.[7] Negative responses echoed those we had heard at IPFW: that granting tenure or promotion based on service "undermines" the foundation of the university and "excuses" faculty from research to produce new knowledge; that it appeals to those whose work "is not highly regarded by the conventional yardstick"; and that it further widens the gap between research universities and other types of higher education institutions. Some of the opposition to the Boyer model is doubtless based on a superficial or an incomplete understanding of his categories and of later work elaborating them. But in fairness, it must be acknowledged that the opposition often touches upon problems that are not easily solved. The gap between research universities and liberal arts colleges or public regional universities is real. Creating standards and policies to reward the work that faculty at such institutions must do might not widen the gap, but it won't lessen it either. What it could do is increase faculty motivation and satisfaction, because faculty are rewarded for all the work they do, not only that which most closely resembles the work of research universities.

Conclusions and Lessons Learned

The IPFW model for integrating service into the university's reward system drew on theories articulated by Boyer, Glassick, and others but stayed rooted in the language and practices of P&T criteria developed by IPFW faculty and approved by the Faculty Senate. Earlier efforts to stimulate discussion about rewarding service work had fallen on deaf ears, at least in part because they lacked connections to local policies and practices. The guidelines were written by members of the vice chancellor's staff with input from faculty, chairs, and deans who are steeped in the campus culture and alert to any action that could be interpreted as misuse of administrative authority. Numerous drafts were published for comment, and most comments were incorporated into subsequent versions before being published as OAA 04-2. Faculty reactions ran the gamut from strongly worded objections to affirmations along the lines of "It's about time!" On the one hand, the vehemence of some of the negative reactions reflects the fact that the project was led by academic administrators rather than faculty. On the other hand, positive reactions show that faculty who stood to benefit from OAA 04-2 had not felt empowered to claim excellence in service without some kind of authorization from the administration. The document helped make service visible so that it could be talked about, analyzed, and evaluated.

The IPFW project did not address gendered aspects of service specifically, but it was initiated by a vice chancellor with feminist convictions that were shared by the authors of OAA 04-2. It is noteworthy that the first faculty members to make use of the examples and rubrics for defining and evaluating service were women associate professors serving as department chairs or associate deans. To my knowledge, none based her case for promotion to professor solely on excellence in service; however, it is highly likely that without OAA 04-2, which provided a model for claiming excellence in service in addition to good performance in teaching and research, they may not have presented cases for promotion at all. Creating a framework for integrating service into an institution's reward system certainly does not solve the problems of gendered service that have been identified by the other contributors to this volume. However, by making the work visible and deserving of reward, it is perhaps a small step toward theorizing service as a component of the political economy of academe.

Notes

1. Part-time faculty members teach approximately 35 percent of the credit hours generated at IPFW.

2. A predecessor to IPFW's guidelines for valuing service was an academic affairs memorandum that was created and promulgated to encourage more systematic evaluation of teaching (OAA Memo No. 03-2, online at http://www.ipfw. edu/vcaa/promotion/default.shtml). Faculty reactions to OAA 03-2 had ranged from enthusiastic approval to vocal opposition. Departments that placed a high value on teaching drew on OAA 03-2 to reinforce criteria they already used (one department even voted to incorporate the entire document into its P&T criteria). Opposition came from some self-styled faculty leaders who saw publication of the document as usurpation by the administration of faculty rights to define standards. In general, though, OAA 03-2 had generated useful discussions about documenting and evaluating teaching.

3. Strategic Directions was a comprehensive, change-oriented initiative launched by then-president of Indiana University Myles Brand, who served from 1994 to 2002. The project on defining, documenting, and evaluating service was only one part of a much larger whole.

4. Indiana University Purdue University Indianapolis (IUPUI) takes a similar position: "University service is necessary for promotion and/or tenure. It qualifies as professional if it is documented as intellectual work that relates to the discipline or to the mission of the university. For example, the economist on the task force charged with revising university revenue distribution policies may be performing professional service but the English professor would be engaged in university citizenship." See IUPUI Dean of the Faculties *Guidelines for Preparing and Reviewing Promotion and Tenure Dossiers* 2007–2008, Appendices pp. 22–31. Online at http://www.faa.iupui. edu/common/uploads/library/FAA/APPD735652.doc.

5. Much as feminists in the 1970s needed to create language for identifying practices that systematically disadvantaged women, the humanities disciplines needed to create language for making visible the work they are increasingly expected to do. See MLA Commission 2002.

6. Since my retirement from IPFW in 2006, I am of course no longer involved in P&T deliberations and cannot comment on more recent responses to OAA 04-2.

7. That comment came from St. Norbert's College. The other institutions cited as having adopted the Boyer model are Northeastern State University, New Century College at George Mason University, Daniel Webster College, Alcorn State University, and Utah State University.

Works Cited

Boyer, Ernest L. 1990. *Scholarship Reconsidered: Priorities of the Professoriate*. Princeton, NJ: Carnegie Foundation for the Advancement of Teaching.

Driscoll, Amy, and Ernest A. Lynton. 1999. *Making Outreach Visible: A Guide to Documenting Professional Service and Outreach*. Washington, DC: American Association of Higher Education.

"Examples for Documenting and Evaluating Teaching." 2003. IPFW Office of Academic Affairs Memorandum No. 03-2. http://www.ipfw.edu/vcaa/promotion/default.shtml.

"Examples for Documenting and Evaluating Faculty Service." 2005. IPFW Office of Academic Affairs Memorandum No. 04-2. http://www.ipfw.edu/vcaa/promotion/default.shtml.

Glassick, Charles E., Mary Taylor Huber, and Gene I. Maeroff. 1997. *Scholarship Assessed: Evaluation of the Professoriate*. San Francisco, CA: Jossey-Bass.

Indiana University Purdue University Fort Wayne. 1989. Senate Document SD 88-25, Criteria for Promotion and Tenure. http://www.ipfw.edu/senate/document/promtenu.htm.

Indiana University Purdue University Fort Wayne. 1994. Document SD 94-3, Promotion and Tenure Guidelines. http://www.ipfw.edu/senate/document/promtenu.htm.

Indiana University Purdue University Indianapolis Dean of the Faculties. 2007–2008. *Guidelines for Promotion and Tenure Dossier Preparation and Review*. http://www.faa.iupui.edu/common/uploads/library/FAA/APPD735652.doc.

Jaschik, Scott. 2007. " 'Scholarship Reconsidered' as Tenure Policy." *Inside Higher Ed* (October 2). http://www.insidehighered.com/news/2007/10/02/wcu.

MLA Commission on Professional Service. 2002. "Making Faculty Work Visible: Reinterpreting Professional Service, Teaching, and Research in the Fields of Language and Literature." *Profession 2002*. New York: MLA, 172–86.

National Review Board for the Scholarship of Engagement. 2002. http://www.scholarshipofengagement.org/.

Western Carolina University Faculty Handbook. 2007–2008. http://www.wcu.edu/facsenate.

17

Curb Service or Public Scholarship To Go

Teresa Mangum

Trying to decide which aspects of one's work belong in the category "service" can complicate even the most routine occasions of academic life. At my university, for example, February is marked not only by flowers and chocolates but by a request that my colleagues and I submit a CV for an annual salary review. That academic CV accommodates innovative professional activities about as well as Hallmark expresses unconventional sentiments.

If I have been foolish enough to sit on a committee that reviews protests of parking violations, then that detail obviously belongs in the category "service." But what if a silver-tongued dean has lured me onto a committee reviewing the general education curriculum? This charge would require hours of research, collaboration, evaluation, analysis, argument, and pages of written conclusions—all about curricular matters. Can such labor be swept under the inevitably denigrated rubric *service*? Perhaps I have been elected an officer of a professional organization or asked to serve on the editorial board of a press or journal. A scholar in that position helps determine the future of a field and its standards for scholarship, publication, and hence indirectly the promotion and tenure of countless colleagues. Yet that too is service.

No wonder studies of faculty work use synonyms like *catchall* for service or define the category through negation, as Robert Blackburn and Janet Lawrence (1995) do when they characterize service as "everything that is neither teaching, research, nor scholarship" (222). Even in a clear, accessible guide like Christopher Lucas and John Murry's (2002) *New Faculty: A Practical Guide for Academic Beginners*, service remains a mystery. This handbook, which also uses the term *catchall* (181), clarifies how that mystery imperils faculty members. Because references to service are "vague, ill-defined mandates" marked by "ambiguity and uncertainty" (183), faculty members have no idea when it is appropriate to accept and refuse service requests. And lacking consensus about performance criteria, administrators avoid evaluating service, only noting its most egregious absences at crucial moments of tenure and promotion.

The categorical confusion escalates for scholars who participate in what is variously called "community-based," "engaged," or "public" teaching and scholarship. In my own case, I recently co-directed an interdisciplinary faculty seminar focused on the emerging field "Critical Animal Studies." Our conventional scholarly discussions in the semester-long seminar fanned an anticipated glow of ideas into an unexpected bonfire. Funded by a public engagement grant, we organized "The Animals among Us," two competitive photo-essay exhibits hosted by local museums (and now online) in addition to a third fine arts exhibition. We labored long and hard to create visual displays, juxtapositions, and accompanying texts that would invite spectators to reflect on questions about human-animal relations we were exploring in our research. When I asked an administrator where these activities belonged in the annual salary CV, I was advised to classify these projects, which had involved intellectual stretching and illuminating interactions with judges from presses, galleries, and museums, along with hours of debate, a community-based course, and a statewide exchange of ideas as—*service.*

This essay drills down to the double entendre of my title. I agree with others writing for this volume that faculty members must curb participation in work for which our particular areas of expertise have not prepared us and which do not take advantage of what each of us can do effectively or productively. At the same time, I would argue that we need to protest the indiscriminate ubiquity of the category "service." Imprecision not only poorly serves faculty members and their institutions, it also imperils work that I and others, including a disproportionate number of women, want to do and want to have acknowledged, evaluated, and rewarded.

A glimpse at the many definitions of "service" in the *Oxford English Dictionary* locates the trouble at the root. Few of us want to be in the "condition, station, or occupation of being a servant," while many of us, as state employees, acknowledge that we are in the "condition or employment of a public servant." I might willingly undertake "the action of serving, helping, or benefiting; conduct tending to the welfare or advantage of another" while preferring not to engage in the "act of waiting at table or dishing up food." In fact, I even feel ambivalent about being "at one's disposal, ready or available for one to use," much less paying fealty to an employer (a definition that comes to mind when my university sends out the annual United Way call, despite my usual off-duty impulses to be charitable).

The "catchall" character of service imposes particular burdens on scholars in the humanities, disciplines that outsiders see as already vague and incomprehensible. Certain fields in the sciences and all of the professional schools and health professions include forms of applied research: fieldwork, clinical research, and even that problematic category "outreach." The activities that comprise these forms of work render the subject matter, methods, and products of those disciplines somewhat comprehensible to outsiders—from deans to legislators, from parents to donors. On the other hand, the interpretive, analytical, and epistemological emphases of the humanities inspire deep thought, but not necessarily action. Despite the fact that many of us plant our research and teaching in very grounded political literature, "the humanities" as a category can seem oddly ethereal. At best, most non-academics conjecture that "the humanities" are "good for you" in some uncertain, impractical fashion. Even when we try to be accessible, we describe our work in abstract terms such as analysis, critique, or interpretation, words that offer no vision, smell, or taste of what we do. Perhaps after working hard for decades to secure legitimacy for their fields through affiliation with theories that require highly specialized knowledge, some scholars fear that any form of outreach, which would necessitate accessibility, might dilute and even undermine their disciplines. In any case, most of us are better at articulating what we are against than what we *are*. Our potentially most valuable tendencies—being skeptical, attending to language in all of its nuances, questioning authorities and conventions—can turn us into our own worst enemies when irony and critique dissipate into evasiveness and inaction. Small wonder that deans and provosts assume we have the time to serve on endless committees and task forces. They compare us to scientists conducting clinical trials, law faculty doing pro bono work, and nursing faculty staffing free medical clinics, while we have difficulty locating any common core in what we do.

Humanities departments have long been havens for solitary scholars with a passion for private, contemplative thought; the most successful (and privileged) often experience their careers as a kind of vocation that may soon be almost unimaginable in the increasingly corporate, assessment-driven culture of higher education. The traditional image in the humanities of the solitary scholar also goes hand in hand with an emphasis on individual labor. Articles and books written by single authors are still the only seriously valued accomplishment in the humanities at those colleges and universities with aspirations to be highly ranked as research institutions, and often even at schools that otherwise take special pride in undergraduate teaching. Today, even as changes in the autonomous role of the scholar are signaled by organizations such as the American Association of Universities, the Association of American Colleges and Universities, the American Council on Education, the Carnegie Foundation for the Advancement of Teaching, CASE (the Council for Advancement and Support of Education), and the Pew Charitable Trust, which focus on "reinvigorating the humanities" (the title of a 2004 AAU report), often through calls for civic engagement, a leader in the humanities like Stanley Fish can still assert: "I find that as a general rule the higher the aims of an academic, the lower the level of his or her performance in those duties for which he or she is actually paid" (Fish 2005, 43). Fish's dismissal of all forms of "service" seems justified by his success in the profession and access to its rewards. At the same time, his expressed distrust of engaged research and teaching contradicts observations he made as a dean, when he criticized faculty work habits, as in the online *Chronicle* piece "What DID You Do All Day?" (Fish 2004). Nevertheless, his charge that service—including experiments with engaged pedagogy and scholarly—simply is not our work deserves serious reflection.

The problem for those who are writing for this collection and you who find yourself motivated to peruse these pages is that obviously we/you are asking whether our intellectual lives and our professional obligations extend beyond the limited body of knowledge in which we originally trained, beyond the walls of our classrooms, even our departments, sometimes even beyond our contractual duties. The very act of writing this kind of essay in this kind of book suggests that a significant number of us may be negotiating with public as well as traditional professional claims upon scholars. Bruce Robbins (2007) addresses these public claims in a pragmatic response to Fish, also published in *The Chronicle*:

> Whatever our political preferences and commitments as individu-als, collectively speaking we cannot afford not to make claims to some sort of social value or purpose and to back up those claims as convincingly as possible. The question that must be debated is which claims—which legitimizing statements or strategies we scholars should choose to adopt, which of these extremely different projects of change deserve or deserves our allegiance. (Robbins 2007, 314)

Our training as readers and writers prepared those of us in the humanities to understand that the "public," that is, our audiences, can be surprisingly fluid. Working alongside traditional solitary scholars, humanities professors are sometimes inspired by that vaster sense of a reading public to produce textbooks, publish with trade presses, edit journal issues and book collections, and even write in collaboration with partners. This book, for example, is first addressed to colleagues, but then also to students, junior women whom we mentor, administrators, legislators, and even general readers who want to understand what faculty members in universities do and what best practices suggest they should (and should not) do. I suspect the writers of the essays in this volume have done more service than anyone should have asked them to do, which is why we are experts *on* service, which is only rarely paid the compliment of scholarly analysis. (Paradoxically, of course, writing about the service dilemma may be perceived by those who evaluate us as yet another form of service.)

Moreover, the disposition of some humanities scholars is changing. While the majority feel well served by traditional forms of individual scholarship and classroom-based teaching, a growing number of faculty members long to take their intellectual work to the curb, to the boundaries of colleges and universities, where ideas, projects, and talents might genuinely nourish rather than merely serve a few of those millions. In order to make these crucial choices wisely, we need much more concrete language, definitions, and administrative endorsement for the different types of work we do, work that currently disappears into the service abyss. How, we need to ask, does "service" differ from what is increasingly referred to as "engagement"? Where does bureaucracy end and collaboration begin? What qualitative differences distinguish managerial labor from intellectual leadership? And before many of us put energy into answering those questions, we need to know how committed colleges and universities are to making these distinctions meaningful. We need to believe administrators will reward both the service and the engaged scholarship and teaching of faculty members whose work has potential impact beyond traditional university and disciplinary enclaves.

Faculty members who envision a more public role for scholars and scholarship have been trying since at least the early 1990s to distinguish among the kinds of work still routinely collapsed together as service. Ernest L. Boyer's (1990) influential report for Carnegie, *Scholarship Reconsidered: Priorities of the Professoriate*, has had an enormous impact on thinking, if not practice, in higher education administrative circles. Boyer argued that conventional research (scientific breakthroughs, humanities published scholarship) was merely one form that new knowledge could take. He advocated giving equal weight to what he called "the scholarship of *discovery*; the scholarship of *integration*; the scholarship of *application*; and the scholarship of *teaching*" or pedagogy (16, emphases in original); in a later article, he added the scholarship of engagement (Boyer 1996). While discovery and integration are tied to the more familiar academic research methods of investigation and synthesis, the scholarship of application prompts questions seldom demanded of humanities scholarship, such as: " 'How can knowledge be responsibly applied to consequential problems? How can it be helpful to individuals as well as institutions?' " and " 'Can social problems themselves define an agenda for scholarly investigation?' " (Boyer 1990, 22). These questions could give new urgency and meaning to our scholarly work. But the continuing confusion about service, linked with the tendency in the humanities to classify (and denigrate) work associated with practical application *as* service, means that

Boyer's influence has had a price. Studies that revisit his vision and try to assess its impact reach the same conclusion: faculty members who have taken up Boyer's charge rarely transform their scholarship or their institutions. They just work harder. In 1995, *Inside Higher Ed* writer Scott Jaschik reviewed online two major studies of Boyer's impact and found that "the dominant change in tenure in the decade following the publication of *Scholarship Reconsidered* may have been more demands that faculty members be better in everything, including traditional models of research" (Jaschik 2005).

Nonetheless, many faculty members keep fighting the good fight. In *Faculty Service Roles and the Scholarship of Engagement*, Kelly Ward (2003) provides a clear, instructive history, literature review, and assessment of the challenges separating public scholarship from service, "outreach," volunteer work, and even civic participation—categories that most universities will never seriously reward and that even the best-hearted of us would not confuse with "disciplined" intellectual work. Ward divides and then subdivides forms of service as she works carefully toward a distinction between service and forms of public scholarship and engaged teaching. She describes internal service as that required "to conduct institutional business and service to the discipline" through professional associations. External service, on the other hand, is "a means for institutions to communicate to multiple external audiences what it is that higher education does to meet societal needs" (iv). Collectively, in these senses, service refers to the activities that comprise the service role—from that parking committee to a position on a journal advisory board (4).

In varying degrees, faculty tend to perceive such labor, especially for the home institution, as a distraction from their "real" work. The more research intensive the college or university, the more likely administrators are to view such service as "institutional housework"—necessary but only at the least possible cost to the institution. As many of us who say yes too often painfully learn, the devaluation of this labor can actually taint those who perform it. Praise for good citizenship morphs quickly into rebuke for poor judgment. In fact, the parallel between devalued domestic and institutional labor is one of the reasons, Dale Bauer (2004) argues in "Academic Housework," that women end up doing such a disproportionate part of all kinds of service.

Rather than criticizing either women faculty or this kind of labor, Ward joins Boyer in urging greater dignity (and reward) for institutional service, which among other things she sees as the price of faculty governance. But she is most intent on distinguishing between service activities and the intellectual inquiry and methods—the "concepts"—that she associates with "engagement." Her maneuver at first seems to participate in the obfuscation that is apparently endemic to service when she argues that "engagement" emphasizes *connections* among "scholarship, faculty disciplinary expertise, and campus missions" (Ward 2003, 4). But her further distinctions between service and engagement free faculty members from the catchall service trap by encouraging individuals to match their intellectual interests to opportunities for application. More precisely, she says, after surveying wide-ranging literature on the subject, engagement refers to "a relationship with the community that is grounded in mutuality and respect, while acknowledging the complexities that exist in campus community relationships" (4). Engagement also refers to the connections between the "service" provided by a faculty member and her or his disciplinary expertise. For Ward, the crucial questions asked of engagement, as opposed to service, are "not only how expertise is useful to a larger public but how involvement with that public profoundly affects scholarship" (4). This last crucial feature of "engagement," its inherent reciprocity, profoundly contrasts with expectations for "service" in ways particularly relevant to humanities scholars.

Earlier I noted that the humanities as a body of disciplines is still distinguished from the social sciences by claims that our methods are necessarily abstract. But that claim contradicts the fact that many scholars' work has been deeply affected by the U.S. political struggles of the 1960s. All across campus, women and minorities still push for changes in "worklife" as well as the curriculum. Critiques posed by feminist theory, race- and ethnic-based theory, disability studies, age studies, and cultural studies have changed subject matter, texts, methods, syllabi, and research priorities first on the margins of humanities disciplines but now in a more encompassing fashion. As only one example of the diverse paths to these curricular and institutional changes, many faculty members of my generation remember confrontations when lines were drawn between feminist theorists and feminist activists in the 1970s, 1980s, and early 1990s. Those collisions often ended in painful partings when frustrated activists turned their backs on the academy. But activists' demands of theory and of scholars deeply affected many who remained committed to academe, and that legacy is palpable in most humanities disciplines.

As one result of that activist period, research in the humanities has become more engaged in investigating how cultural forms—from historical documents to novels, from art to popular culture—participate in attitudes and practices that affect, to take a few examples, undocumented laborers, trade unions, gender- and race-based oppression, imperial conquest, and postcolonial struggle. Yet even this scholarship generally remains interpretive, analytical, and epistemological rather than action based. The reward structures in universities and in humanities disciplines still discourage scholars from working with and on behalf of nonacademic organizations that represent the very people and cultures being studied, especially if collaboration would interfere with publication.

The scholarship of engagement seems poised to bridge such chasms. Collaborative engagement demands intellectually rigorous exchanges in which all parties acknowledge each others' varying forms of knowledge and mutually create new knowledge. The success of an exchange is measured by genuine breakthroughs of understanding in the academy and by actual solutions to problems in the larger world. Some faculty will, quite reasonably, argue that their *teaching* is engagement. And yes, teaching can powerfully affect students' thinking, which may lead them to put their knowledge and skills to work in the interest of their communities. Still, traditional teaching methods require little direct contact with the world outside the academy for humanities scholars. So does the claim that "teaching" is the best form of "service" (another blurring of categories) have to be the final word for all of us?

The answer of one organization that is devoted to offering a more capacious understanding of the forms that scholarship might take and to recovering "public scholarship" from the blanket category we know as service would be no. Imagining America: Artists and Scholars in Public Life is a growing consortium of colleges and universities that has the ambitious goal of transforming higher education into a space that values and rewards the myriad forms that public scholarship might take. The organization has launched a nation-wide "Tenure Team Initiative" (TTI) with the goal of "Valuing Public Scholarship in the Cultural Disciplines," using the working definition, "Public scholarship is scholarly or creative work integral to a faculty member's academic area. It is jointly planned, carried out, and reflected on by co-equal university and community partners. And it yields one or more public good products" (Imagining America 2007, online).

The TTI report focuses on the "project" rather than a book or an article as the "unit of work" for designing and evaluating public scholarship. The characterization of a "project" helps explain another reason "service" is so disparaged (and depressing). Service generally demands intense coordination and collaboration, yet it is treated as idiosyncratic, fairly mindless *individual* labor for which an individual is left with almost nothing to show. The report explains that engagement "organizes knowledge production around a project" in which work is conducted by a "purpose-built team" that seeks solutions to problems or creates "things of lasting value and significance" (from ideas to institutes, from museum exhibitions to literacy programs). The project model firmly shifts attention to the diverse forms that scholarship might take, the complex labor and intellectual transformations required, and the significance of context as well as collaboration in knowledge formation. The model of the project also offers a way to restructure the humanities in concert with Cathy Davidson and David Theo Goldberg's (2004) call for a new interdisciplinary humanities model that would be "problem- or issue-based rather than field-specific" (45). Scholars and artists would be able to define the nature of cultural work in reference to the explicit objectives and time frame set out for any given project. In the context of the humanities, this process offers us an opportunity to explain far more convincingly what we do and why it matters. To find collaborating partners, we would have to explain the value of humanities scholarship, which is so often unfathomable and unarticulated, even to and by humanities scholars themselves.

The Imagining America tenure report also offers explicit guidelines for evaluating public scholarship along with a wealth of examples from existing projects and policies. To summarize quickly, the report recommends the use of public scholarship portfolios. These would open with a framing statement in which faculty members explain the progress of their public scholarship, the nature of projects and collaborations, the projects' importance for the discipline and the public good, and future directions of a scholar's work. The portfolio would include evidence of the project and its impact: news clips, material from presentations, single-authored or collaborative publications, teaching materials, project reports, participant interviews, responses, and so forth. The report also argues that one of the reviewers should be a seasoned public scholar or community leader. The report and the public scholarship movement offer those of us with the desire to use our scholarly work as a bridge across the town/gown divide to accomplishment, contribution, discovery, and usefulness. Good citizenship could be not only good judgment but good scholarship.

The opportunity to develop and co-direct a week-long "Institute for Graduate Engagement and the Academy" at my institution's Obermann Center for Advanced Studies brought home for me all of these questions in very concrete ways. Many of our departments prepare graduate students for a scholarly career; the most responsible departments also mentor graduate teachers (though the devaluation of pedagogical scholarship means that neither faculty nor graduate students necessarily learn much about pedagogy before entering a classroom). While graduate students sometimes serve on textbook or search committees or as teaching mentors to their peers, we do little if anything to prepare them for the choices that confront faculty members daily about service expectations and distinctions.

Even with the inspiring model of the Institute on the Public Humanities for Doctoral Students at the University of Washington's Simpson Center for the Humanities before us, planning an interdisciplinary graduate institute on "engagement" raised endless problems of terminology. The group spent an entire session on the implications of language being used by a range of scholars such as Nancy Cantor, Evan Carton, Cathy Davidson and Theo Goldberg, Julie Ellison, Stanley Fish, Sylvia Gale, Edward Said, and David Scobey. We wanted the institute students to distinguish clearly between service and engagement. We trusted that together we would discover connections among our various intellectual projects and our teaching, on one hand, and the needs that both might serve in the larger public, on the other. We also

felt obligated to clarify the career risks that students might take in becoming public scholars and engaged teachers—rather than scholars and teachers
who limited themselves to the routine committee work and departmental
tasks that would come with their future employment. We were well aware
that many colleagues would resist what one friend wryly called "do-gooder
desertion of the classroom."

When KerryAnn O'Meara (2002) interviewed administrators in 2002
to assess the degree to which Boyer's arguments had changed American
colleges and universities, she frequently encountered the claim that engaged
scholarship was an "abdication of the appropriate faculty role as expert" and
therefore did not deserve rewards (72). As one dean explained, "There were
faculty involved in the schools who had, in many people's view, gone sort
of native in terms of service; you get involved with the troops out there
and you become one of them, forgetting that you are part of the university
community and that role has responsibilities in a different way" (73). The
"raced," if not racist, image is telling. Numerous studies have found that
by far the majority of faculty members participating in engaged scholarship and teaching are women and/or minorities (Antonio, Astin, and Cress
2000; Bellas and Toutkoushian 1999; Rice, Sorcinelli, and Austin 2000; Sax,
Astin, Arredondo, and Korn 1996). In 2002 O'Meara found that 90 percent
of faculty undertaking "service scholarship" were women, and 25 percent
were faculty of color. As she concluded, "*The first challenge is acknowledging
that reward systems are about who we value as well as what we value*" (2002,
75, emphasis in original). As we designed and led the institute for fifteen
graduate students, we repeatedly asked ourselves and later the students how
engaged research and community-based teaching reproduced or differed from
"service." Is the phrase "service learning" itself indicative of an intellectual
promise or yet another capitulation to devalued labor, we mused? Were we
transforming the university with our students, or were we marginalizing
them and ourselves through association with what many would insist on
seeing as "service"?

I met my faculty codirector, David Redlawsk, in a week-long institute
where faculty members revised a conventional course in light of service
learning or similarly "engaged" pedagogy and practice. Obviously we shared
particular values despite our different disciplines. As we visited groups on
campus to publicize the graduate institute, I realized I was grateful that Dave
is a respected political scientist (and so from the social sciences) and, well,
a man. The gender balance of the codirectors, the institute students, and
the panelists who periodically visited the institute suggested that progress
was being made in diversifying engagement (this time to include more men
and white people). Despite the reassuring presence of a social scientist at
the forefront, however, by far the greatest number of applicants and so of

institute students were in the humanities. That brings us back to the question of whether the humanities is ready to invest cultural capital in public scholarship rather than constraining its "service" options to internal, conventional, career-irrelevant, and largely devalued labor on campus.

The Institute on Graduate Engagement and the Academy, in fact, succeeded because so many academics and community partners generously shared their time and expertise. We heard from panels composed of faculty members from across campus, administrators who evaluate faculty for tenure and promotion, graduate students, and community leaders.

Most of our speakers simply refused to countenance the boundaries that usually separate teaching from service and engagement. At the University of Iowa, as in many locations, pedagogical practices even outside of the "professional" fields have been undergoing remarkable transformations for some time. Whether called "community-based learning," "experiential learning," or "service learning," these new pedagogies challenge conventional classroom geographies and power relations. The single teacher-as-authority often gives way to collective learning rooted in problem solving. Concepts are tested in community settings, and teachers collaborate with community partners and with students themselves to produce rather than disseminate knowledge. Does that mean our teaching is becoming service? Or are these multitiered attempts at engagement simply evasions of our "true" responsibilities as scholars and teachers, as Fish would have it? While many faculty members, in partnership with community groups, have forged ahead in creating new forms of "action research" for their students and new structures for experiential learning, they do so knowing that their work will be probably be considered (and disregarded) as "service." No one acknowledged these impasses more ruefully during our institute than the UI associate provost for faculty.

The speakers who visited the institute also reminded us of another way to think about the distinctions among teaching, scholarship, service, and engagement. Repeatedly, we realized that *practices* have changed despite the fact that most college and university *policies* for promotion and tenure have not kept up with the ways many faculty members are choosing to do their work. A fascinating picture of secret "service" lives began to emerge under the pressure of the graduate fellows' questions. We learned of teachers like art education professor Rachel Williams, who has been involving her students in community projects for years with only her commitment to student learning as reward. We heard from administrators like law professor and associate provost for diversity Marcella David, who had cobbled together grants and funding to bring minority students to a summer legal seminar in order to convince them—through engaged research—to apply to law school. We met engineering graduate student Marcelo Mena, who led the UI branch of Engineers for a Sustainable World in a campus energy audit that has saved thousands of dollars and watts of electricity. His faculty mentor, Craig Just, has created his own "study abroad" program, convincing students to take their hydraulics "homework" to villages in Mexico with no running water. Their research-in-action in collaboration with townspeople has produced life-saving public water pumps. An MFA student, Austin Bunn, started the Patient Voice Project. He designed a writing workshop curriculum for chronically ill patients at the local hospital. He has graduated, but fellow MFA students have followed in his footsteps, working with over 100 patient-writers since 2005. Over and over we heard stories of artists, scholars, and researchers who looked beyond conventional service to find places and partners with whom to share their talents and knowledge. With community partners, they were creating genuinely new knowledge even as they were helping to solve painfully old problems.

Many faculty members ignore these changes and calls for change in higher education, but even those who are not experimenting with new forms of scholarship and teaching are being shaken by these seismic shifts. As the labor of higher education becomes more complex, varied, collaborative, and interdisciplinary, the category "service" is only becoming more difficult to identify, much less to curb. That perplexity leads us back to those calls for faculty members to serve on the parking committee (which might suddenly seem important to a colleague who feels she has received an unjust parking fine) or to the need for faculty members to shepherd curricular change or lead the Faculty Senate or chair a provost search committee. To have the kind of institution in which any of us want to work, we have to accept these responsibilities. In any case, that is part of what we are paid to do. But finer discriminations among types of work will give us far more power to make good judgments about which assignments are appropriate to an individual faculty member's knowledge, rank, and both work and life demands in a given semester or year. Finer discriminations would also help us grasp what the "norms" are for service. Many women have probably had the experience I had several years ago. After years of assuming that the service I agreed to do was in line with others' contributions, I found myself on the department salary review committee, reading my colleagues' annual self-reports. The disparities among service portfolios were stunning. I realized not that my colleagues were slackers, but that I was far out of balance. Does anyone need to serve on more than one major university committee each year? Should a faculty member chairing a departmental search committee get a pass on other assignments for a semester? While it feels ungracious to refuse a provost's request that you give "just two hours" to an awards committee meeting, serving on three such "undemanding" committees in a year is a significant interruption. Careful distinctions between engaged work and service should encourage a faculty member to define which activities meet which expectations, but those distinctions should also help an individual decide when those expectations are unreasonable and excessive. Being competent should not provoke a life sentence to committee work. Such distinctions are all the more crucial for women because—true confessions—some of us may be drawn to service more than is actually good for us.

The plain truth of the matter is that some of us—women in particular—may not want to avoid "service" that is deeply collaborative, intellectually engaging, and genuinely good for the larger community. Instead, many of us want clear distinctions among types of "service"; we want respect for forms of work that generate ideas, inspire learning, and facilitate change; and we want reward systems and promotion policies that evaluate "engagement" rather than demanding and then dismissing "service." These distinctions will only become more important as documents advocating changes in the evaluation of professors' work, such as Imagining America's Tenure Team Initiative, begin to be debated.

These issues are of particular importance to women faculty because we keep being asked and being too willing to take on such a disproportionate amount of the work. While I respect and learn much from Marxist and other systemic analyses of the inequities of labor relations, years of experience also argue that a great number of women are particularly susceptible to service demands because they share the values upon which service work ideally depends: collegiality, citizenship, and community. I confess that serving on a well-run committee composed of a cross-campus group of intelligent, tough-minded, imaginative, innovative, witty colleagues who are deeply committed to analyzing and solving a problem that affects thousands of people can be a real pleasure. Such "service" is not unlike the pursuit of a new explanation for a literary phenomenon, but the work is a collaboration in challenging and collegial company. Having been socialized to facilitate such exchanges—both as women and as teachers—many women are extraordinarily talented at this kind of work. That is one reason they get asked to carry such an unfair burden of service in higher education, where very few are the least bit prepared to lead, to orchestrate group dynamics, to run meetings, to mediate, or to facilitate collective action. How often do women wearily accept another "service" assignment—from committee chair to placement director to essay prize organizer to associate chair or dean or provost—because they know their contribution will ensure that the process will be thoughtful, fair, consultative, innovative, and successful? So if I and others are going to "serve," then why not let us develop collaborative, engaged projects that enhance our research rather than inhibit our progress?

Perhaps in the best-case scenario, at least one of the directions in which higher education is heading will lead to recognition of the value of "engagement" and of those who excel at translating scholarship into practice, learning into the collaborative production of knowledge that addresses community needs, and service into engagement. Of course, that will not happen

unless some of us, yet again, serve on the committees that have the power
to change promotion requirements, to rewrite policies to reflect reality, and
to persuade administrators and colleagues to open their minds as well as
their new ops manuals.

Even as we faculty members clarify terms, resist bureaucratic nonsense,
and dignify engagement at multiple levels of higher education, graduate
students like those who participated in the Obermann Institute are setting
their own agendas for the future. From the Publicly Active Graduate Education (PAGE) Fellow program of Imagining America (founded by graduate
student Sylvia Gale) to graduate engagement institutes at the University
of Washington and the University of Iowa to the new community-based
MA in cultural studies at the University of Washington at Bothell or the
MA in public humanities offered by the John Nicholas Brown Center for
the Study of American Civilization at Brown University, graduate students
are using the "three-legged" stool of academic work as kindling. They are
dismantling dichotomies that separate teaching, scholarship, and "service."
Good luck convincing them to sit on the parking committee. In just a few
years, I suspect they will create educational institutions different from and
better than the ones in which they studied. I'm with them. It's time to
curb service to its proper proportions and instead consider ways to nourish
ourselves, our students, our institutions, and our communities with "scholarship to go."

Note

I would like to thank Katie J. Hogan and Michelle A. Massé for their helpful
suggestions. I am, as always, grateful for the suggestions of my writing group—Kathleen
Diffley, Kim Marra, and Leslie Schwalm, who know all too much about service.

Works Cited

"Animals Among Us." 2007. Online Exhibition. The Obermann Center for Advanced
    Studies. The University of Iowa. http://www.uiowa.edu/obermann/animals/
    exhibits.html.
Antonio, A., H. Astin, and C. Cress. 2000. "Community Service in Higher Education:
    A Look at the Nation's Faculty." *Review of Higher Education* 23:4: 373–97.
Bauer, Dale. 1998. "The Politics of Housework." *Women's Review of Books* (Febru-
    ary): 19–20.
Bauer, Dale. 2004. "Academic Housework: Women's Studies and Second Shifting."
    In *Women's Studies on Its Own: A Next Wave Reader in Institutional Change*, ed.
    by Robyn Wiegman, 245–57. Durham, NC: Duke University Press.

Bellas, M., and R. Toutkoushian. 1999. "Faculty Time Allocations and Research Productivity: Gender, Race, and Family Effects." *Review of Higher Education* 22:4: 367–90.

Blackburn, Robert T., and Janet H. Lawrence. 1995. *Faculty at Work: Motivation, Expectation, Satisfaction.* Baltimore, MD: Johns Hopkins University Press.

Boyer, Ernest. 1990. *Scholarship Reconsidered: Priorities of the Professoriate.* New York: The Carnegie Foundation for the Advancement of Teaching.

Boyer, Ernest. 1996. "The Scholarship of Engagement." *Journal of Public Outreach* 1: 1: 11–20.

Cantor, Nancy. 2003. "Transforming America: The University as Public Good." In *Foreseeable Futures: Working Papers from Imagining America # 3.* http://www.imaginingamerica.org/foreseeFutures.html.

Cantor, Nancy, and Steven Lavine. 2006. "Taking Public Scholarship Seriously." *Chronicle of Higher Education* (June 9). Posted on Syracuse University News Web site, http://www.sunews.syr.edu/cantoroped.cfm.

Davidson, Cathy N., and David Theo Goldberg. 2004. "Engaging the Humanities." *Profession*, 42–62.

Ellison, Julie, Committee Chair. "The Tenure Team Initiative on Public Scholarship" of Imagining America: Artists and Scholars in Public Life. Draft Report. Online at http://www.imaginingamerica.syr.edu/documents/tti-background-study%20DRAFT.pdf. [Note: Now published as: J. Ellison and T. K. Eatman. *Scholarship in Public: Knowledge Creation and the Engaged University.* Syracuse, NY: Imagining America, 2008.]

Fish, Stanley. 2004. "What DID You Do All Day?" *Chronicle of Higher Education* (December 11). http://www.chronicle.com/jobs/2004/11/2004112401c.htm.

Fish, Stanley. 2005. "An Interview with Stanley Fish: Aiming Low in the Ivory Tower." *National Civic Review* (Summer): 41–45.

Gayle, Sylvia, and Evan Carton. 2005. "Toward the Practice of the Humanities." *The Good Society* 14:3: 38–44. http://www.muse.jhu.edu/journals/good_society/v014/14.3gale.html.

Imagining America: Artists and Scholars in Public Life. 2007. Consortium Web site. Online at http://www.imaginingamerica.syr.edu/.

Jaschik, Scott. 2005. "Has Scholarship Been Reconsidered?" *Inside Higher Ed* (October 4). http://www.insidehighered.com/news/2005/10/04/tenure/.

Lucas, Christopher J., and John W. Murry Jr. 2002. *New Faculty: A Practical Guide for Academic Beginners.* New York: Palgrave.

Mathae, Katherine B., and Catherine Birzer, eds. 2004. *Reinvigorating the Humanities: Enhancing Research and Education on Campus and Beyond.* New York: Association of American Universities.

O'Meara, KerryAnn. 2002. "Uncovering the Values in Faculty Evaluation of Service as Scholarship." *The Review of Higher Education* 26:1: 57–80.

Rice, E., M. D. Sorcinelli, and A. E. Austin. 2000. *Heeding New Voices: Academic Careers for a New Generation. New Pathways Working Paper Series,* Inquiry No. 7. Washington, DC: American Association for Higher Education.

Robbins, Bruce. 2007. "Epilogue: The Scholar in Society." 3rd ed. In *Introduction to Scholarship in Modern Languages and Literature,* ed. David G. Nicholls, 313–30.

New York: Modern Language Association. Excerpted in *The Chronicle of Higher Education,* June 8, 2007, B16.

Said, Edward. 2002. "The Public Role of Writers and Intellectuals." *The Nation* (September 17). http://www.thenation.com/doc/20010917/essay. (This article originally appeared in *The Nation,* September 17, 2001.)

Sanchez, George. 2004. "Crossing Figueroa: The Tangled Web of Diversity and Democracy." Foreseeable Futures: Working Papers from Imagining America #4. https://www.ctools.umich.edu/access/content/group/1106364909396-12033726/Sanchez_G_CrossingFigueroa.pdf.

Sax, L. J., A. Astin, M. Arredondo, and W. S. Korn. 1996. *The American College Teacher: National Norms for the 1995–96 HERI Faculty Survey.* Los Angeles: Higher Education Research Institute, University of California.

Scobey, David. 2002. "Putting the Academy in Its Place." *Place* 14:2 (Spring): 50–55.

The Simpson Center for the Humanities. University of Washington at Seattle. Institute on the Public Humanities for Doctoral Students. Online at http://www.depts.washington.edu/uwch/research_graduate_Connecting.htm.

Ward, Kelly. 2003. *Faculty Service Roles and the Scholarship of Engagement.* ASHE-ERIC Higher Education Report 29:5.

18

"Pearl was shittin' worms and I was supposed to play rang-around-the-rosie?"

An African American Woman's Response to the Politics of Labor

Valerie Lee

It is Friday, December 9, 2007, at The Ohio State University. Classes for the quarter are over, so no one expects to see faculty in the halls. Yet all the tenured and tenure-track faculty members in the Department of English—all seventy of us on the Columbus campus—sit in a room, some on top of tables, some in the windowsills, waiting for a meeting to start that has the potential to change how we define, reward, and do service. Although as a department we were used to having, and indeed expected, all the senior faculty to show up for promotion and tenure meetings and junior and senior faculty to show up for hiring meetings, no one would have suspected that the topic "academic service" would be enough of a magnet to attract everyone. After all, service always pales in comparison to research and teaching. Service never gets anyone tenure. It is the Clydesdale in a race run and won by thoroughbreds.

We were assembled to vote on a "workload plan." When asked by the university to institute differential teaching loads based on research productivity (allowing the mostly white male group of full professors in each college to be in a greater position to do more of what they already were doing quite well), I solicited the assistance of an associate professor and a full professor who were young enough to think creatively but experienced enough to know how to craft an argument tailored for our colleagues.[1] They went to work, creating a document that performed several functions: (1) The document made visible the fact that differential loads already existed in our unit. Many among us had course reductions for journal editing, course directorships, and internal administrative positions, such as director of undergraduate studies, graduate studies, digital media studies, and so forth. Others had contracts that gave them a course release or two, and several had private deals with the chair and/or the dean; (2) The document presented a plan whereby, without losing student enrollments, indeed increasing enrollments, everyone in the department could go on a 2-2-0 workload, which under our quarter system means six months in the classroom and six months out of the classroom; (3) The document targeted service, academic labor, and not research as the great equalizer; and (4) The document asked that we identify all activities that we value, and anyone whose civic engagement met the threshold outlined in the plan could elect the six months in the classroom, six months out the classroom model. Against the backdrop of a very bureaucratic institution, we had created our own in-house sabbatical.

As we sat in the room that December day, we were at a crossroads, deciding whether the historical way of doing service was in fact a model we wished to continue to institutionalize, or whether we wanted to try doing service in a way that carried weight and honor. It was time for the vote. As chair of the Department of English, I had to draw upon my background as a former chair of the Department of Women's Studies to ask those most invested in our current hierarchical distribution of course releases to be willing to give up those releases so that we could vote a system where everyone had an equal chance at a more desirable work/life policy. Senior white male full professors who were prolific scholars faced a tough situation. They enjoyed many opportunities that afforded them course releases, while others who taught more classes and performed as much or more service did so without the accompanying perks. The plan called for the redistribution of teaching and service expectations across the department. But to get there, the most rewarded ranks of our community had to give up some of their privileges. Of course in the bathrooms and around the water fountains, those of us who are feminist scholars had already predicted that at heart the issue would be about patriarchy and white privilege, however masked. But if ever there was a time when the greater good prevailed, then this meeting was the moment. Although there was some oration about meritocracy, some grandstanding about having earned an elite or a distinguished status, in the end every person present voted for the plan. It was the first time in my career that I saw colleagues teary-eyed with joy over a conversation about academic labor. Currently the department has an environment where people are eager to do academic labor, for the rewards are vital and visible. In a College of Humanities, where everyone was on a five-course load, we had claimed our future. We voted ourselves a life.

I would like to think that this moment in time owes much to my two colleagues who bravely and dutifully drafted the plan and a little to the fact that I am the first woman and the first African American chair of a department whose roots go back to the 1880s. Moreover, I am doing this chairing at a time when my dean, who had to approve the workload plan, is an African American male with specialties that I share in African American literature and folklore. Here I am claiming a particular attitude about service that is heavily influenced by the mores of black communities, African American folklore traditions, and African American women's literature. Academic service has been the stumbling block for many African American tenure candidates because academe has been slow in recognizing (and the candidates have been slow in relinquishing) a social contract that emphasizes the rhetoric of "reach back," "come back," and "pay back." Many African American faculty grow up hearing proverbs about service: Shirley Chisholm, "Service is the rent we pay for the privilege of living on this earth"; Marian Wright Edelman, "Service is the very purpose of life and not something you do in your spare time."[2] We hear these sayings and sentiments in the pews of churches, the halls of community centers, and the kitchens of our homes.

Those who receive opportunities and never make those same opportunities available to others in the community lose respect. Alice Walker, in her poem *For My Sister Molly Who in the Fifties*, describes the daughter who goes away to college, reads much, learns much, and picks up "accents never heard / in Eatonton"; the family is in awe of Molly because she is the one "Who found another world"—a world beyond her provincial upbringing. But the poem announces, Molly "*left us*" (emphasis added). As I mention in an essay "Smarts," "the poem does not fault Molly because her education took her to many different places; it faults her because she did not know how to travel to those places and still travel home again."[3] The desire to reach back, come back, and pay back always has been at the forefront of what some would call responsible citizenship and engagement in the black community.[4]

Even so, other African American faculty hear the communal voice more as an intrusion on their personal rights, subtracting from them time that their white colleagues are not asked to surrender. In a "First Person" column from the October 12, 2007, *Chronicle of Higher Education,* an assistant African American professor bemoans the pressure placed on him to attend campus Kwanzaa celebrations, Martin Luther King Breakfast celebrations, and Black Commencement celebrations.[5] The essay describes how "pressured to be seen at certain college events, a black professor decides to redefine his role on campus." At some point most African American professors ask themselves the question that this professor raises in his essay: What do the pouring of libations, the speaking of Swahili, and the beating of drums have to do with the advancement of my academic career? The professor relents and attends

his campus version of a black graduation ceremony, and it does turn out to
be, as he describes it, a "bizarre performance," helping him recognize that
he does not want to assume that type of blackness:

> That bizarre performance led to a decision. I would attend no
> more kente-cloth breakfasts. I would not attend a Kwanzaa cel-
> ebration. Never again would I applaud speeches that celebrated
> the myth of black defeat, and I would not participate in events
> simply because of the color of my skin. And if people questioned
> my absence, I would not tell them a lie.
>
> I intend to be visible, I would tell them, but only in ways
> I wish to be seen. (C3)

For some, service to one's home community, whether on campus or off
campus, is a distraction; for others, such as African American Professor
of Family Studies April L. Few,[6] service is what she feels she must do to
"nurture the soul," "to provide voice to the values [she] holds," to maintain
a commitment to social justice and activist pedagogy (49–58). Few's essay,
jointly written with her chair of tenure and promotion and her department
chair, argues that academe's conceptions of scholarship should be broadened
and offers to tenure-track faculty of color ten recommendations that include
such motivational advice as "Do not give up who you are. Live your commitments, your passion. Be strategic. Fit your commitment for service into
your research and teaching" (62). The earlier mentioned *Chronicle of Higher
Education* essay and the essay in the *NWSA Journal*, where the Few article was
published, demonstrate the ends of the spectrum—African American faculty
who resent how their presence is always already racialized, and those on a
mission to "deconstruct which [institutional] values should matter" (62).

Many misunderstand why African American faculty are complicit in
their own service enslavement, not realizing that African American cultural
beliefs, literature, and folklore shape a service ethic that makes it difficult to
say no. How does one determine which work is more important and what
constitutes too much work? In African American folklore there are many
jokes about mules who did not want to work because they were not the ones
defining and evaluating "work." There are many variations of these folk jokes,
but they all center on how much work a mule (read the black underclass;
those who are marginalized; those in the lowest ranks) is supposed to do.
One such joke describes a white man who cannot get his mule to work, so
he asks a black farmer to help him. Confident, the black farmer tells the
white man that he can definitely get the mule to work. The black farmer
has a way with mules. One variation of the joke has the conversation running along these lines:

> *Black farmer*: Watch me get this ole mule working. Okay, [turning to the mule], Obadiah, start working.
>
> [The mule does not move.]
>
> *Black farmer*: Okay, Zechariah, start working.
>
> [The mule does not move.]
>
> *Black farmer*: Okay, Zephaniah, start working.
>
> [The mule does not move.]*Black farmer*: [turning to white man] Now watch the mule start working *this time*. Malachi, start working.
>
> All of a sudden, the mule starts working
>
> *White man*: If you knew his name was Malachi all along, why did you call him by all those other names?
>
> *Black farmer*: I couldn't let that ole mule think he was the only one working.

The joke is playing upon the stereotype that black people do not want to work. It is a stereotype that has been particularly troubling because of its roots in the slave economy. Throughout the tales of ex-slaves, the slaves complain that no matter how hard they work, no matter how much cotton they pick, their masters think they are lazy.

Other mule stories decry how much work mules are expected to do. A variation of this tale is called "The Talkin Mule" tale.[7] An "ole feller" wants to sleep late so he sends his son to fetch the mule, Ole Bill, and get the day's work started. The son runs into trouble because the mule does not want to start working. Ole Bill rolls his eyes, and after the boy keeps pressuring him to work, Ole Bill says, "Evah mawnin it's 'Come round, Bill! Come round, Bill!' Don hahdly git no res fo it's 'Come round, Bill!'" Needless to say, the boy is shocked that the mule is talking. He runs home, shares the news with his "ole man," but his father accuses him of telling lies. The father tells his "ole lady" that he's going to get to the bottom of this, and with his dog, "Lil fice," running behind him, he goes to see the mule. Again the mule complains about every morning having to work: "Evah mawnin, it's 'Come round, Bill!'" The ole man runs back to share the shocking news with his wife:

Ole man say to de ole lady, "Dat boy ain lyin. He telling da troof.
Dat mule is talking. I ain nevah heard a mule talk befo."

[The dog], Lil fice say, "Me neither."

If mules (and dogs) could truly speak on behalf of themselves, then what
constitutes labor would have to be reconfigured.[8]

In addition to African American folklore, work issues also figure promi-
nently in African American women's literature, and voices from the community
pass judgment on its worth. Zora Neale Hurston's "Sweat" describes the life
of Delia Jones, a washwoman with a "great hamper in the bedroom," that
she uses to sort white folks' soiled clothing to the dismay of her philandering
husband, Sykes. Doing white folks' laundry for over fifteen years has paid
for Delia's horse and house, items that Sykes wants to take from her and
give to his mistress. Readers sympathize with Delia's hard work ethic, her
"knotty, muscled limbs, her harsh knuckly hands" (128). Sykes, an abusive
husband, dismisses Delia's work ethic as being too Christian and too white.
The other men in the community, however, denigrate Sykes for his choice
of a mistress and for his lack of understanding that honest labor helps the
community and raises Delia's stature in their eyes.

Community is central to the story. The men sit around on their
porches and talk about how they treat their wives, how they define beauty,
and what they think of housing a snake in the home. It is the community's
conversation that drives and clarifies the narrative, and the reader must
listen to the community, for its folk sayings and jokes shape how readers
are to judge the characters. Delia's religious values and the folk talk on the
porch condemn Sykes's behavior. Hurston's characters often find themselves
in situations where voices from the community comment on whether they
are working too much or not enough. In a reference to "Sweat," Critic
John Lowe points out that "the appearance of the communal comic chorus
in the personages of the loiterers on Joe Clarke's porch constitutes another
significant development in Hurston's craft."[9] When the community speaks
in Hurston's narratives, they assume judgmental roles. The story ends with
Sykes placing a rattlesnake in the hamper so it can kill Delia, but in a case
of situational irony, the snake crawls in their bed and is there when Sykes
jumps in. Delia knows that the snake will kill Sykes and watches his final
moments but does not help.

The pull of the community's voice is strong, and many African American faculty want to respect that voice. For some, it is a matter of what is
at stake by saying no. Who can afford to say no and to whom? When the
community calls, it is not easy to "Just say no." Mildred, the maid in Alice
Childress's *Like One of the Family: Conversations from a Domestic's Life* (1956),

says yes when her girlfriend Marge wants her to do community activities and says no when her white employer wants her to refrain from doing so. The whole time that Mildred is working in the white folks' homes, she is spending her few hours outside of work politically engaged in Jim Crow issues, "Negro History" events, independence issues for African countries, and so forth. One of Mildred's white women employees, Mrs. B., disapproves of Mildred spending time reading "the colored newspaper" and worries that Mildred might be planning to attend a Paul Robeson concert advertised in the paper. Knowing that the employer thinks of Robeson as a radical race man, Mildred tries to avoid responding to the question about her activities outside of work; however, Mrs. B. insists on warning about how these community events can bring trouble to Mildred, presumably the loss of her job. Exasperated, Mildred tells Mrs. B. a lengthy story that begins with an old slave master and his slave Jim. The tale is an allegory of all of black history with the master exploiting Jim through every era, ending with the master vowing never to let Jim's children profit from the 1954 *Brown v. Topeka* Board of Education Supreme Court case. Mildred uses the tale of historical and ongoing discrimination to announce that going to see Robeson is a task that is more important than cleaning Mrs. B's house. Rattled by the story, Mrs. B. does what Mildred tried to do when first asked about attending a Paul Robeson event: Mrs. B. changes the subject to a more neutral topic: "Yes, it sure is a nice sunshiny day, and I hope it doesn't rain."[10]

Alice Childress uses Mildred to show how presumptuous it is on the part of the white employer to pit the value of the community event against the need to maintain one's employment, employment controlled by masters and mistresses. Toni Morrison too has a story that vexes the relationship between the labor of the marginalized and the expectations of the privileged. In Morrison's *Sula*, Hannah, yearning for what she views as the normalcy of nuclear family life, asks her eccentric, sassy, and economically poor mother Eva about "quality time." The mother responds by describing how she took good care of Hannah and her siblings, Pearl and Plum, under the worst of circumstances. Not satisfied with this response, Hannah retorts, ". . . I know you fed us and all. I was talking' 'bout something else. Like. Like. Playing' with us. Did you ever, you know, play with us?"[11] Eva responds, "Play? Wasn't nobody playin' in 1895. Just 'cause you got it good now you think it was always this good? 1895 was a killer, girl. Things was bad. Niggers was dying like flies" (68). Eva keeps working, and Hannah keeps pressing her for an adequate response. Given their poverty-stricken status, Eva calls Hannah a "snake-eyed ungrateful hussy" for expecting her to go "leapin' 'round that little old room playin' with youngins with three beets to [her] name" (69). Eva, who never wanted to engage in this conversation in the first place, details all that she did to help her children survive. She responds to her daughter's need for play by asking, "Pearl was shittin' worms and I was supposed to play rang-around-the-rosie?" (69). Eva is arguing that her position in life shapes her philosophy of labor and love. Pain places pressure on play. Aesthetics tug against mere survival. Eva's response is a more raw rendering of the voice in Gwendolyn Brooks's "kitchenette building," where a poor couple bemoans that " 'Dream' makes a giddy sound, not strong / Like 'rent,' 'feeding a wife,' 'satisfying a man.' " For the poor, the poem argues, dreams must fight onion fumes. Therefore, the speaker dares not take too long mulling over the relationship between the aesthetic and the mundane, for if she is to take care of her personal needs, she would do better to listen for the flushing sound of the shared bathroom toilet: "Since Number Five is out of the bathroom now, / We think of lukewarm water, hope to get in it."[12] Those who live in kitchenette buildings must attend to the physical before spending too long contemplating the philosophical. As do all faculty, African American faculty want to advance in the academy. But how does one get faculty of color to be cautious about their service obligations without being dismissive of their home communities? In addition to whatever aesthetic project the scholar may be doing, these communities want a return on their emotional and spiritual investment. Who can afford "to play rang-around-the-rosie" if "Pearl was shittin' worms"? If the community is still under siege, if the numbers of those males of college age are more populous in jail than in the college classroom, if the disparity in health care, housing, and job opportunities remains unacceptable, then how is it that the scholar can afford to do only that work that will give himself or herself tenure? Again, a Gwendolyn Brooks's poem advises to "First Fight, then Fiddle." The sonnet ends with the couplet, "For having first to civilize a space / Wherein to play your violin with grace" (54).

Perhaps the time has come in the academy when faculty of color should not have to choose between fiddling and fighting. If there is one thing to be learned from black feminist criticism, it is what Toni Cade Bambara calls "wasteful and dangerous splits."[13]

Even as all faculty members must choose how to balance their lives and will be held accountable for doing so, the solution to the problem of too many service responsibilities for faculty of color can only partly be solved by ourselves. One solution rests on the shoulders of academe. Why not hire clusters, cohorts, cadres of faculty so that individual faculty of color can choose to be invisible, visible, or hypervisible? Why not initiate what the ADE Ad Hoc Committee on the Status of African Americans Faculty Members in English calls "affirmative activism"?[14] Affirmative activism calls for action steps on the part of chairs and their undergraduate and graduate program coordinators, hiring committees, and leadership at the institution's highest levels. Collectively, the action steps seek to change the climate in which faculty and students of color are expected to thrive. Some of the suggestions are calls for aggressive action: "Identify targets of opportunity instead of always waiting for candidates to surface in a national pool; start building curriculum and scholarly strength in African American literature and culture, whether or not your department already has African American faculty members in place and whether or not African American faculty members you may hire will be specialists in that area." Some of the suggestions are calls for equitable action: "Assign new course preparations to African American junior faculty members in the same proportion as to other junior faculty members, even when they have been hired to develop a new curricular area." And some of the suggestions are calls for a redistribution of priorities and resources: "Reallocate internal resources to create 'topping off' fellowships for graduate students from underrepresented groups, as is commonly done in senior faculty searches or for hires in highly competitive fields." The essay proceeds with detailing close to fifty suggestions that in the end seek to alleviate a problem that the academy helped create: the numbers of faculty of color are so few that they are not allowed to have a range of professorial identities. Without a critical mass, faculty of color will always be more constrained by service commitments than their peers.

I would like to think that as a product of a home community that expects its scholars to be willing to advise the Black Student Union, attend the rally for the latest political injustice, speak at the local black bookstore about the Black Arts Movement, explain Toni Morrison's work to the black women's local reading groups, and so forth, my attitude about service is more expansive than that of many of my colleagues. As a chair, I have been caught between protecting all of my junior faculty from service tasks, while at the same time giving greater recognition to the various types of service that my senior faculty do. I have added "Community Building" as a new heading on the Annual Activity Report, allowing my colleagues to define community and name any activity that they can justifiably argue enriches their professional or work/life career. To give service value, it needs to be in the reward structure, and faculty must have the kinds of teaching workloads that allow service to inform teaching and research, as well as all three informing each other, rather than "wasteful, dangerous splits."

At the same time that many more women are chairing departments, I believe that the job has become more difficult, given uncooperative state legislatures, corporate models of funding of higher education, litigious students and faculty, the pressure to be entrepreneurial, the never-ending quest to advance beyond one's benchmark and affinity schools, and so forth. When my colleagues see me working late at night, they sympathetically ask me to give up something. "Go home; you do not have to do all that you do," they advise. So I sit and ponder which university committee I should stop chairing—the University Diversity Council, or the University Compensation Committee for Faculty Governance? Do I step down from major committees just when I have the power and authority to make structural changes? Or, perhaps, which lecture should I not do—the one for the Women's Leadership panel? The lecture for the common text written by an African author? Or, which program review can I afford not to do? Which Department of English is doing so well with diversifying its curriculum, faculty, and graduate student body that I need not worry about adding my voice to the critique? Or, which department should I say no to when asked if I will be an external reader for a promotion to full case—certainly, not the case of the candidate whose field is African American literature, with a focus on race, gender, and sexuality? If I say no, then how many full professors are there who do precisely this work at a comparable school? Is the group that I am in large enough that I can say no to several of the cases and still remain the kind of mentor that I choose to be for the next generation? Or, which summer institute do I say no to—the one for recruiting more underrepresented students to graduate programs in English?[15] The one for recruiting more underrepresented students to graduate programs in the arts and humanities?[16] The Summer Research Opportunities Program[17] at the consortium level? How should I calibrate, weigh, or measure these many demands? As Few mentions, one must be "strategic about the kinds of service" that one takes on (58), as well as creative in using service as a handmaiden for one's scholarship. For my own calibrations, I subtract the amount of "reach back" that my home community asks of me from the amount of "fall back" that they have given to me throughout the years and continue to give. That is, when asked to speak at yet another Martin Luther King Jr. Day celebration, I subtract from my effort all the times when I was at a loss to finish the next book chapter and the church sisters prayed and fasted on my behalf. Many of these women, these othermothers, are like the mother in Alice Walker's poem "Women" who "knew what we must know / without knowing a page / of it / themselves."[18] I subtract from whatever perceived burden that the "reach back" costs those times when, weary of writing the dissertation, I found encouragement in the question asked curiously but supportively every time that I returned home: "What degree are you working on *now*?" I subtract from the burden of having to read their poorly written poems, their pride when introducing me as "Dr. Valerie Lee, PhD." Every time that I tried to explain the redundancy of their titling of me, I heard them repeat, "But we haven't called you out of your name."

There is no denying that I am among the generation of African American scholars very much influenced by what Marilyn Mobley McKenzie describes as those who inherited the legacy of "lifting while we climb," those with "a cultural orientation to service."[19] As Mobley McKenzie so astutely observes, "When a black woman has a predisposition to serve, an activist sensibility to make a difference, and a heightened sense of responsibility to marginalized communities of which she is a part, she is particularly vulnerable to expectations that she will contribute over and above what is expected of others and that she will do the service that others have elected not to do" (241). In the early 1990s, I collaborated with seven other African American faculty and professional staff members under the collective name of "Andrea" to write about humanizing academic service. The essay details how as Third World women we felt that we were working a third shift, the graveyard shift, but even so, we saw ourselves creating a third space, a space we created for "humanizing change." Looking back over a decade, I still affirm our final words in that essay: "Sweet grass baskets woven with our voices hold a collection of third-space ideas. We go to work. *We are Andrea*. At the day's end we remain Third World women living in a third space working a third shift. But we have learned that working the third shift has one irrevocable advantage: we are awake while others sleep, and in that wakefulness, we safeguard dreams" ("Andrea's Third Shift: The Invisible Work of African American Women in Higher Education," 403).

Granted, I do have a sense of mission that is affecting how I see my own politics of labor. Early in my career I attended a women's studies conference called "Transforming the Academy," and I have never given up that project. Indeed, as a full professor at a Research I institution, chairing one of the nation's largest departments of English during the time when the Modern Language Association is calling for a "more capacious conception of scholarship," serving under a dean and under an executive dean who are both African Americans in identity and scholarship, and currently presiding over ADE, I feel more like the position of the biblical Esther: "Who knows that thou art come to the kingdom at such a time as this?"[20]

There are times when I wistfully sit back and imagine what it would be like to have a professional life where my ethnicity and sex do not place added demands on me. After all, the work that needs to be done inside and outside the academy should be a shared enterprise, especially among feminist scholars. Mobley McKenzie pinpoints part of my worry: "When our fellow women scholars can analyze race in texts but shy away from doing so in everyday life interactions outside of the texts they study, we have a tangible manifestation of the politics of labor" (237). Can I trust those who have an intellectual interest in racial discourse to hear and heed the community's call, to understand that intellectual work need not stop at the campus gate?

In determining when to say yes and when to say no, I weigh how I want the climate of my return visits to the community to be. I choose not to return as Gloria Naylor's Reema's boy, who with his technology in hand returns home to do "extensive fieldwork," but his academic notion of fieldwork falls short of how his community defines work in the fields: Reema's boy "ain't never picked a boll of cotton or head of lettuce in his life" (7).[21] I choose not to return as Dee in Alice Walker's "Everyday Use," parading the new relationships that I have formed, the new words acquired, and the new foods eaten, and arguing that she needs to take with her some of her grandmother's quilts, apt symbols of folkness, to decorate her walls. Her fear is that her sister, who did not receive a college education, would "be backward enough to put [the quilts] to everyday use" (33). I choose not to return as the college-educated young people in Toni Cade Bambara's, "My Man Bovanne," who exploit "the folks" as grassroots specimens for their political agendas. As someone for whom social justice is still an important cause, I choose not to return as someone "playing rang-around-the-rosie when Pearl is shittin' worms."

Notes

1. I am indebted to Professors Jared Gardner and Sebastian Knowles for crafting the workload plan.

2. These phrases can be found in the speeches and writings of Shirley Chisholm (1972 Democratic Convention) and Marian Wright Edelman. See Edelman, *The Measure of Our Success: A Letter to My Children and Yours* (New York: HarperCollins, 1993).

3. Valerie Lee, "Smarts: A *Cautionary* Tale," in *Calling Cards: Theory and Practice in the Study of Race, Gender, and Culture*, ed. Jacqueline Jones Royster and Ann Marie Mann Simpkins, 104 (Albany: State University of New York Press, 2005).

4. There is no monolithic black community. Here I am speaking of the community as it has been spoken of and romanticized in black churches, community centers, folklore, and African American literature. My point is that however debatable these notions may be, they have had an effect on many of the African Americans who assume professional jobs whether in the academy, law firms, or corporations.

5. Jerald Walker, "Visible Man," *The Chronicle of Higher Education*, October 12, 2007, C2–C3.

6. April L. Few, Fred P. Piercy, and Andrew Stremmel, "Balancing the Passion for Activism with the Demands of Tenure: One Professional's Story from Three Perspectives," *NWSA Journal* 19:3 (Fall 2007): 47–66.

7. This particular variation is told in *Black Writers of America: A Comprehensive Anthology*, ed. Richard Barksdale and Keneth Kinnamon, 457 (New York: Macmillan, 1972).

8. The historical connection between mules and African American women is best summarized by Nanny in Zora Neale Hurston's *Their Eyes Were Watching God* (1937: Philadelphia, PA: J.B. Lippincott, University of Illinois Press, 1978), 29. "De nigger woman is de mule uh de world so fur as Ah can see. Ah been prayin' fuh it tuh be different wid you. Lawd, Lawd, Lawd!"

9. John Lowe, "From *Jump at the Sun: Zora Neale Hurston's Cosmic Comedy*," in *Sweat: Zora Neale Hurston*, ed. and intro. Cheryl A. Wall, 184. Women Writers Texts and Contexts Series (New Brunswick, NJ: Rutgers University Press, 1997).

10. Alice Childress, *Like One of the Family: Conversations from a Domestic's Life* (Boston, MA: Beacon Press, 1956; rpt. 1986), 119–22.

11. Toni Morrison, *Sula* (New York: Alfred A. Knopf, 1976), 68.

12. Gwendolyn Brooks, "kitchenette building," in *Selected Poems*, 3 (New York: Harper & Row, 1963).

13. Toni Cade Bambara, "What It Is I Think I'm Doing Anyhow," in *The Writer on Her Work*, ed. Janet Sternburg, 165 (New York: W.W. Norton, 1980).

14. See "Affirmative Activism: Report of the ADE Ad Hoc Committee on the Status of African American Faculty Members in English," *ADE Bulletin* 141–142 (Winter–Spring 2007): 70–74. In this essay the team of Dolan Hubbard (Morgan State University), Paula Krebs (Wheaton College), David Laurence (ADE), Valerie Lee (The Ohio State University), Doug Steward (ADE), and Robyn Warhol (University of Vermont) looks at some alarming statistics, such as "of the approximately 400 institutions that have graduated African American undergraduates who have gone on to complete a PhD in English, 192 produced only one in the past thirty-three years" (70). The essay outlines a number of strategies to address a range of issues faced by African American graduate students, undergraduate students, and faculty.

15. The Summer Institute for Literary and Cultural Studies (SILCS) is a four-week institute at Wheaton College that targets students from ethnic or racial groups who are underrepresented in the field of English studies. For more information, see their Web site at http://www.wheatoncollege.edu.silcs.

16. The Program for Arts and Humanities Development (PHD) is a two-year research and mentoring program that targets students from historically underrepresented groups, focusing on providing summer classes, mentoring, and year-long financial support for graduate work in the Arts and Humanities. For more information, see their Web site at http://www.humanities.osu.edu/studentinfo/undergrad/phd.

17. The Summer Research Opportunities Program (SROP) is an initiative sponsored by the Committee on Institutional Cooperation (CIC—the Big Ten schools) that targets undergraduate minorities for doctoral programs in the Arts and Sciences. For more information, see their Web site at http://www.cic.uiuc.edu/programs/srop.

18. Alice Walker, *Her Blue Body Everything We Know: Calling Earthling Poems 1965–1990* (San Diego, CA: Harcourt Brace Jovanovich, 1991), 160.

19. Marilyn Mobley McKenzie, "Labor above and beyond the Call: A Black Woman Scholar in the Academy," in *Sister Circle: Black Women and* Work, ed. Sharon Harley and the The Black Women and Work Collective, 243 (New Brunswick, NJ: Rutgers University Press, 2002). As Mobley McKenzie mentions in her essay, there is a long history of racial uplift formally dating back to the motto of the National Association of Colored Women, "Lifting as We Climb." As I was finishing my essay, I read her essay. Had I not been so busy with academic service and read it earlier, I would not have felt a need to write my piece. Her story resonates with my story. That is, we are senior professors looking back on our careers—a very different posture from the young professor that I quote at the beginning of this essay.

20. In Esther 4:14, Mordecai, representing his community, warns Esther: "For if thou altogether holdest thy peace at this time, then shall there enlargement and deliverance arise to the Jews from another place; but thou and thy father's house shall be destroyed: and who knoweth whether thou art come to the kingdom for such a time as this?"

21. Gloria Naylor, *Mama Day* (New York: Ticknor and Fields, 1988).

Selected Bibliography

Antonio, Anthony L., Helen S. Astin, and Christine M. Cress. "Community Service in Higher Education: A Look at the Nation's Faculty." *Review of Higher Education* 23, no. 4 (2000): 373–97.

Arreola, Raoul A. *Developing a Comprehensive Faculty Evaluation System*. Boston, MA: Anker, 1995.

"Balancing Faculty Careers and Family Work." Special issue of *Academe: Bulletin of the American Association of University Professors* 90, no. 6 (November–December 2004).

Bauer, Dale. "Academic Housework: Women's Studies and Second Shifting." In *Women's Studies on Its Own: A Next Wave Reader in Institutional Change*, ed. Robyn Wiegman, 245–57. Durham, NC, and London: Duke University Press, 2002.

———. "The Politics of Housework." *Women's Review of Books* (February 1998): 19–20.

Bellas, M., and R. Toutkoushian. "Faculty Time Allocations and Research Productivity: Gender, Race, and Family Effects." *Review of Higher Education* 22, no. 4 (1999): 367–90.

Bird, Sharon, Jacquelyn Litt, and Yong Wang. "Creating Status of Women Reports: Institutional Housekeeping as 'Women's' Work." *NWSA Journal* 16, no. 1 (2004): 194–206.

Blackburn, Robert T., and Janet H. Lawrence. *Faculty at Work: Motivation, Expectation, Satisfaction*. Baltimore, MD: Johns Hopkins University Press, 1995.

Bousquet, Marc. *How the University Works: Higher Education and the Low-Wage Nation*. New York: New York University Press, 2008.

———. "The Rhetoric of 'Job Market' and the Reality of the Academic Labor System." *College English* 66, no. 2 (2003): 207–28.

———, Tony Scott, and Leo Parascondola, eds. *Tenured Bosses and Disposable Teachers: Writing Instruction in the Managed University*. Carbondale: Southern Illinois University Press, 2003.

———. "The Waste Product of Graduate Education: Toward a Dictatorship of the Flexible." *Social Text* 70, no. 1 (2002): 81–104.

Boyer, Ernest L. "The Scholarship of Engagement." *Journal of Public Outreach* 1, no. 1 (1996): 11–20.

———. *Scholarship Reconsidered: Priorities of the Professoriate*. San Francisco, CA: Carnegie Foundation/Jossey-Bass, 1997.

Braskamp, Larry A., and John C. Ory. *Assessing Faculty Work: Enhancing Individual and Institutional Performance.* San Francisco, CA: Jossey-Bass, 1994.

Breznau, Anne, Charles Harris, David Laurence, James Papp, and Patricia Meyer Spacks. "Report of the ADE Ad Hoc Committee on Governance." *ADE Bulletin* 129 (Fall 2001): 1–13. Rpt. *Profession 2002*, 211–28. New York: MLA, 2002.

Burgan, Mary. *What Ever Happened to the Faculty?: Drift and Decision in Higher Education.* Baltimore, MD: Johns Hopkins University Press, 2006.

Caesar, Terry. *Traveling through the Boondocks: In and Out of Academic Hierarchy.* Albany: State University of New York Press, 2000.

Cantor, Nancy, and Steven D. Lavine. "Taking Public Scholarship Seriously." *Chronicle of Higher Education* (June 9, 2006): B20.

Denham, Robert et al. "Making Faculty Work Visible: Reinterpreting Professional Service, Teaching, and Research in the Fields of Language and Literature." Rprt of the MLA Commission on Professional Service. *Profession 1996*, 1–56. New York: MLA, 1996.

Fish, Stanley. "An Interview with Stanley Fish: Aiming Low in the Ivory Tower." *National Civic Review* (Summer 2005): 41–45.

———. "What DID You Do All Day?" *Chronicle of Higher Education* (December 11, 2004). http://www.chronicle.com/jobs/2004/11/2004112401c.htm (accessed May 16, 2008).

Fogg, Piper. "So Many Committees, So Little Time." *The Chronicle of Higher Education* 50, no. 17 (November 19, 2003); (December 19, 2003): A14. See also http://www.chronicle.com/colloquy/2003/collegiality for discussion of the article.

Furman, Andrew. "Measure Professors' Real Service, Not Lip Service." *The Chronicle of Higher Education* 51, no. 11 (November 5, 2004): B20.

Gappa, Judith M., Ann E. Austin, and Andrea G. Trice. *Rethinking Faculty Work: Higher Education's Strategic Imperative.* San Francisco, CA: Jossey-Bass, 2007.

Glassick, Charles E., Mary Taylor Huber, and Gene L. Maeroff. *Scholarship Assessed: Evaluation of the Professoriate.* San Francisco, CA: Jossey-Bass, 1997.

Golde, Chris M., and George E. Walker, eds. *Envisioning the Future of Doctoral Education: Preparing Stewards of the Discipline-Carnegie Essays on the Doctorate.* New York: Jossey-Bass, 2006.

Guillory, John. "Valuing the Humanities, Evaluating Scholarship." *Profession 2005.* New York: MLA (2005): 28–38.

Hall, Donald E. *The Academic Community: A Manual for Change.* Columbus: Ohio State University Press, 2007.

———. *The Academic Self: An Owner's Manual.* Columbus: Ohio State University Press, 2002.

Harney, Stefano, and Frederick Moten. "Doing Academic Work." In *Chalk Lines: The Politics of Work in the Managed University*, ed. Randy Martin, 154–80. Durham, NC: Duke University Press, 1998).

Hogan, Katie J. "Superviceable Feminism." *The Minnesota Review* 63/64 (2005): 95–111. http://www.theminnesotareview.org/journal/ns6364/iae_ns6364_superserviceablefeminism.shtml.

Hutcheon, Linda, et al. "Professionalization in Perspective." MLA Ad Hoc Committee on the Professionalization of PhDs. In *Profession 2002*. New York: MLA (2002): 187–210.

Imagining America: Artists and Scholars in Public Life. Consortium Web site. Online at http://www.imaginingamerica.org (accessed December 13, 2008).

Jaschik, Scott. "Committee Equities and Inequities." *Inside Higher Ed* (April 10, 2006). http://www.insidehighered.com/news/2006/04/10/service (accessed May 16, 2008).

———. "The Evolving (Eroding?) Faculty Job." *Inside Higher Ed* (May 1, 2006). http://www.insidehighered.com/news/2006/05/01/faculty (accessed May 16, 2008).

———. "Has Scholarship Been Reconsidered?" *Inside Higher Ed* (October 4, 2005). http://insidehighered.com/news/2005/10/04/tenure/ (accessed May 16, 2008).

Jenkins, Rob. "The Service Question." *Chronicle Careers* (June 21, 2006). http://www.chronicle.com/jobs/news/2006/06/2006062101c.htm (accessed May 16, 2008).

Kerber, Linda K. "We Must Make the Academic Workplace More Humane and Equitable." *Chronicle of Higher Education* (March 18, 2005): B6–9.

Lemuel, John (pseudonym). "Death by Committee." *Chronicle of Higher Education* (January 9, 2007). Careers section. http://www.chronicle.com/weekly/v53/i19/19c00301.htm.

Lucas, Christopher J., and John W. Murry Jr. *New Faculty: A Practical Guide for Academic Beginners.* New York: Palgrave, 2002.

Martin, John Jeffries. "Letter to the Editor." *The Chronicle Review* (April 18, 2005): B17.

Martin, Randy, ed. *Chalk Lines: The Politics of Work in the Managed University.* Durham, NC: Duke University Press, 1998.

Mason, Mary Ann, and Eve Ekman. *Mothers on the Fast Track: How a New Generation Can Balance Family and Careers.* New York: Oxford University Press, 2007.

———, and Marc Goulden. "Do Babies Matter? The Effect of Family Formation on the Lifelong Careers of Academic Men and Women." *Academe: Bulletin of the American Association of University Professors* 88, no. 6 (November–December 2002): 21–27.

Massé, Michelle A. "Higher Ed, A Pyramid Scheme?" http://www.youtube.com/watch?v=TXHzzvWyKLQ.

———. "Melodramas of Beset (Real) Womanhood: Women Narrating Feminism in Academe." *Concerns: A Publication of the Women's Caucus for the Modern Language Association* 27, no. 1–2 (Spring 2000): 36–43.

———. "Ten Million Served!" http://www.youtube.com/watch?v=ig18SWwh6g&feature=related.

Mathae, Katherine B., and Catherine L. Birzer, eds. *Reinvigorating the Humanities: Enhancing Research and Education on Campus and Beyond.* New York: Association of American Universities, 2004.

McCaskill, Barbara, et al. "Women in the Profession, 2000." Committee on the Status of Women in the Profession. In *Profession 2000*. New York: MLA (2000): 191–215.

Midler, Frank (pseudonym). "Service Masochists." *Chronicle of Higher Education* (January 27, 2006). http://www.chronicle.com/jobs/news/2006/01/2006012701c/careers.html (accessed May 16, 2008).

Modern Language Association Committee on the Status of Women in the Profession. "Women in the Profession, 2000." *Profession 2000.* New York: MLA (2000): 191–215.

Murphy, Lynne (pseudonym). "At Your Service." *Chronicle of Higher Education* (February 23, 2007). http://www.chronicle.com/jobs/news/2007/02/2007022301c/careers.html (accessed May 16, 2008).

Nelson, Cary. *Office Hours: Activism and Change in the Academy.* New York: Routledge, 2004.

———. "What Hath English Wrought? The Corporate University's Fast Food Discipline." In *Disciplining English: Alternative Histories, Critical Perspectives*, ed. David R. Shumway and Craig Dionne, 195–211. Albany: State University of New York Press, 2002.

Nerad, Maresi. *The Academic Kitchen: A Social History of Gender Stratification at the University of California, Berkeley.* Albany: State University of New York Press, 1999.

O'Meara, Kerry Ann. "Uncovering the Values in Faculty Evaluation of Service as Scholarship." *The Review of Higher Education* 26, no. 1 (2002): 57–80.

———, and R. Eugene Rice, eds. *Faculty Priorities Reconsidered: Rewarding Multiple Forms of Scholarship.* New York: Jossey-Bass, 2005.

Porter, Stephen R. "A Closer Look at Faculty Service: What Affects Participation on Committees?" Presentation, Annual Meeting of the American Educational Research Association, San Francisco, CA, April 7–11, 2006.

Rauch, Alan. "Great Work: You're Fired." *Chronicle of Higher Education* (April 1, 2005): B15.

"Rethinking Faculty Work." Special issue of *Academe: Bulletin of the American Association of University Professors* 91, no. 4 (July–August 2005).

Rhoades, Gary. *Managed Professionals: Unionized Faculty and Restructuring Academic Labor.* Albany: State University of New York Press, 1998.

Rice, E., M. D. Sorcinelli, and A. E. Austin. *Heeding New Voices: Academic Careers for a New Generation.* New Pathways Working Paper Series, Inquiry No. 7. Washington, DC: American Association for Higher Education, 2000.

Rothberg, Michael, and Peter K. Garrett, eds. *Cary Nelson and the Struggle for the University: Poetry, Politics, and the Profession.* Albany: State University of New York Press, 2008.

Sax, L. J., A. Astin, M. Arredondo, and W. S. Korn. *The American College Teacher: National Norms for the 1995–96 HERI Faculty Survey.* Los Angeles: Higher Education Research Institute, University of California, 1996.

Schuster, Jack H., and Martin Finkelstein. *The American Faculty: The Restructuring of Academic Work and Careers.* Baltimore, MD: Johns Hopkins University Press, 2006.

Stanton, Domna C. "The Labor of Service." In *MLA Newsletter* (Summer 2005): 3–4.

Tighe, Thomas J. *Who's in Charge of America's Research Universities? A Blueprint for Reform.* Albany: State University of New York Press, 2003.

Tokarczyk, Michelle M., and Elizabeth A. Fay, eds. *Working-Class Women in the Academy: Laborers in the Knowledge Factory.* Amherst: University of Massachusetts Press, 1993.

Ward, Kelly. *Faculty Service Roles and the Scholarship of Engagement.* ASHE-ERIC Higher Education Report. San Francisco, CA: Jossey-Bass, 2003.

Williams, Jeffrey. "Brave New University." *College English* 61, no. 6 (June 1999): 742–51.

———. "The Other Politics of Tenure." *College Literature* 26, no. 3 (Fall 1999): 226–41.

Wright, Mary C. *Always at Odds: Creating Alignment between Faculty and Administrative Values.* Albany: State University of New York Press, 2008.

Contributors

Andrea Adolph is associate professor of English and coordinator of service learning at the Stark campus of Kent State University. Her work in areas of civic engagement was honored in 2008 with the David Hoch Memorial Award for Excellence in Service from Ohio Campus Compact. She is the author of *Food and Femininity in Twentieth-Century British Women's Fiction* (Ashgate) and is at work on a study of intersections of austerity and female desire during and after World War II.

Margaret Kent Bass is associate professor of English and director of the Center for Diversity and Social Justice at St. Lawrence University. Her areas of specialization and interest are autobiography studies, Caribbean literature, and creative non-fiction. She is presently completing a manuscript on the misinterpretation of the perceived homophobia in African American communities. Bass continues to be an uneasy sojourner in academe.

Marc Bousquet is associate professor of cultural studies and writing with new media at Santa Clara University. He is the author of *How the University Works: Higher Education and the Low-Wage Nation* (New York University Press). He serves on the national council of the American Association of University Professors and was the founding editor of *Workplace: A Journal for Academic Labor.*

Mary Burgan has served as professor of English at Indiana University-Bloomington, as distinguished visiting professor at Marquette University, and as general secretary of the American Association of University Professors. Her publications include *What Ever Happened to the Faculty?* and *Illness, Gender, and Writing: The Case of Katherine Mansfield* (both from Johns Hopkins University Press). At Indiana she served as director of composition, as associate dean of arts and sciences, as chair of the English Department, and as chair of the Faculty Council. She received the Distinguished Service Award from Indiana and the Frances Andrew March award for service to the profession from the Association of Departments of English.

Myriam J. A. Chancy's first novel, *Spirit of Haiti* (Mango), was a finalist in the Best First Book Category, Canada/Caribbean region, of the Commonwealth Prize 2004. Chancy is the author of *Framing Silence: Revolutionary Novels by Haitian Women* (Rutgers), *Searching for Safe Spaces: Afro-Caribbean Women Writers in Exile* (Temple; Choice OAB Award), a second novel, *The Scorpion's Claw* (Peepal Tree Press), and, forthcoming, *The Loneliness of Angels* (Peepal Tree Press). Her work as editor of *Meridians* garnered the CELJ Phoenix Award for Editorial Achievement. She is professor of English at Louisiana State University.

Kirsten M. Christensen is associate professor of German at Pacific Lutheran University. Christensen teaches all levels of German language, literature, and culture at Pacific Lutheran University. A medievalist by training and passion, her publications examine the mystical and devotional writings of women from Germany and the Low Countries. She teaches courses on the Middle Ages whenever she can, along with courses on literature and film produced in the former East Germany and since Unification. She also has an abiding interest in and has written about labor issues in higher education. She was a member of the MLA's Committee on the Status of Women in the Profession, and served as its co-chair.

Jeanette Clausen is professor of German and chair of the Department of International and Second Language Studies at the University of Arkansas at Little Rock (UALR). Prior to joining UALR, she was a faculty member in modern foreign languages and women's studies at Indiana University Purdue University Fort Wayne (IPFW), where she also held a series of administrative posts. Her colleagues at IPFW used to comment that she never met a committee she did not like (not quite true). Besides faculty roles and rewards and faculty development, Clausen is interested in German women writers, minority voices in German literature, and graphic novels. She is the translator of Irmtraud Morgner, *The Life and Adventures of Trobadora Beatrice as Chronicled by Her Minstrel Laura: A Novel in Thirteen Books and Seven Intermezzos* (University of Nebraska Press).

Donald E. Hall is Jackson Distinguished Professor and chair of the Department of English at West Virginia University (WVU). Prior to his arrival at WVU, he spent thirteen years as a professor and administrator at California State University, Northridge. He has published widely in the fields of gender studies, higher education studies, and Victorian cultural studies. His books *The Academic Self: An Owner's Manual* (Ohio State University Press) and *The Academic Community: A Manual for Change* (Ohio State University Press) have been used as faculty development manuals around the nation.

His latest book is *Reading Sexualities: Hermeneutic Theory and the Future of Queer Studies* (Routledge).

Katie J. Hogan is professor of English and director of women's studies at Carlow University. The author of *Women Take Care: Gender, Race, and the Culture of AIDS* (Cornell), Hogan is also coeditor of *Gendered Epidemic: Representations of Women in the Age of AIDS* (Routledge). A former member of the MLA Committee on the Status of Women in the Profession and Elections Committee, Hogan is currently a member of the MLA Delegate Assembly representing women in the profession.

Paula M. Krebs teaches English at Wheaton College, in Norton, Massachusetts. She edits *Academe*, the magazine of the American Association of University Professors, and directs the Summer Institute for Literary and Cultural Studies, a Mellon Foundation-funded program designed to encourage students from underrepresented groups to pursue doctorates in English.

Valerie Lee is professor and the most recent chair of the Department of English and a former chair of the Department of Women's Studies at Ohio State University. She has published in the areas of African American literature, folklore, American literature, feminist theory, and multicultural pedagogy. The author of *Invisible Man's Literary Heritage: Benito Cereno and Moby Dick, Granny Midwives and Black Women Writers: Double-Dutched Readings*, and *The Prentice Hall Anthology of African American Women's Literature*, Lee is also the recipient of Ohio State University's highest teaching award, as well as its highest service award. She holds courtesy appointments, teaches, and serves on committees in African American and African Studies, the Center for Folklore Studies, the Department of Comparative Studies, and the Center for Interdisciplinary Law and Policy Studies.

Shirley Geok-lin Lim, professor of English at the University of California, Santa Barbara, has published two critical studies and has edited and coedited many critical volumes, including *Reading the Literatures of Asian America; Approaches to Maxine Hong Kingston's The Woman Warrior; Transnational Asia Pacific; Power, Race and Gender in Academe*; and *Transnational Asian American Literature*. Winner of the Commonwealth Poetry Prize, Lim has also published short stories, a memoir (*Among the White Moon Faces*, an American Book Award winner), and two novels, *Joss and Gold* and *Sister Swing*.

Teresa Mangum is associate professor of English at the University of Iowa (UI). Besides serving on innumerable committees there, she serves on the

Delegate Assembly Organizing Committee of the MLA and on several national advisory boards, and she co-directs the UI Obermann Graduate Institute on Engagement and the Academy. Her publications include *Married, Middlebrow, and Militant: Sarah Grand and the New Woman Novel* (Michigan) and articles on Victorian novels and representations of both human-animal relations and aging. Mangum has received the Michael J. Brody Award for Faculty Excellence in Service to the University and the state of Iowa.

Michelle A. Massé directs Women's and Gender Studies at Louisiana State University. She is the author of *In the Name of Love: Women, Masochism, and the Gothic* and essays on psychoanalysis, feminism, and fiction. The series editor of State University of New York Press's Feminist Theory and Criticism series, she has also been the ex-, co-, or acting chair of MLA's Prose Fiction Division's Executive Committee, the Committee on the Status of Women in the Profession, Psychological Approaches to Fiction, Nominating Committee, and Delegate Assembly Organizing Committee. She is working on a project entitled *Great Expectations: Gendering Age, Narcissism, and the Bildungsroman* as well as on a monograph on Louisa May Alcott.

Sharon O'Dair holds a PhD from the University of California, Berkeley, and is professor of English at the University of Alabama and director of the Hudson Strode Program in Renaissance Studies. She coedited *The Production of English Renaissance Culture* (Cornell) and is the author of *Class, Critics, and Shakespeare: Bottom Lines on the Culture Wars* (Michigan). O'Dair has published many essays on Shakespeare, literary theory, and the profession of English studies, and she currently is working on two manuscripts, *Elitist Equality: Class Paradoxes in the Profession of English* and *The Eco-Bard: The Greening of Shakespeare in Contemporary Film*.

Colleen Ryan-Scheutz is associate professor of Italian and director of Italian language instruction at Indiana University. Her publications include *Sex, the Self and the Sacred: Women in the Cinema of Pier Paolo Pasolini* (Toronto), and she is coeditor of *Set the Stage! Teaching Italian through Theater: Theories, Methods, and Practices* (Yale). Ryan-Scheutz has published articles on Italian women writers, Italian cinema, and various aspects of Italian language and culture pedagogy. She is currently working on a collection of essays about teaching different languages through theater and a book-length study of illness and disability in Italian cinema.

Patricia Meyer Spacks is Edgar Shannon Professor of English Emerita at the University of Virginia, the author of eleven books, and the editor of six books. Her numerous honors and awards include the Association of Departments of English's Francis Andrew March Award for service to the profession, service as vice president of the American Academy of Arts and Sciences, and president of the Modern Language Association. Her most recent publications include *Boredom: The Literary History of a State of Mind, Desire and Truth: Functions of Plot in Eighteenth-Century English Novels* and, most recently, *Novel Beginnings: Experiments in Eighteenth-Century English Fiction.*

Donna Strickland is assistant professor of English at the University of Missouri-Columbia. Her previous work on the politics of writing programs has appeared widely, including in *College English, Works and Days,* and *JAC.* She coedited the forthcoming *The Writing Program Interrupted: Making Space for Critical Discourse* (Heinemann-Boynton/Cook).

Phyllis van Slyck is a professor in the English Department of LaGuardia Community College, City University of New York. Her articles on pedagogy, learning communities, and Henry James have appeared in *College English, Profession, Change Magazine,* and *Criticism: A Quarterly for Literature and the Arts* and the *Henry James Review* as well as anthologies on James and monographs on learning communities. Her service activities at LaGuardia have included co-directing the Writing Program, co-coordinating the Writing across the Curriculum Program, and coordinating and developing learning communities and related professional development and assessment initiatives.

Index